Cy...o

rio

Third Edition

John Lynes

Travel better, enjoy more

ULYSSES

Travel Guides

Offices

Canada: Ulysses Travel Guides, 4176 St. Denis Street, Montréal, Québec, H2W 2M5, ☎(514) 843-9447, ⚏(514) 843-9448, info@ulysses.ca, www.ulyssesguides.com

Europe: Les Guides de Voyage Ulysse SARL, 127 rue Amelot, 75011 Paris, France, ☎01 43 38 89 50, ⚏01 43 38 89 52, voyage@ulysse.ca, www.ulyssesguides.com

U.S.A.: Ulysses Travel Guides, 305 Madison Avenue, Suite 1166, New York, NY 10165, info@ulysses.ca, www.ulyssesguides.com

Distributors

U.S.A.: Hunter Publishing, 130 Campus Drive, Edison, NJ 08818, ☎800-255-0343, ⚏(732) 417-1744 or 0482, comments@hunterpublishing.com, www.hunterpublishing.com

Canada: Ulysses Travel Guides, 4176 St. Denis Street, Montréal, Québec, H2W 2M5, ☎(514) 843-9882, ext.2232, ⚏514-843-9448, info@ulysses.ca, www.ulyssesguides.com

Great Britain and Ireland: Roundhouse Publishing, Millstone, Limers Lane, Northam, North Devon, EX39 2RG, ☎1 202 66 54 32, ⚏1 202 66 62 19, roundhouse.group@ukgateway.net

Other countries: Ulysses Travel Guides, 4176 St. Denis Street, Montréal, Québec, H2W 2M5, ☎(514) 843-9882, ext.2232, ⚏514-843-9448, info@ulysses.ca, www.ulyssesguides.com

Canadian Cataloguing-in-Publication Data (see p 4)
© May 2004, Ulysses Travel Guides.
All rights reserved. Printed in Canada
ISBN 2-89464-702-6

When I see an adult on a bicycle,
I do not despair for the future of the human race.

– H.G. Wells

Author
John Lynes
Additional research
Amber Martin

Publisher
André Duchesne

English Editing
Cindy Garayt

Page Layout
Isabelle Lalonde

Cartographers
Julie Brodeur
Christian Lapointe

Computer Graphics
André Duchesne

Artistic Director
Patrick Farei
(Atoll Direction)

Illustrations
Vincent
Desruisseaux
Lorette Pierson

Photography
Cover page
EyeWire (Photodisc)

Acknowledgements: We would like to thank Rey Stephen and the
Ontario Tourism Marketing Partnership as well as the local tourism
representatives for their generous assistance.

We acknowledge the financial support of the Government of
Canada through the Book Publishing Industry Development Program (BPIDP) for our publishing activities. We would also like to
thank the government of Québec for its SODEC income tax program for book publication.

National Library of Canada cataloguing in publication

Lynes, John Allan, 1956-
   Cycling in Ontario
   3rd ed.
   (Ulysses green escapes)
   Includes index.
   ISBN 2-89464-702-6
   1. Bicycle touring - Ontario - Guidebooks. 2. Ontario - Tours.
   I. Title II. Series.
GV1046.C32O57 2004b   796.6'4'09713   C2003-942089-2

Write to Us

The information contained in this guide was correct at press time. However, mistakes can slip in, omissions are always possible, places can disappear, etc. The authors and publisher hereby disclaim any liability for loss or damage resulting from omissions or errors.

We value your comments, corrections and suggestions, as they allow us to keep each guide up to date. The best contributions will be rewarded with a free book from Ulysses Travel Guides. All you have to do is write us at the following address and indicate which title you would be interested in receiving (see the list at the end of the guide).

Ulysses Travel Guides
4176 St. Denis Street
Montréal, Québec
Canada H2W 2M5
www.ulyssesguides.com
E-mail: text@ulysses.ca

Map Symbols

⚑	Golf course	?	Tourist information
◎	Beach	⊨	Accommodation
►◄	Lock	▲	Camping
✈✚	Airport, airfield	⌁	Rest area
🛄	Train station	🔆	Lookout
CN CP	Canadian National Railway / Canadian Pacific Railway	★	Start of the tour
⇥⊦	Tunnel	═══	Paved trail
)(	Bridge	▦▦▦	Unpaved trail
🚲	Bicycle shop	▥▥	Rail bed

Table of Contents

Cycling in Ontario **11**
    Ontario: An Overview 12
    Money 15
    Holidays 15
    Emergencies 16
    Travelling to Ontario 16
    Road Signs 20
    Ontario Cycling Laws 21
    Canadian Cycling Attitudes 21
    Equipment 22
    Types of Cycling Tours 23
    Rail Trails and Off-Road Cycling 24
    Accommodations 25
    Tour Preparation and Training 26
    Cycling With Children 28
    The Tours 29
    How This Guide Works 30
    On The Road 30
    Additional Reference Materials 31

Southwestern Ontario **35**
    1. Magical Pelee Island 38
    2. Sarnia Circle Tour: Bluewater Discovery 42
    3. Lake Erie's North Shore: Woodstock, Port Dover
        and Tillsonburg 47
    4. Shakespeare's Stonetown: Stratford and St. Marys 55
    5. Two Sunsets, a River and a Trail: Goderich and
        Scenic Huron County 62
    6. Down by the Old Mill Stream: London and Dorchester ... 67
    Off-Road Cycling 75

Festival Country **79**
    7. Quarries and Cataracts: Elora to Cataract Rail
        Trail Adventure 81
    8. Dundas Valley and the Niagara Escarpment
        (including Webster and Tew's Falls) 86
    9. Elmira and St. Jacob's Countryside Tour 92
    10. Elora Gorge Adventure (Guelph to Elora) 96
    11. Paris to Cambridge Rail Trail 100
    12. Welland Canal Explorer: Port Dalhousie, St. Catharines
        and Welland 103
    13. Myths, Miracles and Pathways 110
    14. Wineries and Vineyards 115
    Off-Road Cycling 120

Table of Contents *(continued)*

The Georgian Lakelands **123**

15. Breweries, Sulfur Springs and Boxing: Cycling in the
Queen's Bush 125
16. Cycling the Bruce Peninsula: Owen Sound, Tobermory
and Sauble Falls 130
17. Beaver Valley Explorer: Thornbury, Meaford
and Markdale 139
18. Cycling to the Big Chute and Back: Midland, Port Severn
and Severn Falls 145
19. Lake of the Bays and Muskoka Hills 149
Off-Road Cycling 154

The Greater Toronto Area **157**
20. Toronto Islands, Lakeshore and Beaches 158
21. Olde Town Toronto 163
Off-Road Cycling 168

Central Ontario **169**
22. Peterborough: The Heart of the Kawarthas 171
23. Kawartha Lakes Adventure: Peterborough, Fenelon Falls
and Lindsay 175
24. Kawartha Cycling and Spelunking Adventure: Peterborough,
Lakefield and the Otonabee River 181
25. Port Hope to Cobourg and Back (including Part of
the Waterfront Trail) 185
26. Kent Portage: The Oldest Road in Ontario 190
27. Lake on the Mountain Adventure: Picton and
Prince Edward County 193
28. Lighthouse and Lookouts 197
29. Athol Bay, Sandbanks and Sand Dunes 200
Off-Road Cycling 204

Eastern Ontario **207**
30. Limestone and Black Powder: Discovering Kingston 208
31. The Rideau Canal and the 1000 Islands Parkway:
Kingston, Ottawa and Brockville 216
32. Ottawa Explorer: A Full Day in Under Two Hours 228
33. Gatineau Hills Leg Warmer 234
34. To Hog's Back Falls and Back: Ottawa's Rideau Canal
Recreational Trail 238
Off-Road Cycling 242

Rainbow Country **243**
35. Sudbury: Nickel Capital of the World 245
36. Manitoulin Day Tripping: Lake Mindemoya,
the Bridal Veil Falls and the Cup and Saucer Lookout ... 248
Off-Road Cycling 253

Index **255**

List of Maps

Where is Ontario? 9
Ontario 10
Southwestern Ontario 36
   1. Magical Pelee Island 39
   2. Sarnia Circle Tour 43
   3. Lake Erie's North Shore 49
      Oxford Centre 50
   4. Shakespeare's Stonetown 57
      Stratford 58
   5. Two Sunsets, a River and a Trail 65
   6. Down by the Old Mill Steam 68
      Dorchester 71
      London – Downtown 72
Festival Country 80
   7. Quarries and Cataracts 83
   8. Dundas Valley and the Niagara Escarpment 88
   9. Elmira and St. Jacobs Countryside Tour 93
  10. Elora Gorge Adventure: Guelph to Elora 97
  11. Paris to Cambridge Rail Trail 101
  12. Welland Canal Explorer 105
  13. Myths, Miracles and Pathways 111
  14. Wineries and Vineyards 117
The Georgian Lakelands 124
  15. Breweries, Sulphur Springs and Boxing 127
  16. Cycling the Bruce Peninsula 131
  17. Beaver Valley Explorer 141
  18. Cycling to the Big Chute and Back 147
  19. Lake of the Bays and Muskoka Hills 151
The Greater Toronto Area 156
  20. Toronto Islands, Lake Shore and Beaches 159
  21. Olde Town Toronto 165
Central Ontario 170
  22. Peterborough: The Heart of the Kawarthas 173
  23. Kawartha Lakes Adventure 177
  24. Kawartha Cycling and Spelunking Adventure 183
  25. Port Hope to Cobourg 187
  26. The Kent Portage (Trenton) 191
  27. Lake on the Mountain Adventure 195
  28. Lighthouse and Lookouts 199
  29. Athol Bay, Sandbanks and Sand Dunes 200
Eastern Ontario 200
  30. Limestone and Black Powder (Kingston) 210
      Kingston – Downtown 212
  31. The Rideau Canal and the 1000 Islands Parkway 217
  31. Ottawa – Leg 2 220
  31. Ottawa – Leg 3 22
  32. Ottawa Explorer 22
  32. Ottawa – Near 24 Sussex Drive 230
  33. Gatineau Hills Leg Warmer 23
  34. To Hog's Back Falls and Back 24
Rainbow Country 24
  35. Sudbury: Nickel Capital of the World 24
  36. Manitoulin Day Tripping 24

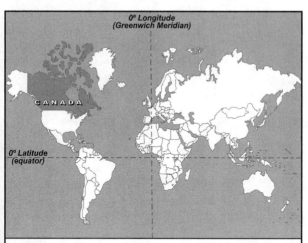

 Where is Ontario?

ONTARIO
Capital: Toronto
Population: 11,669,300 inhab.
Area: 1,068,630 km²
Currency: Canadian dollar

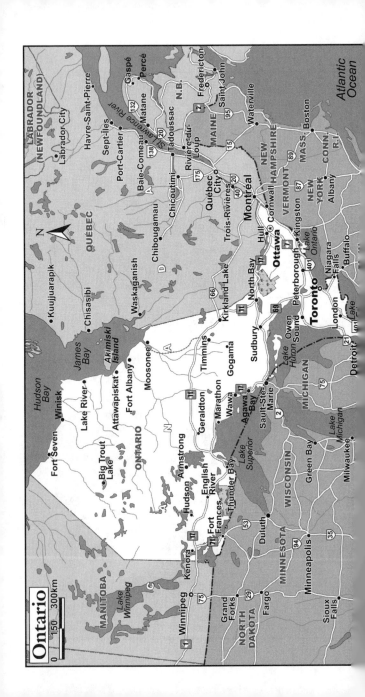

Cycling in Ontario

Ontario's immense size
and geological variety offer cyclists a lifetime of adventure.

Whether you cycle along Highway 141, one of the province's most scenic roads, down an abandoned jeep trail to a long-forgotten gold mine, or along a stretch of world-class single-track, you are in for a powerful experience. Like a good wine, Ontario offers the cyclist a different experience each time it is explored.

In addition to the scenic hills and dales, you can be assured of a friendly smile, lots of questions and a helping hand at each stop along the way. Whether cycling by yourself, as a group or as a family, this guide will lead you along some of Ontario's most fascinating paths. Paths to unique communities, intriguing individuals and lifelong friendships.

It is our hope that you will be able to experience the pleasure, satisfaction and sense of accomplishment that can only come from taking your favourite two-wheeled vehicle to the roads, greenways and trails of one of Canada's most interesting provinces—Ontario.

Ontario: An Overview

Ontario is as rich in human resources as it is in natural ones. As Canada's melting pot, Ontario continues to develop a healthy society by successfully mixing many unique peoples, cultures and traditions, past and present, with an exciting countryside. There are festivals throughout the year that celebrate the province's ancestry, its love for music and dancing and its appreciation of the skilful talents of local artists and crafts people.

Ontario is a province with one hand steadily holding onto the traditions, architecture and community values of the past, while the other hand stretches forward in anticipation and hope for the future.

Geography

"Ontario" is derived from an Iroquois word meaning "sparkling water." It is appropriately named, since over 20% of the province's area is taken up by nearly 250,000 lakes and rivers that sparkle brightly and blend harmoniously with a landscape of extensive forests, rocky outcrops, rolling hills and lush farmlands. Miles of shoreline are found within Ontario's borders, which encompass four of the five Great Lakes Superior, Huron, Erie and

Ontario as well as the St. Lawrence Seaway and the connecting waterways of the Trent-Severn and Rideau canal systems. Home to the largest provincial population over 11 million in Canada, it is second only to Québec in geographical size, covering an area of 1.6km^2 (412,582 sq mi). Ontario stretches 1,680km from its most southerly point, which lies on the same latitude as northern California, to the cool arctic waters of Hudson Bay in the north where the land is almost at sea level. In breadth, the province just falls short of its height, covering some 1,600km from east to west.

Flora and Fauna

Ontario's provincial flower and tree grow profusely in wooded lots and forests throughout the province. Delicate, white and three-petalled, the trillium is easily recognizable and is a welcome sight in May and early June. The provincial tree, the eastern white pine, can be identified by its long, slender needles and continues to be a valuable resource in the lumber and tourist industries. Ontario's abundance of water has also bestowed on it the enormous responsibility of caring for its many natural wetland areas. These areas provide habitat for many forms of wildlife, and opportunities to investigate, study and promote the management of the land, birds, reptiles and other aspects of nature.

Tourist Information

Ontario Travel
10th Floor, Hearst Block, 900 Bay St, Toronto, ON M7A 2E1
☎ *800-668-2746*
www.ontariotravel.net

Ontario Travel Associations

There are currently 11 Regional Tourism Associations (RTA) in Ontario.

Southern Ontario
☎ *800-267-3399*
www.soto.on.ca

Metropolitan Toronto
☎ *800-363-1990*
www.torontotourism.com

Getaway Country
☎ *800-461-1912*
www.getawaycountry.com

Ontario East
☎ *800-567-3278*
www.realontario.ca

Ontario's Near North
☎ *800-387-0516*
www.ontariosnearnorth.on.ca

Northern Ontario
☎ *800-603-3837*
www.getnorth.com

Rainbow Country
☎ *800-465-6655*
www.rainbowcountry.com

Algoma Country
☎ *800-263-2546*
www.algomacountry.com

James Bay Frontier
☎ *800-461-3766*
www.jamesbayfrontier. com

North of Superior
☎ *800-265-3951*
www.nosta.on.ca

Sunset Country
☎ *800-665-7567*
www.ontariossunsetcountry.ca

Central Ontario
no RTA; contact local tourism offices

The Regions

We have divided the province of Ontario into seven different areas, travelling from west to east. This guide concentrates on the six southern and most popu-lated areas, which offer cyclists a host of touring opportunities. Note that "Festival Country" and "The Lakelands" are officially part of the Southern Ontario RTA; we have chosen to retain their for-mer appellations as they are still in common use strongly associated with these regions.

Area A	*Southwestern Ontario*
Area B	*Festival Country*
Area C	*The Lakelands*
Area D	*Toronto Area*
Area E	*Central Ontario*
Area F	*Eastern Ontario*
Area G	*Ontario's North*

For descriptions of the regions, see the first page of the corre-sponding chapter.

Climate

Ontario's climate is moderate and consistent. From the middle of May until the last week in Octo-ber, temperatures are generally pleasant, the average provincial temperature being 20 degrees Celsius. Clothing should be of light to medium weight. In July and the first part of August, the roads are much busier, as this is peak vacation time. However, this should not deter you from travelling. In September and October, there is considerably less daylight, most attractions are only open on the weekends and the temperatures are much cooler. Waterproof clothing is advisable throughout the year.

Weather Information on the Internet

Weather Channel
www.weather.com

Environment Canada
www.msc-smc.ec.gc.ca

Weather Network
www.theweathernetwork.com

Weather Information by Telephone

Road Conditions
☎ *800-268-1376*

Weather Network
☎ *900-565-9328*

Canadian Broadcasting Corporation

Web address: *www.cbc.ca*

CBC Radio Frequencies:

Atikokan	*90.1 FM*
Bancroft	*600 AM*
Chatham	*88.1 FM*
Cornwall	*95.5 FM*
Dryden	*100.9 FM*
Elliot Lake	*90.3 FM*
Fort Frances	*90.5 FM*
Fort Hope	*101.5 FM*
Haliburton	*92.3 FM*

Hearst	*91.9 FM*
Huntsville	*94.3 FM*
Kapuskasing	*105.1 FM*
Kenora	*98.7 FM*
Kingston	*107.5 FM*
Kirkland Lake	*90.3 FM*
Kitchener-Waterloo	*89.1 FM*
Little Current	*97.5 FM*
London	*93.5 FM*
Moosonee	*1340 AM*
Niagara-Crystal Beach	*90.5 FM*
Nipigon	*98.9 FM*
North Bay/Timmins	*96.1 FM*
Orillia	*91.5 FM*
Ottawa	*91.5 FM*
Owen Sound-Wiarton	*98.7 FM*
Parry Sound	*89.9 FM*
Pembroke	*92.5 FM*
Penetanguishene	*89.7 FM*
Peterborough	*98.7 FM*
Sarnia	*90.3 FM*
Sioux Lookout	*1240 AM*
Sudbury	*99.9 FM*
Temagami	*1340 AM*
Thunder Bay	*88.3 FM*
Toronto	*99.1 FM*
Wawa	*88.3 FM*
White River	*1010 AM*
Windsor	*1550 AM*

Money

Currency

One Canadian dollar equals 100 cents. Bank notes come in denominations of $1,000, 500, 100, 50, 20, 10 and 5. Coins come in denominations of 1 and 2 dollars and 50, 25, 10, 5 and 1 cents.

Banking

All international credit cards are accepted. Travellers cheques are best purchased in Canadian dollars. All Ontario financial institutions, banks, credit unions, and trust companies have auto-

matic teller machines (ATMs); you will also find ATMs located in large and small shopping centres, airports, train stations, and even many gas stations and corner stores. There are two international networks operating in Canada: the Plus Network (affiliated with the Visa credit card) and Cirrus (affiliated with MasterCard). All Canadian financial institutions are members of one or the other; the Bank of Montreal and Royal Bank are members of both.

Taxes

Ontario has two taxes on goods purchased within the province. An 8% provincial sales tax (PST) and the 7% Federal Goods and Services Tax (GST) are charged on most products and services sold or provided in the province. Foreign visitors to Canada can apply for a rebate on GST paid for accommodations and on goods purchased in Canada that are subsequently exported.

For information:
☎ *800-668-4748 in Canada*
☎ *(902) 432-5608 outside Canada*
www.ccra-adrc.gc.ca/visitors

Holidays

New Year's Day
January 1

Good Friday
date varies, late March to late April

Easter Monday
Monday after Good Friday; most shops open

Victoria Day
Monday on May 19 or closest prior Monday

Canada Day
July 1

Civic Holiday
1st Monday in August

Labour Day
1st Monday in September

Thanksgiving
2nd Monday in October

Remembrance Day
November 11

Christmas Day
December 25

Boxing Day
December 26

Emergencies

In case of an accident, fire or other emergency dial ☎**911** or **0**.

Police

Ontario is policed by three levels of government: federally, by the Royal Canadian Mounted Police; provincially by the Ontario Provincial Police and municipally, most often by local law enforcement officers.

Travelling to Ontario

Travel Documents

From the United States: American visitors crossing the Canadian border (either way) may be asked to prove their citizenship with a document such as a passport or a birth or baptismal certificate. Naturalized US citizens should carry a naturalization certificate. Permanent US residents who are not citizens are advised to bring their Alien Registration Receipt Card.

From all other countries: Citizens of all other countries, except Greenland and residents of St. Pierre et Miquelon, must have a valid passport. Travellers from some countries may be required to obtain a visitor's visa: for details, consult the nearest Canadian embassy or consulate serving your home country or the Canadian Citizenship and Immigration Web site *(www.cic.gc.ca)*.

Transporting Your Bicycle

Each form of transportation has its own idiosyncrasies when you are travelling with a bicycle. It is recommended that you contact your transportation company several weeks ahead of departure to verify fares and special requirements (by booking in advance you may also enjoy a reduced fare). If shipping containers are required, they can be ordered and made available to you several days before departure. Always pack your own bike. Tightly secure (use extra padding) everything inside the shipping container. Make sure no parts are rattling around as they could easily get lost or damage your bicycle. Wrap duct tape around the box to prevent the case from being split open. One of the best ways to ship your bicycle is to purchase or rent a commercial bicycle case. It will provide

Table of Distances (km)
Via the shortest route

	Chicago (Il.)	Hamilton	Kingston	Kitchener-Waterloo	London	Montréal (QC)	New York (N.Y.)	Niagara Falls	Ottawa	Sault Ste. Marie	Sudbury	Toronto	Thunder Bay
Hamilton	788												
Kingston	1100	338											
Kitchener-Waterloo	767	69	369										
London	661	140	451	110									
Montréal (QC)	1383	621	299	650	738								
New York (N.Y.)	1294	765	583	838	911	618							
Niagara Falls	896	77	408	156	227	689	690						
Ottawa	1242	480	203	511	600	202	719	544					
Sault Ste. Marie	780	748	894	777	699	1003	1498	814	806				
Sudbury	1079	460	609	490	572	700	1212	529	508	302			
Toronto	855	75	263	123	198	547	829	144	410	696	411		
Thunder Bay	1058	1469	1623	1496	1414	1638	2212	1534	1516	723	1019	1421	
Windsor/Detroit (Mi.)	460	318	626	306	191	912	1018	413	773	584	751	386	1310

Example: The distance between Montréal and Toronto is 547km.

additional protection and you can rest assured that your bicycle will arrive at its destination safely. If your arrival and departure gateways are different, or if you have no place to leave the container (most hotel/motels will gladly store your bicycle box if you are staying there on the first and last night), the commercial bicycle case will most likely be out of the question and you will have to use one of the boxes offered by your chosen carrier. Finally, if you do not want to travel with your bicycle, it is possible to ship it by commercial parcel carrier. The disadvantages are that you need a final shipping address and some flexibility on delivery time, but if you can allow three to four days for delivery, the savings on transporting your bicycle by parcel carrier can be quite significant.

Courier Companies

Federal Express
☎800-463-3339
www.fedex.ca

United Parcel Service
☎800-742-5877
www.ups.ca

DHL Worldwide
☎800-225-5345
www.dhl.ca

Airborne Express
☎800-247-2676
www.airborne.com

By Car

There are bridges connecting Canada to the United States at Baudette International Falls, Point Edward and Niagara Falls. Two tunnel connections are located in the Windsor-Detroit and Sarnia-Point Huron areas. Ontario can also be accessed from northern Michigan at Sault Ste. Marie, from Minnesota at Grand Portage and Fort Frances, from Manitoba at Granite Lake, and from Québec at Hull and Montréal.

By Plane

Ontario has a network of 13 regional and national airlines transporting travellers to and within the province. Over 50 international airlines land at Ontario's main international airport, Toronto's Lester B. Pearson International Airport. Ottawa, Windsor, Hamilton and London (Ontario) also have international airports. In addition, there are local airports in over 50 of Ontario's smaller communities. Most airlines have a policy for transporting bicycles. All require your bicycle to be partially disassembled and placed in a cardboard box or similar container. It is strongly suggested that you check with the airline before departure to find out what is required, what they supply and what their rates are, as they vary dramatically.

Airlines

Air Canada
☎888-247-2262
www.aircanada.ca

WestJet Airlines
☎888-937-8538 or 800-538-5696
www.westjet.com

By Train

VIA Rail

It is still possible to go all the way from Vancouver to Halifax with

Canada's national passenger rail service. VIA Rail links most of Ontario's major cities, and in southern Ontario trains between major centres run several times a day. The train service connects with rail lines from the United States (Amtrak) at various border crossings. Its schedules include express, frequent-stop and (on some lines) request-stop services. VIA is flexible when it comes to transporting your bicycle. One condition set by VIA is that the train must have a baggage car. If you have a direct connection (no transfers), you do not have to box your bike but you are responsible for damage; if there is a transfer, you must box the bicycle (provided free) as per standard packing instructions; turn the handlebars and remove the pedals; remember that tools are not provided. Rates for transporting bicycles by rail are quite reasonable, making it one of the most economical ways for you and your bicycle to reach your destination.

VIA Rail Canada Inc.
☎ *(416) 366-8411 or 888-842-7245*
www.viarail.ca

Amtrak

Amtrak's Maple Leaf route takes travellers from New York to Toronto, with several stops along the way, including Niagara Falls.

Amtrak
☎ *800-872-7245*
www.amtrak.com

Toronto & Area Rail Service (Subway and Commuter Trains)

Toronto and its immediate surroundings are served by a complex network of subways, streetcars, light rail transit (LRT) lines, and suburban (GO) trains. GO Transit operates trains over six routes. The Lakeshore line has all-day service between Pickering and Oakville, seven days a week. This service is extended to Oshawa and Hamilton on weekdays at rush hours. The other five lines are named for their suburban terminal points: Milton, Georgetown, Bradford, Richmond Hill and Stouffville. Bicycles are allowed on non rush-hour GO Trains. Cyclists may take bikes on board all trains on Saturdays, Sundays and statutory holidays, and on weekday trains except those arriving at Union Station, Toronto's main station, between 6:30am and 9:30am, or departing from Union Station between 3:30pm and 6:30pm. Bicycles will only be carried in the two vestibules just inside the doors of each train car—two bicycles are allowed per vestibule. Stow your bicycle on either end of the handrail posts. Bicycles exceeding 173cm (68") in length or 41cm (16") in width will not be carried. Bicycles are prohibited in all handicapped-equipped coaches (the fifth car from the east end of the train). Rates for transporting bicycles with Go Transit are quite reasonable, offering a viable and economical way to get to your destination around the Toronto area.

GO Transit
☎ *(416) 869-3200 or 888-438-6646*
www.gotransit.com

By Bus

Greyhound is the nation's largest intercity bus company and the only nationwide provider of intercity bus service. It is the most economical way to travel across the country. Greyhound will transport bicycles as freight, provided that the bicycle is partially disassembled and placed in a cardboard box or similar container. Greyhound offers shipping cartons at reasonable rates, but the depots in smaller communities generally do not carry them in stock, so they must be ordered ahead. Another alternative is to get a box at your local bike shop. However, it will be smaller and you will have to remove your handlebars, seat, front wheel and pedals. Since the bicycle is considered freight, it will also be your responsibility to move it from bus to bus if you are travelling with it and transfers are required.

Greyhound Canada
Passenger Sales Centre (fares and schedules)
☎ *800-661-TRIP (8747)*
GCX (Courier Express)
☎ *800-661-1145*
www.greyhound.ca

Road Signs

Distance/Direction Signs: Ontario road signs come in all shapes, sizes and colours.

Information/Direction Signs: Green background/white letters, rectangular shape indicate distance and destination.

Regulatory Signs: White or black background, vertical/rectangle or square shape. These signs must be obeyed. They indicate highway numbers, speed limit and local traffic directions. When these signs are used in a permissive situation and have a green ring-shaped band displayed, they indicate that whatever is depicted

within the ring-shaped symbol is mandatory or permitted. When the sign displays a red circle and a diagonal red stroke, this indicates whatever is depicted within the symbol is prohibited.

Warning Signs: Yellow with black lettering, diamond shape warn of dangerous or unusual conditions ahead, such as a curve, turn, dip or side road.

Temporary Conditions: Orange/black letters warn and provide directions on road conditions ahead.

School Crossing: Blue, rectangular or pentagon in shape indicate crossing for children going to school.

Facilities: Brown or blue with white lettering, square or rectangular indicate facilities where fuel, food, accommodations or camping is available.

No Bicycles

Bicycles are not allowed on Ontario highways in the 400 series, the Queen Elizabeth Way and other multi-lane, divided routes with controlled access.

Bicycles Allowed

All roads numbered from 2 up are conventional highways of two or more lanes (some also include a cycling lane). Highways in the 500-600 series (pavement and loose surface) are Secondary Highways and roads in the 800 series are Tertiary Roads located in northern Ontario. County and regional roads have local number and name designations. Recently the Government of Ontario has undertaken a project to rename many of the roads to facilitate the

Cycling Associations

Ontario Cycling Association
1185 Eglinton Ave E, suite 408
North York, ON M3C 3C6
☎*(416) 426-7416*
www.ontariocycling.org

Canadian Cycling Association
702-2197 Riverside Dr
Ottawa, ON K1H 7X3
☎*(613) 248-1353*
www.canadian-cycling.com

province-wide 911 emergency action plan. Many of the roads have been renamed, but some

of them still retain their old designations. Be aware that some road names may have changed since the publication of this guide.

Ontario Cycling Laws

1. Your bicycle must have a warning device such as a bell or horn that sounds loud and clear.

2. When riding half an hour before sunrise and half an hour after sunset or when the light is poor, your bicycle must have a white or amber light on the front and a red light on the rear. Also, reflective material at least 25cm (10 inches) long and 2cm (1 inch) wide should be visible (white in the front, and red in the back).

3. All riders under the age of 18 must wear a government-approved cycling helmet.

4. Bicycles are prohibited on expressways and freeway-type highways such as the 400 series, the Queen Elizabeth Way and on roads where "no bicycle" signs have been posted.

5. Cyclists are required to obey all traffic laws under the Highway Traffic Act.

General Information

Road Conditions
☎*800-268-1376*

Directory Assistance
Canada and USA
☎*411*

Signals and Other Peculiar Traffic Rules

Right Turns: Unless there are signs indicating the contrary, in Ontario a right turn may be made on at a traffic light when it is red. The turn can be completed if there is no oncoming traffic and it is safe.

Single File Only: Toronto is currently the only city in Ontario that has a bylaw prohibiting riding two abreast.

Canadian Cycling Attitudes

Although cycling is an internationally recognized form of transportation, Canada is still a relatively young country where cycling is concerned. Over the last few years, the province has made great strides in public education and people who share the roads with bicycles are gradually becoming more aware of and considerate towards cyclists. On the less travelled backroads where traffic is light, it is legal to ride two abreast, but it's common courtesy to get into single file when traffic approaches from the front or rear. Use your hand signals to let others know your intentions and keep at least one bicycle length between you and the rider in front of you. This is especially true when travelling with children who constantly wander off and on the road. If you do go off the road, ride on the shoulder for a bit until you have regained control, then return to the pavement once the way is clear. Be aware of what is going on in front and behind you at all times. If you find yourself in an uncomfortable situation, always yield the right of way, take to the shoulder, walk your bike, or stop until the situation has improved and you are comfortable riding your bicycle, again.

Equipment

The Bicycle

Racing bicycles are lightweight, quick-handling (road or track) and have high-quality components: narrow, lightweight wheel rims and tires, a short wheelbase, and either close-ratio gearing or a fixed gear.

Road bicycles/randonneur bicycles are lightweight and designed to carry at least 9kg (20lbs) of supplies in cargo packs. They have a long wheelbase for stability (42 inches or more), long chain stays, generous fork rake, heavy-duty but narrow wheels, and cantilever brakes. Head tube and seat tube angles are shallow, usually 72 to 73 degrees. The bottom bracket is set low for stability.

Touring bicycles are more robust versions of road bicycles. They have heavy-duty components and construction. They offer a wide range of gears, and often have triple chain rings for hill climbing. A touring bicycle is designed to carry 8 to 23kg (40 to 50lbs) of cargo.

Hybrid bicycles are often referred to as all-purpose adventure bikes. These bicycles are essentially a cross between a mountain bike and a road bicycle. They have cantilever-style brakes, triple chain rings, wide-range gearing, and flat handlebars similar to mountain bikes. On the other hand, they have somewhat larger diameter wheels (700 cc instead of 26 inch) and narrower tires (1.5 inches instead of 2). The frames are more like those of road bikes. They commonly have 72-degree head tube angles and 73-degree seat angles, and 17-inch or shorter chain stays.

The **mountain bike** is a sturdily built bicycle specially designed for off-road or rough-terrain riding. Mountain bikes have flat handlebars, cantilever-style brakes, triple chain rings, wide-range gearing, and knobby tires, approximately 2-inches wide. Most mountain bikes now have a 70- to 72-degree head angle, 1.5 to 2 inches of fork rake, and a 68- to 74-degree seat-tube angle. On a good road, a mountain bike is about 10% slower than a road bike. When used for touring, the offer stability, load-carrying ability and long-distance comfort. They have a long wheelbase with a generous fork rake and long chain stays. The handlebars are wider than on other bikes, and there are rack mounting bosses near the front and rear wheels.

Bicycle Panniers and Loading

As the majority of the tours in this guide are planned as day trips or weekend getaways, a medium-sized, rear top-rack bag and two rear side panniers (1,500-1,800 cc), with enough room for both the essentials and food, are adequate. For the best handling, a bicycle should carry 60% of its load in the rear, 35% in the front panniers, and 5% in the handlebar bag. The front panniers should be mounted low and centred fore and aft on the axle. Great care should be taken to keep this load balanced, or the bike will become unsafe. One new idea that offers cyclists a better way to transport gear is the single-wheel tag-a-long trailer that easily attaches to the rear wheel quick-release mechanism. These trailers give you increased luggage capacity and more control over the bicycle handling when fully loaded.

Types of Cycling Tours

Independent Cycling

Independent cycling in this manner means that you plan and

create your own cycling tour. Generally, this allows your dollar to stretch a little further. Often you will determine your own route, use a route travelled by others or rely on written instructions and mapping from books such as this one. You can either travel in the lap of luxury by staying in deluxe accommodations or camp along the road. This type of cycling lets you travel at your own pace, allowing time to enjoy the countryside and interact with locals and travelling companions.

In a Group

Travelling with a group of cyclists can be a rewarding experience. It's a fun and easy way to learn the ropes and it offers an excellent venue for the exchange of information and ideas. Travelling on group tours also provides companionship and moral support along the way. Some discussion with travelling companions at the beginning of a tour is important, however; there is nothing wrong with a bit of friendly competition throughout the day, but you don't want the tour to turn into an endurance race.

Organized Group Tours

If you are a single rider or are concerned about doing your first bicycle tour, one option is to join an organized group outing. Ontario has a number of reputable bicycle tour operators providing quality tour packages.

Rail Trails and Off-Road Cycling

Multi-Use Trails

Multi-use trails are the most popular trail used by cyclists today. Their surfaces vary from asphalt paths to unsurfaced, man-made nature trails and reconditioned rail beds. These trails are shared by hikers, cyclists, horseback riders and, in winter, snowmobiles; in some cases the trail will share a roadway with car as well.

Trans Canada Trail

The Trans Canada Trail, an exciting new multipurpose trail, was inaugurated on September 9, 2000. Upon completion, it will be the longest such trail in the world, spanning a stunning 16,000km across Canada from St. John's, Newfoundland, to Victoria, British Columbia; from Calgary, Alberta, it heads north to Tuktoyaktuk, Northwest Territories, and Chesterfield Inlet, Nunavut.

The trail will be used for walking and hiking as well as cross-country skiing, cycling, horseback riding and snowmobiling, drawing on both existing and newly converted trails. Nearly 18,000km have thus far been completed. The trail is being funded by corporate sponsors, public donations and governmental contributions.

Trans Canada Trail Foundation
43 Westminster Ave N, Montréal, QC
H4X 1Y8
☎ *(514) 465-3636 or 800-465-3636*
www.tctrail.ca

"Rails to Trails" in Ontario

Ontario's abandoned rail lines are increasingly being turned into scenic cycling paths. The surface of redeveloped rail beds varies depending on the character and needs of the communities through which it passes. Local terrain, the frequency of use, the type of use and the amount of funds, labour and local governmental support all dictate what the trail will look like. Currently, there are about 250km of designated rail trails in southern Ontario.

Ontario Trails Council
8 Garrett St, PO Box 190, Sharbot Lake,
ON K0H 2P0
☎ *877-ON-TRAIL (668-7245)*
www.ontariotrails.on.ca

Single and Double Track Trails

Single Track Trails are hard-packed routes that are found in natural areas. Generally, bicycles can only travel in single file, and the terrain demands a higher skill level from the cyclist.

Double Track Trails are unsurfaced, hard-packed routes wide enough to accommodate two riders abreast, and are generally preferred by less experienced cyclists.

Resort and Conservation Trails

These trails are well maintained and thoughtfully designed, and in most cases are privately owned or operated by a local conservation authority. There may be a user fee at some of these locations.

Accommodations

Once your route and travel dates are set, you need to arrange your accommodations. Always book your accommodations before you leave. Never assume that there will be a vacancy when you arrive in the evening.

Hotels and Motels

Generally, these are the most expensive types of accommodations and are not found in all areas. If you decide to stay in these places, try to get a room on the ground floor so that you can take your bicycle into your hotel room more easily.

Bed and Breakfasts

A unique way to enjoy Ontario's hospitality, bed and breakfasts are family homes that rent out rooms to visitors. They can provide a relaxing experience that gives you a glimpse into the local community. When booking, remember to ask if they have a garage to store your bicycle. Upon request, some bed and breakfasts will even allow you to camp in the backyard and provide breakfast in the morning. For reviews of some of Ontario's best bed and breakfasts, pick up a copy of *Bed and Breakfasts in Ontario*, published by Ulysses Travel Guides (ISBN: 2894643071).

Camping

The most economical form of accommodation, camping also brings you closest to nature. One drawback is that it always takes longer to dismantle a tent in the morning than to walk out of a hotel room. Generally, however, the flexibility and the fresh air afforded by this type of accommodation outweigh any drawbacks encountered.

Camping Information

Ontario Parks
☎ *800-668-2746 or 888-668-7275*
www.ontarioparks.com

Ontario Private Campgrounds
☎ *(519) 371-3393*
www.campgrounds.org

Showers

Showers or simply a place to wash up can be hard to find when camping. Most towns usually have a public pool where showers offer cyclists an economical way to clean up and relax after a long day's ride. Most private campgrounds have shower facilities.

Bicycle Camping Equipment

Tent

Your tent should be a lightweight (one- or two-person) backpacking tent with a fly, and not more than 60cm (24 inches) wide when rolled up. Make sure that the tent has an extendable foyer or enough room inside for your panniers. Tip: get some plastic, cut a ground sheet the same size as the bottom of your tent and put it under the tent, as it will extend the life of the tent floor.

Gas Camping Stoves

There are a number of excellent products on the market that are reasonably priced. An important consideration is size and weight. A stove (single burner) designed for white gas naphtha and backpacking will do.

Warning: never start a stove or any other flammable product in a tent or enclosed area.

Cooking & Other Equipment

Travel as light as possible. Lightweight cookware (stainless steel is recommended) is available in the camping department of most major retail outlets. A Swiss Army knife can always come in handy, especially for camping and emergencies. Lastly, take along some grey duct tape. If all else fails, this stuff won't let you down—it repairs everything! Step on the roll and flatten it out so that it does not take up too much room.

Food

Plan your daily menu before you go on tour. This will also help you budget for your trip. Most groceries should be picked up along the way, but some items will have to be purchased before departure. Fresh fruit is a must and can be complimented by cereal or granola bars as these items will help you keep your energy level up throughout the day. Your menus

should also include food high in carbohydrates; a combination of milk and pasta will satisfy this daily requirement. Try to include easy-to-carry, lightweight instant food, which can be purchased at your local grocery store before departure. You'll be surprised at the variety and quality (excellent taste and very nutritious) of instant foods that are available today. Most important is WATER! Keep your body constantly hydrated and you will be fine.

Food and Wildlife

Wildlife is also a concern. Racoons, skunks and black bears are attracted to food and garbage. When camping, always place food away from your tent, use bear-resistant food storage containers or suspend food 4m off the ground and 1m away from any nearby tree trunks. Keep all garbage until it can be disposed of in the proper manner—don't bury it!

Tour Preparation and Training

Although the tours in this book can be cycled by almost everyone, it is suggested that you take the time to prepare physically and mentally before embarking on a tour. The most important consideration of any trip is to know your equipment: meaning your bicycle and your body.

Make sure you are comfortable on your bicycle. After all, you will be spending many hours in the saddle each day. Your bicycle seat and handlebar position affect your knees, back, neck and wrists. If they are not in the correct position, your trip will be more difficult and uncomfortable. Try adjusting your riding position so that you are as upright as possible, so that about 75% of your weight is on the seat and you grip the handlebars from the top. Take some time to determine your correct riding position. If you're unsure, consult your local bicycle shop. Also, become familiar with how to complete some simple mechanical repairs. Don't rely on someone in your group to fix everything because most problems seem to occur when you become separated for one reason or another. Again, if you are unsure, turn to your local bicycle shop for advice or refer to one of the many repair manuals available.

Physical training is recommended before embarking on any bicycle trip, but don't go to extremes. The more consistent you are in the training program you follow (consult your physician), the more comfortable the cycling experience will be. Included in your exercise program should be daily time on an exercise bicycle and, in good weather, your own

bicycle. This will not only help you become more familiar with your bicycle; it will also help you build some rear-end stamina! As departure day nears, increase your weekend riding, making sure to include some topography that will challenge you physically and mentally. Devote one day a week in your physical training schedule to rest: this will give your body a chance to recuperate.

You should do several weekend training rides with your bike and panniers fully loaded. This will show you the best way to pack, distribute the weight on your bicycle, and make you conscious of the changes in your bike's handling when packed for the tour.

Equipment Checklist

Clothing

- 3 pairs of cotton socks
- 3 pairs of cotton underwear
- 1 pair of pyjamas
- 2 pairs of padded lycra shorts (wash well throughout trip)
- 3 to 4 shirts (brightly coloured for better visibility)
- 1 warm long-sleeved shirt
- 1 pair sweatpants or tights
- 2 pairs cycling shoes (1 pair can be a ridged sole running shoe)
- Rain gear/windbreaker
- Toiletries (towels, etc.)
- bathing suit
- 1 pair cycling gloves

Hardware

- Bicycle (this goes without saying)
- Helmet
- Water bottles (2 minimum)

A Cyclist's Motto

Packing for any kind of tour can be tedious. As you read the list on the next page, keep in mind the Touring Cyclist's Motto: "Take half as much clothing and twice as much money and you'll have a perfect holiday."

- Front/Back Panniers (as required)
- Rear rack top bag (handlebar bags not recommended as they impair steering and balance of your bicycle)
- Rear-view mirror
- Compass
- Mini repair tool kit
- Tire repair kit
- Extra tire tube
- Bicycle pump
- Battery equipped front and rear lights
- Extra brake cable and brake pads
- Light lubricant
- Swiss Army knife
- Duct tape/electrician tape
- Bungie cords or small nylon tie-down straps (bring extras, they always seem to disappear)
- Small first-aid kit
- Pain reliever (Aspirin or Tylenol)
- Wallet (personal identification and currency)
- $5 loose change (in case of emergency)
- Plastic sheet (painters drop sheet to cover bike, keep panniers dry)
- Small binoculars
- Hat
- Camera and extra film
- Bicycle lock and locks for panniers
- Sunscreen
- Sunglasses
- Small flashlight
- Small sewing kit
- Large garbage bags (for clean up; in a pinch can be converted to a raincoat)
- Additional road maps as required
- Durable plastic bags and tie tags (to protect your gear on rainy days)
- This guide and your daily journal

Camping Equipment

The following suggestions are the minimum required equipment for any cycling/camping trip:

- Lightweight tent and fly
- Lightweight sleeping bag (mummy-style preferred)
- Sleeping pad
- Lightweight stove
- Extra fuel tank and fuel for camp stove
- Lightweight cookware and eating utensils
- Matches
- Toilet paper
- Fold up pillow (optional)
- Dehydrated food packages (as per your menu)
- Spices and condiments (as required)
- Lightweight 9" X 12" plastic tarp
- Small whisk

Cycling With Children

Cycling with children of any age can be a very rewarding experience. Listed below are some suggestions that will help make it even more fun.

1. Make sure they know the rules of the road and traffic signs.

2. Make sure they are familiar with their bicycle.

3. Make sure the bike is equipped with a working front light, back light and bell (odometer is optional but can be helpful when setting targets).

4. Make sure they keep at least one bicycle length between

them and the rider in front—young eyes tend to wander when experiencing new sights and sounds.

5. Set time goals for stops—this will keep them pedalling in anticipation of an upcoming stop.

6. Provide them with a set of panniers (large or small, at your discretion) so that they feel they are contributing to the cycling adventure by carrying their own gear.

7. Provide a disposable camera so they can create their own memories of the cycling trip.

8. Allow them time to play; after all, they are children. Pack a card game, a frisbee and a small toy.

9. Involve them in pre-trip preparations and map reading. Ask them from time to time in what direction they are travelling on route.

10. Relay the local information found in this guide—this will help entertain them, keep their minds off the chore at hand and may lead to questions that, together, you can find answers to.

Lastly, when choosing a tour for children, take into consideration that they will require more breaks and a lower average speed. Therefore, when doing your pretour calculations on the length of your day, remember to add at least one to two hours.

The Tours

As you leaf through this book deciding which area of Ontario is of interest to you, you will notice that most regions have a tour of five or more days, a number of single-day outings and several two- and three-day looped itineraries.

Generally, the tours begin in fairly large cities and each tour provides the necessary information for you to arrange your own cycling excursion. Suggested touring days accommodate all levels of riding ability, from ages eight to 80, from the skilled to the occasional cyclist. Most of the overnight tours can be completed as day outings, expanded or combined with other tours in this guide by making a few simple changes, so you can design a tour that accommodates your availability and preferred destinations. Tours have been carefully planned so you have enough time to get off your bike to explore and experience the province's many attractions and unique features.

In an effort to accommodate the needs of all cyclists, maximum daily cycling distances of 70km a day are suggested. The roads chosen are primarily paved secondary roads. Wherever possible, the use of abandoned rail lines and off-road trails are incorporated into the itinerary. Routing has been designed to accommodate all cyclists and bicycle types. Alternative routing suggestions are included in most itineraries for those who prefer to remain on familiar roadways.

How This Guide Works

Bicycle Types

Listed in order of preference; when in parentheses( ), some sections of the route may require more physical effort for this type of bicycle.

Level of Difficulty

Each tour in this guide can be completed by all cyclists regardless of riding ability, by simply extending daily riding time.

Easy, flat terrain

Easy/medium flat and slightly rolling terrain

Medium, rolling terrain

Medium/hard, rolling terrain including 2 or 3 good climbs

Difficult, rolling terrain, numerous long climbs

Abbreviations

Intersection	[I]
Junction	[J]
Right	[R]
Left	[L]

Rail bed	[RB]
Side Roads, gravel or Loose Surface Roads	[SR]
Asphalt Roads	[Apht]
County Road	[CTY]
Highway	[HWY]
Township Road	[TWP]

Road	Rd
Street	St
Drive	Dr
Avenue	Ave
Boulevard	Blvd
Crescent	Cr
Highway	Hwy
Parkway	Pkwy
County	Cty
Route Road One	RR 1

North	N
South	S
East	E
West	W
Ontario	ON

Kilometres	km
Metres	m
Hectares	ha
Kilometres per hour	kph

On The Road

Directions

To help you decide which area of Ontario to visit, a brief description and indication of difficulty precede each tour itinerary. The guide has been designed to meet the needs of the independent cyclist. Detailed written directions, including distance and tidbits of local information, complement the maps, making the guide easy to use. This book also includes contact information for local tourist centres, unique attractions, bicycle shops and interesting local events. This guide has tried to keep that sense of adventure alive in each

Cycling in Ontario

tour while providing you with all the essential information.

Dehydration

Dehydration is the cyclist's greatest concern. Drink plenty of water throughout the day. A good way to make sure that you stay hydrated (even if you are not thirsty) is to follow this simple rule: every 5km, drink at least one quarter of your water bottle, and more on hot days.

Circle Checks

Do a circle check of your bicycle and equipment each morning, beginning with a quick look at your tires, spokes, rack bolts and brakes. An early morning start is always recommended because the sun is low in the sky and the temperatures are cooler and more comfortable. An early morning departure is even more important if you are camping, as it always seems to take more time to repack your gear and get going. Review the day's itinerary and maps before setting out; never try to read a map while riding.

Theft

Whenever you leave your bicycle unattended, *lock it up!* It is a good idea to lock your panniers as well. Never leave your wallet or expensive camera equipment unattended. They, like your bike, may be just too tempting to curious eyes.

The Environment

When on tour, it is important to remember that you are only an observer and should therefore respect all that Mother Nature

Some Advice

The old saying "the faster I go... the farther behind I get" is applicable to cycling as well. It is important that you set and stick to a comfortable cycling speed to make your touring experience a pleasant one.

has provided for us. The old Boy Scout adage of "leaving a place visited in a better condition than one found it in" is an excellent way to treat this world and more particularly the communities that you are cycling through. After all, the impression you leave will affect others that follow.

Each tour provides ample time to stretch and explore. Don't be afraid to stop. Take some time to visit and enjoy the natural beauty of your surroundings and the area's many amenities. By doing so, you will find that your trip will be a relaxing and rewarding experience.

Additional Reference Materials

Internet Sites

Here are a few of the many cycling sites available on the net:

Bicycling Magazine
www.bicyclingmagazine.com

Canadian Cycling Association
www.canadian-cycling.com

Cyber Cyclery
www.cyclery.com

Ontario Cycling Association
www.ontariocycling.org

Ottawa Cycling Club
www.ottawabicycleclub.ca

Rail Trails
www.railtrails.org

Trans Canada Trail
www.tctrail.ca

UCI- Union Cycliste Internationale
www.uci.ch

VeloNews
www.velonews.com

Cycling Magazines

Here are some interesting cycling magazines:

Bicycling Magazine
Bike
Mountain Bike
Off Camber
Pedal
Velo News

Ontario Cycling Publications

Backroads & Railbeds, A Grand Adventure
Lynes Bicycle Adventures
ISBN 0-9683000-0-6

Backroads & Railbeds - North Shore Lake Erie Book
Lynes Bicycle Adventures
ISBN 0-9683000-1-4

Backroads & Railbeds - North Shore Lake Erie Book 2
Lynes Bicycle Adventures
ISBN 0-9683000-2-2

Backroads and Railbeds - Pelee Island & Marsh Trails
Lynes Bicycle Adventures
ISBN 0-9683000-3-0

Bicycle Day Trips In and Around London
Wallis and Gordon
ISBN 0-9699594-0-0

Bicycle Guide to Eastern Ontario
Gary Horner
ISBN 1-895591-00-7

Bicycling the Bruce
Tom Hakala
ISBN 0-921773-22-6

Cycling Around the Sound
Tom Hakala, Owen Sound Area
ISBN 0-921773-32-3

The Canadian Cycling Association Complete Guide to Bicycle Touring in Canada
Elliot Katz
ISBN 0-385025415-6

The Bicycle Guide to Southwestern Ontario
Gary Horner
ISBN 0-9698297-0-1

Day Trips on Bike Trails
The Valley Girls
☎*(519) 599-6290*

Lakeshore Cycle Guide - Toronto to Belleville
Donna McNeil
ISBN 0-9681255-0-6

Pioneer Cycle Guide - Haliburton to Lake Ontario
Donna McNeil
ISBN 0-9681255-1-4

The Waterfront Trail
Waterfront Regeneration Trust
ISBN 0-7778-4082-0

Maps of Ontario

Surveys and Plans Office
Ministry of Transportation
1201 Wilson Ave
Downsview, ON M3J 1J8
☎ (416) 235-4686
www.mto.gov.on.ca

Other Publications

Scouting for Boys
Baden-Powell, Lord of Gilwell
National Council Boy Scouts of Canada

Discover Southern Ontario
Beck, David
Learnxs Press, 1978

My Country - The Remarkable Past
Berton, Pierre
McClelland & Stewart, 1976

Ghost Town's of Ontario Vol. 1
Brown, Ron
Cannon Books, 1987

Ghost Railways of Ontario
Brown, Ron
Broadview Press, 1995

Ghost Towns of Ontario Vol. 2
Brown, Ron
Cannon Books, 1983

Ghost Towns of Ontario Vol. 3
Brown, Ron
Cannon Books, 1983

The Governor's Road
Byers, Mary and Margaret McBurney
University of Toronto Press, 1982

Tourist Guide Book of Ontario
Canadian Automobile Association

Ontario
Couture, Pascale
Ulysses Travel Guides, 2004

Ottawa–Hull
Couture, Pascale
Ulysses Travel Guides, 2001

Old Oxford is Wide Awake
Dawe, Brian
William Brian Dawe, 1980

Bicycling the Bruce
Hakala, Tom
The Ginger Press, 1994

Toronto
Ulysses Travel Guides, 2002

Circle Tours of Festival Country
Ontario Ministry of Industry and Tourism

Exploring Manitoulin
Pearen, Shelley J.
University of Toronto Press, Revised ed. 1996

Canadian Book of the Road
Readers Digest, 1979

Ontario Place Names
Scott, David E.
Vancouver, Toronto: Whitecap Books, 1993

Ontario Mountain Bike Guide
Seca, Ron
Stoddart Press, 1994

Cycling in Ontario

Canada Handbook
Statistics Canada
Canadian Government Publishing
Centre

A Bicycle Guide to Pelee Island
Tiessen, Ronald
Ronald Tiessen, Pelee Island Heritage
Centre, 1994

Bicycle Day Trips In and Around London
Wallis, Susan and Mindy Gordon
Forward Publications, 1996

The Waterfront Trail
Waterfront Regeneration Trust, 1995

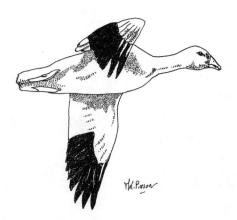

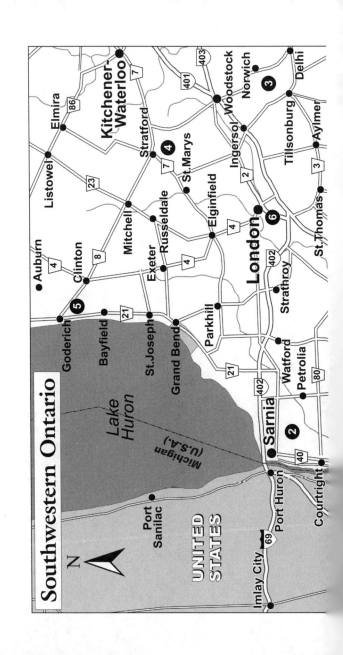

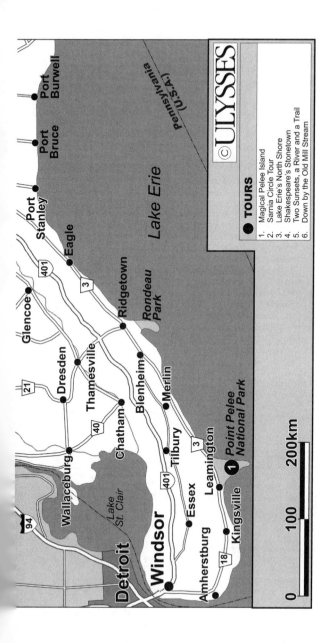

© ULYSSES

● TOURS

1. Magical Pelee Island
2. Sarnia Circle Tour
3. Lake Erie's North Shore
4. Shakespeare's Stonetown
5. Two Sunsets, a River and a Trail
6. Down by the Old Mill Stream

Port Burwell

Port Bruce

Port Stanley

Eagle

Lake Erie

Pennsylvania (U.S.A.)

Glencoe

401

Dresden

21

Thamesville

40

Ridgetown

Rondeau Park

3

Blenheim

Merlin

Chatham

Wallaceburg

401

Tilbury

3

Leamington

Point Pelee National Park

1

Lake St. Clair

Essex

94

Detroit

Windsor

Amherstburg

18

Kingsville

0   100   200km

Southwestern Ontario

stretches eastward from Windsor to Woodstock, the Dairy Capital of Canada, and from the shipping port of Goderich in the north to Pelee Island, the most southerly tip of Ontario.

1. Magical Pelee Island

This island glistens like an emerald amid the blue waters of Lake Erie. Upon disembarking at the west dock, you immediately get the feeling that time has stood still on this resort island. Much of the island's history is intact, waiting to be discovered as you begin to explore every nook and cranny. The romance of the wine industry wafts through the air, beckoning you to sample its wares. And you can enjoy all this simply by taking a bicycle ride.

Return Distance:
54km of road on the island

No. of recommended legs:
1

Level of Difficulty:

Surface:
Asphalt and some gravel

Villages/Towns/Cities:
Leamington (mainland, north of the island), Pelee Island

Local Highlights:
John. R. Park Homestead, Pelee Island Museum, Pelee Island Winery, Fish Point Nature Reserve, Glacial Groves, Indian Grinding Stone, the restored Pelee Lighthouse, Huldah's Rock, Vin Villa Ruins, Point Pelee National Park, Jack Miner Bird Sanctuary, Colasanti's Tropical Gardens, Wheatley Provincial Park and Rondeau Provincial Park are nearby on the mainland.

● ATTRACTIONS

1. Restored lighthouse
2. Scudder Marina
3. Gwendolyn's Ice Cream
4. Township of Pelee Offices & Opp
5. Pelee Island Medical Clinic
6. Canada Customs
7. Pelee Island Transportation
8. Heritage Centre Museum
9. Pelee Island Winery Pavilion
10. Pelee Art Works
11. Star of the Sea R.C. Church
12. Pelee Island Pheasant Farm
13. Airport
14. Fish Point Nature Reserve
15. Postal Station
16. Vin Villa Ruins (private)
17. The Pelee Club (private)
18. Sarah Ann McCormick House (private)
19. J.McCormick Quarry (private)
20. Pelee Quarry (private)
21. Harris House (private)
22. Pegg Mission (private)
23. Finlay Winery ruins (private)
24. Tin Goose Inn
25. Customs House (private)
26. South End School (private)
27. William Stewart House (private)
28. Location of the "Battle of Pelee Island"

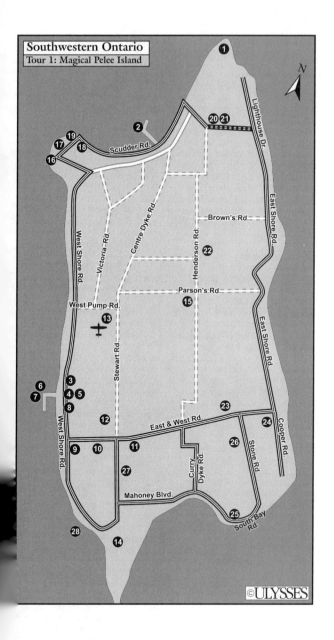

N

Lighthouse Dr.

Scudder Rd.

West Shore Rd.

Victoria Rd.

Centre Dyke Rd.

Brown's Rd.

Henderson Rd.

Parson's Rd.

West Pump Rd.

Stewart Rd.

East Shore Rd.

East & West Rd.

Curry Dyke Rd.

Stone Rd.

Cooper Rd.

Mahoney Blvd.

South Bay Rd.

©ULYSSES

Recommended Bicycles:
Touring/Hybrid/Mountain

Tour Suggestions:
To make the trip more enjoyable, try to spend at least one night on the island. Take the early morning ferry (1.5hr one way) across, spend the day exploring, and then return to the mainland the next day to visit Point Pelee National Park. The island's roads are narrow and must be shared with motorized vehicles. Also, book your accommodations well ahead of time as the island's many bed and breakfasts are in popular demand.

How to get there:
From April 1 to August 1, the ferry departs from the city of **Leamington**; from August 1 to December 7, it departs from **Kingsville**. To get there from the north, take Hwy 401 to Hwy 77 S. From the east, follow County Rd 20 or Hwy 3, and from the west, take Hwy 3. From the south, the island may be reached by taking a ferry across the lake from neighbouring Sandusky, Ohio. A good way to ensure a spot on the ferry is to call ahead to make reservations.

From the earliest times, the French referred to the islands of Lake Erie collectively as the "Isles des Serpents à Sonnelles," translated as Rattlesnake Islands. The name may have been a contributing factor in delaying exploration of **Pelee Island** which, despite its natural amenities, has only a few truly noteworthy historical treasures. It is perhaps best known for its famous wine, which has been produced on the island since 1866.

Itinerary:
The Ontario Northland ferry, the *M.V. Jiimann*, is the largest on the lake. It is 80m long, weighs over 6,350 kilograms and docks at the island's West Dock. Once you put your wheels on dry land, locate the tourist information booth, just north of the ferry dock in the municipal office (summer only), and stock up on information. Then stop by the Pelee Island Heritage Centre, operated by historian Ron Tiessen, located across from the ferry dock. If you are looking for a more formal island bicycle tour, it can be booked here. For more detailed historical information while cycling on the island, pick up a copy of *A Bicycle Guide to Pelee Island*, available at the Heritage Centre and elsewhere on the island.

By cycling the island in a clockwise direction, you will finish the day at the Pelee Island Winery Pavilion and Vineyards. The winery is one of only three "Designated Viticultural Areas" in Ontario, and it boasts over 200ha of vines.

Several of the island's sights are difficult to get to and not so easy to find. One that is not to be missed is the Vin Villa ruins. It can be found through a grove of trees to the left of where Sheridan Point Rd swings right and turns into North Shore Dr. Cycle through the natural gateway of overgrown trees, ride a few metres down the trail (which is, in fact, a private driveway; leave your bicycle by the road) and look to the left. Vin Villa was the home of the Thaddeus Smith family, which had a wine cellar built 3.5m into solid rock. Today not much is left of the estate; some of the walls have collapsed and those that are still standing are held together by creeping vines. Be careful as you explore, as there is an open hole in the middle of the ruins that drops down into the old wine cellar. It is prohibited to enter the building. At the end of the driveway, Huldah's Rock rises out of the water.

As you continue your ride around the island on North Shore Rd, you'll see an empty field just opposite the Calvary Anglican Church. On the other side of the field is the lake, but note that the beach here is private. (Those who feel the need for a swim should instead head to the East Park Campground, Sunset Beach on the west side of the island, Lighthouse Point, Fish Point or Brown's Point on the east side.)

The second sight on the island that is not to be missed is a short distance down the road from Scudder Dock. While at the dock, take the time to ride your bicycle out onto the pier. Take a look around the old grain elevator, but be careful to avoid stepping on the remains of fileted fish. From the marina, follow Harris Garno Rd over to Lighthouse Dr. Turn [L] and cycle north along the road, which travels through Lake Henry Marsh.

The wetlands are filled with many wonderful sights, including hundreds of turtles sunning themselves on logs and numerous water snakes. Leave your bicycle at the top of the trail.

Riding south along the island's East Shore Rd, you will notice that all of the homes have been built on pillars that protect them from Lake Erie's winter storms, known as Northeasters. Also along the east side of the island, a few kilometres north of the Gla-

cial Grooves, are the warm sands of the island's public beach.

The day will pass quickly as you zigzag across Pelee Island. Remember to pack extra water as East Shore Rd is long and water is scarce. If you happen to run out, however, the locals will be glad to help out. Make sure to leave yourself enough time to hike some of the trails in the Fish Point Nature Reserve before finishing off the day over a glass of fine wine and a "self-cooked" meal at the Pelee Island Winery.

Practical Information

Population:
275 permanent residents, 1,500 in the summer

 Tourist Information

Township of Pelee
1045 West Shore Rd, Pelee Island, ON N0R 1M0
☎*(519) 724-2931*
www.pelee.com

Ferry Information:

Owen Sound Transportation Co. (Ontario Northland), Pelee Island Transportation Co.
1060 West Shore Rd, Pelee Island, ON N0R 1M0
☎*(519) 724-2115 or 800-661-2220*
www.pelee.org/getthereblend.htm

 Bicycle Shops

Dixie Lawn & Cycle
27 Erie St N, Leamington, ON N8H 2Z2
☎*(519) 326-4572*

Special Sights and Events

Relight the Lighthouse Annual Dinner and Auction, Pelee Paddler Canoe and Kayaking, Pelee Island summer theatre, nature bike hikes, Sportsmen's Annual Dinner and Auction, Pelee Island Self-Guided Cyclist Tour, Canada Day celebrations, Monarch and other butterfly migrations, spring and fall annual bird migrations

 Accommodations

Cottages/Inns/B&B

2. Sarnia Circle Tour: Bluewater Discovery

A wonderful ride that combines Sarnia's city streets, industry and extensive park system with the back roads and villages of the Oil Heritage District. It is here that North America's first commercial oil well was discovered and the world's first oil company, the International Mining and Manufacturing Company, had its beginnings.

Return Distance:
115km

No. of recommend legs:
2

Level of Difficulty:
🚲🚲

Surface:
City streets, paved greenways, highways, paved country back roads

Villages/Town/Cities:
Reece's Corners, Wyoming, Petrolia, Oil Springs, Mooretown, Corunna

Local Highlights:
St. Clair River Waterfront and Park System, Walpole Island, Baker Environmental Science Centre, Dow Great Lake Models, Lawrence House, The Petrolia Discovery Oil Museum of Canada, Oil Springs Oil Fields, Victoria Playhouse, Uncle Tom's Cabin, Rock Glen Falls, Rotary Nature Trail-Grand Bend

Recommend Bicycles:
Touring/Hybrid/Mountain

How to get there:
Take Hwy 402, which leads to exit 40B, to Point Edward and downtown Sarnia. A short drive eventually merges onto Front St. Turn [R] onto Front St, cross Exmouth and continue along Front St to Centennial Park; a parking area is located on your right. The parking lot can be used for day parking, but other arrangements should be made if the trip is going to be completed in two days.

What is now the city of **Sarnia** was referred to by the Chippewa First Nation as "The Rapids" in 1831. Extensive hardwood forests and proximity to the St. Clair River helped create an international trade in lumber, which led to the building of sawmills and secondary industries like shipbuilding, fishing and agriculture. In 1836, settlers voted in a referendum to change the village's name to "Port Sarnia," which was shortened to the Celtic name of "Sarnia" in 1855. The town continued to grow with the arrival of the Great Western Railway, the nearby commercial oil fields at

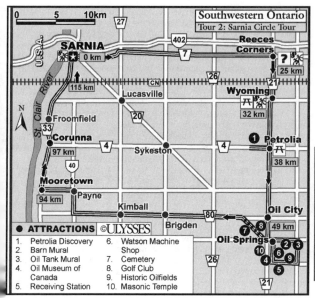

Oils Springs and the completion of the St. Clair River Railway tunnel in 1891. Today, Sarnia is home to Canada's largest complex of petrochemical plants and oil refineries and is connected to the United States by the dual-span Blue Water Bridge at Port Huron, Michigan.

Itinerary:

Before setting out, take some time to explore the area. Look for a picturesque little marina hugging the St. Clair River and Sarnia's chemical valley in the distance. Extending south of the city for approximately 32km, the chemical valley has an impressive fairyland appearance at night with its thousands of twinkling lights. Exit the parking lot by turning [R] into Front St. Watch for the railway tracks. At London Rd turn [R] at the lights, then climb the slight incline to the traffic lights at

Christina St N. Continue along London Rd past the impressive steeple of Our Lady of Mercy Catholic Church. Further along on your right is the St. Joseph Health Centre. London Rd has four lanes and can be quite busy during rush hour until you pass the Murphy Rd Shopping District.

At Lambton College the road curves to the left. Turn [R] at the lights onto old Hwy 27, now Lambton Rd 22/London Rd. Cycle under Hwy 40, cross Wawanosh Creek and ride past Bethel Pentecostal Church. London Rd again becomes two lanes and has an excellent cycling lane past the creative display of man and his buggy, at Blackwell Side Rd.

The route becomes easy as you pass the windmill at Mandaumin Rd and the old headstones of the

Oban Church Memorial Cemetery. Look for the old rusty steam engine at the Jackson Farm. There is a flashing light at **Reece's Corners** and a floating airplane at the Skyview Restaurant and Airport. At Reece's Corners, to the left, is a unique tourist information office, which is a scale reproduction of an 1870 "Canadian Drilling Rig." These rigs were used by local drillers in over 87 countries to discover many prosperous oil fields. At the stoplight, turn [R] onto Oil Heritage Rd/Lambton Rd 21 and continue towards Wyoming.

Wyoming, whose name means "great plain", was founded around 1856 by a group of Pennsylvania settlers. Although oil was never found here, the village acted as a railway shipping centre for oil from Petrolia and Oil Springs in prosperous times. Notice the wooden church spire of Holy Rosary Catholic church on your right. At 528 Broadway/Lambton 21, a local bicycle enthusiast sells rebuilt bikes, and may be of help if you have mechanical problems. Turn [L] at Erie St, following it to a quaint little park that is a good spot for a morning break. In the downtown area, you will find all the amenities of home, including a restaurant and variety store.

Leaving Wyoming behind, cross two sets of railway tracks and Bear Creek No.3, then climb a long grade to arrive at Petrolia. At the flashing light, turn [R] onto Lambton Rd 4/Petrolia St and cycle towards Petrolia Discovery and downtown Petrolia. Bridgeview Park is located on both sides of the road after Bear Creek. The park is an excellent lunch stop. Turn [R] following the entrance road to the Petrolia Discovery grounds. There is a small admission charge to enjoy this tribute to early oil pioneers but it is well worth the visit. Take some time to explore the village of **Petrolia**, ride around its streets, which feature some fascinating architecture, and learn some interesting tidbits of information about the town's incredibly prosperous era.

Resume your journey by retracing your steps to the flashing light at Lambton Rd 21. Turn [R] towards **Oil Springs**. After crossing Bear Creek No. 2, keep your eyes open as you ride pass Rockabye Line. Though its name is impressive, Oil City played a less than impressive role in the development of the region's petroleum industry. This area was continuously bought and sold by speculators in hopes that they could capitalize on the anticipated boom in nearby Oil Springs.

Crossing Lambton Rd 80/Courtright Rd, turn [L] onto Oil Springs' Main St and cycle past a number of commercial buildings, including a white frame building that was formerly the home of the *Oil Springs Chronicle*, Lambton County's first daily newspaper, on the northeast corner of Oil Springs' Line and Kelly. Turn [R], heading south onto Kelly Rd, past Watson's Machine Shop, which was built in 1880 by the Oil Spring Supply Company and used by the company founders to repair and build tools and machinery for the local oilmen. One of Anderson and Murray's significant contributions to the oil industry was the development of a gas-powered engine for oil pumps that made oil production very efficient. The engines ran on natural gas, a by-product of the oil wells. The countryside around the Oil Museum of Canada is littered with abandoned shacks and the rusting steel of discarded oil rigs.

The Oil Museum of Canada, a National Historic Site, is located where James Miller Williams dug the first commercial oil well in 1858. The museum preserves and glamourizes a past that must have been very exciting; there are many open-air exhibits, including a few of the original oil-field drilling rigs and buildings. Continue south and turn [L] onto Gum Bed Rd, where you will see the last remaining oil receiving station in Ontario to your right. As you cycle along, notice the in-ground holding tanks cribbed with logs, and a short distance ahead wooden jerker rods that creak as they sway back and forth, pumping oil.

Turn [L] at the Gypsie Flats, where you will cycle back in time to the 19th century. Jerker lines, pump jacks and frame buildings appear much as they did over 100 years ago. To your left are the salt flats and the Hugh Nixon Shaw "gusher." Just past the bridge on your right is the "Oil Tank Mural" painted in 1983 to commemorate the 125th anniversary of James Miller Williams's commercial oil discovery. Turn [L] onto Oil Springs' Line at the next stop sign. At Duryee St, turn [L] and look for the "Barn Mural" painted on the Fairbank barn. As you continue along Oil Springs' Line towards Lambton Rd 21, the remaining historic buildings are particularly precious, as a fire levelled most of the town after the oil boom.

Cross Lambton Rd 21, then turn [R] onto the hard-packed gravel surface of S Plank Rd. At Lambton Rd 80 (asphalt) turn [L]; when

you pass the Valmack Farm's windmill, the village of Brigden and its bustling downtown core are only 8km away. Once you arrive at the flashing light on Lambton 31/Kimble Rd, you can see the refinery smoke stacks of chemical valley in the distance.

Turning [R] onto Hwy 40, proceed to the lights and turn [L] onto the Moore Line. The road is lined with lilac trees and is a pure joy to ride in early summer. Pass the Moore Union Cemetery and the local golf course, then keep the **Mooretown** Museum complex to your right as you turn [R] onto Emily St and [R] again onto the well-paved bike path along the St. Clair Pkwy. When passing through **Corunna** take some time to walk around the inspiring St. Joseph's Church, built in 1862. There are a lot of good places to take a break along the parkway. Just north of town, the towers of the Shell Oil refinery climb skyward. Past the Shell Oil buildings, look for the Froome and Field Talford historic plaque and the "Welcome to Amjiwnaang" Chippewas of Sarnia First Nation sign.

Follow the parkway into the old chemical valley as it leaves the St. Clair River behind. On both sides of the road are the Dow Chemical facilities, and on your right the familiar Bayer Cross. At this point the parkway turns into Vidal St. Upon crossing the second bridge, move to the left, preparing to make a [L] at the lights onto Confederation St. Proceed to the [T] intersection at Christina, cross the street and join the bike path to the right of Imperial Oil. The path exits onto Johnson St; turn [L] here and follow the road as it changes to Front St S. At the Ferry Dock Hill Rd street lights turn [L], proceed down a steep hill, cross the tracks and turn [R] onto the St Clair Riverbank trail.

The St. Clair River continues to play a vital role in the development of petroleum and chemical industries. At one time, oil was barrelled in Oil Springs and floated down Bear Creek and the Sydenham River to ensure quick delivery, avoiding the difficult land routing. Ships would pick up the barrels and disperse them to ports on the Great Lakes and England. In 1899, barges began to transport crude oil to Ohio, following the construction of the Imperial Oil Refinery.

As you leave the oil refineries and the chemical valley behind, Sarnia's downtown core will be on your right. You are in for a refreshing ride along the waterfront, before the pathway winds its way through numerous small parks that offer a historic perspective on the city through information and memorial plaques.

Practical Information

Population:
Sarnia: 73,000
Petrolia: 5,000
Oil Springs: 775
Mooretown: 410

 Tourist Information

Sarnia

Tourism Sarnia/Lambton
556 N Christina St, Sarnia, ON
N7T 5W6
☎ *(519) 336-3232 or 800-265-0316*
www.tourism-sarnia-lambton.com

Petrolia

Town of Petrolia
Box 1270, ON N0N 1R0
☎ *(519) 882-2350 or 800-717-7694*
http://town.petrolia.on.ca

 Bicycle Shops

Sarnia

The Bicycle Shop
410 Front St N, ON N7T 5S9
☎ *(519) 344-0515*

Centre Ice Sports & Cycle
200 Vidal St N, ON N7T 5Y1
☎ *(519) 337-4545*

 Special Sights and Events

Sarnia

Imperial Oil Centre for the Performing Arts, Discovery House Museum, Uncle Tom's Cabin Historic Site, Duc d'Orleans Cruise Ship, Return of the Swans, Kettle Point Concretions, Arkona Blossom Weekend, Envirofest, Corunna Firefighter's Field Days, Chippewas of Sarnia Pow Wow, Canada Day celebrations, Riverfest, Walpole Island Pow Wow, Highland Games, Air Show Sarnia, Mackinac Boat Race, Snowfest, Easter in the Park, Sarnia Shrine Circus, Dragon Boat Festival

Petrolia

The Petrolia Discovery, The Oil Museum of Canada, Victoria Playhouse Theatre, Petrolia Discovery Auto Show, Canada Day Celebrations, Petrolia Boom Days, Petrolia & Enniskillen Fall Fair, Pumpkin Fest, Rodeo

Oil Springs

Oil Museum of Canada, Spring Kite Fly, Oil Patch Quilt Show, Canada Day Celebrations

Mooretown

Mooretown Strawberry Social, Moore Museum

 Accommodations

Sarnia

Hotels/Motels/B&B/Camping

Petrolia

Motel/B&B/Camping

 Market Days

Sarnia

Farmer's Markets Wednesday and Saturday Tour Suggestions: Strong cyclists can complete in one day. For a shorter excursion, cycle to Petrolia, returning to Sarnia via Cty Rd 4 and 20. Overnight in the Petrolia area where bed and breakfasts and camping are available.

3. Lake Erie's North Shore: Woodstock, Port Dover and Tillsonburg

Beginning in Woodstock, this tour follows the historic Stage Rd into Ontario's tobacco country and completes the first leg in the rural community of Simcoe. Leg two joins the Lynn Valley Greenway and follows it into the fishing village of Port Dover. As the day progresses, the back roads and villages visited along the shores of Lake Erie will be an adventure you'll never forget. The final leg starts off in the marshes of the Long Point Spit and heads north towards Tillsonburg. The highlight of the ride will be cycling on a long-forgotten rail bed into the village of Springford.

Return Distance:
210km (64km, 56km, 89km)

No. of recommended legs:
3

Level of Difficulty:

Surface:
Asphalt, hard-packed gravel, crushed-gravel rail bed

Villages/Towns/Cities:
Woodstock, Oxford Centre, Vanessa, Simcoe, Port Dover, Port Ryerse, Turkey Point, Long Point, Port Rowan, Port Royal, Glen Meyer, Tillsonburg, Springford, Holbrook, Curries

Local Highlights:
Woodstock Little Theatre, Beachville Museum, Woodstock Museum, Ross Butler Studio, Woodstock Art Gallery, Jakeman's Sugar Bush, Dairy Capital Princess, Woodstock Cycling Trails, Simcoe Fall Fair, Port Dover Harbour Museum, Lighthouse Theatre, Nanticoke Thermal Electric Generating Station, Port Ryerse Bakery, Hay Creek Conservation Area, St. Williams Forestry Station, Backus Heritage Conservation Area and cycling trails, Bluevale Witches Gate, Long Point Marsh, Long Point Bird Observatory, Long Point Provincial Park, Big

Creek Wildlife Area, Turkey Point Beach, Coyle's Factory, Annandale House, Tillsonburg's Farmer's Market, Great Western Railway Station, Turkey Point Provincial Park and cycling trails, Normandale Fish Hatchery, McMillen's Iris Gardens, Norwich Historical Archives, Harvard Airplane Association

Recommended Bicycles:
Hybrid/Mountain/Touring

Tour Suggestions:
A nice three-day outing for beginners, as the rides are leisurely. Meals can be obtained as you go since the tour passes through a number of larger centres.

How to get there:
Woodstock has three exits off Hwy 401. It can be reached from the north and south by following Hwy 59 and from the east and west by following Hwy 401. The tour begins at the lower parking lot of the Woodstock Quality Inn, which is at the junction of Hwy 401 and Hwy 59. Parking arrangements can be made with the hotel's management.

Nicknamed the "City Beautiful," **Woodstock** is a unique blend of green areas, traditional buildings and modern facilities. In every corner of the city, private and public buildings have been preserved. Founded by Admiral Henry Vansittart and developed by Captain Andrew Drew, Woodstock was known by many different names over time, like most cities in the province. The first was "Town Plot," which was quickly followed by "Oxford" and "Brighton." In 1852, the city was named Woodstock after a village in Oxfordshire, England. The first church, St. Paul's Anglican Church, was built in 1838 and still stands at the corner of Dundas and Huron Sts.

One of the city's more memorable characters was Thomas "Carbide" Wilson, who in 1892 discovered a commercial process for producing calcium carbide, a chemical compound used in the manufacturing of acetylene gas. This invention had different applications. In fact, it was used to produce a bicycle light that allowed riders of the big-wheeled penny farthings to travel at night.

The area around Woodstock, Oxford County, is largely agricultural, and Woodstock has been known as the Dairy Capital of Canada for the past 50 years.

Itinerary:
Leg 1
(Woodstock to Simcoe, 64km)

Starting at the corner of Hwy 59 and Juliana Dr in Woodstock, turn [R] onto Hwy 59 and follow it south to Old Stage Rd. At the Hillview Farms composting station, turn [L] onto Old Stage Rd. Sometimes known as Thames River Rd, it was first used by Aboriginal people who called it the Detroit Path. During the War of 1812, the road was used by both British and American armies. There's even a chest of stolen payroll gold still hidden somewhere along this section of the road!

Cycling east on this gravel road that was once used by stagecoaches, you will come to the village of **Oxford Centre**. Past the village to the south, look at the rough ground to the right. This area has been identified as the site of an Aboriginal encampment. One kilometre further down the road, you will find the spot where

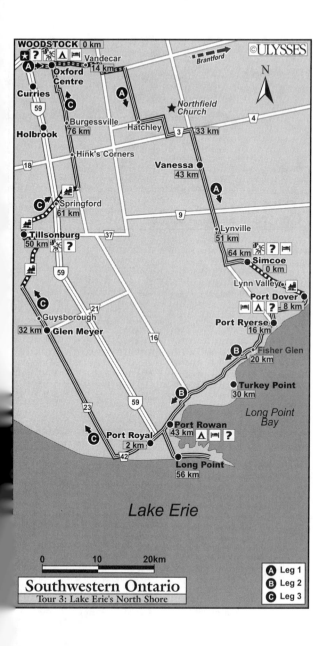

WOODSTOCK 0 km
Vandecar
14 km
Oxford Centre
Curries
59
Holbrook
Burgessville
76 km
Hink's Corners
Vanessa
43 km
Springford
61 km
Tillsonburg
50 km
59
21
Guysborough
32 km ● Glen Meyer
23
Port Royal
2 km
42

©ULYSSES
N
Brantford
Northfield Church
4
Hatchley
3   33 km
9
Lynville
51 km
64 km
Simcoe
0 km
Lynn Valley
Port Dover
8 km
Port Ryerse
16 km
Fisher Glen
20 km
Turkey Point
30 km
Long Point Bay
Port Rowan
43 km
Long Point
56 km

18
37
16

Lake Erie

0   10   20km

Southwestern Ontario
Tour 3: Lake Erie's North Shore

A Leg 1
B Leg 2
C Leg 3

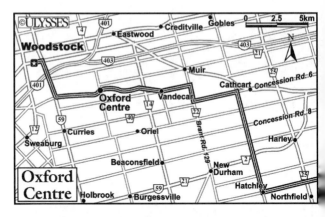

several British Army troops set up camp during the War of 1812. Just before reaching Cty Rd 14 you will come across a historic plaque in front of the school, on your left. The infamous Elizabeth Bigley, or "Gold Brick Cassie" as she was better known, lived near here. She had the distinction of obtaining more money (about $1.5 million) by fraud and deceit then anyone else in the world up until of the Great Train Robbery in England.

Continue riding and cross Cty Rd 14. At Brant Rd 129, turn [R], where you will return to an asphalt surface. Cycle to a [L] turn onto another gravel road known as Sixth Concession Rd. Riding past the large Shur-Gain Research Complex at the West 1/4 Town Line, turn [R] and head to Harley Rd/ Brant Cty Rd 2. At the [T] intersection, turn [L] and pedal a short distance, then make a [R] turn onto West Quarter Town Line and enjoy an easy ride to Hatchley Rd. Turn [L] and cycle through a small wetland area before stopping at Northfield Church for a midday break.

At Brant Cty Rd 24, turn [R] and ride south to Norwich Rd/Brant Cty Rd 3. Turn [R] and at the East Quarter Town Line, make a [L] turn. The landscape here is very flat and the soil is quite sandy. At one time, thousands of acres in Ontario's "Golden Garden" were devoted to producing half of Canada's flue-cured tobacco crop. Today, with the continuing decline in tobacco demand, farmers have been turning to alternatives like ginseng and peanuts.

If you need to refill a water bottle stop at the general store in **Vanessa**; the proprietor will be more than happy to help you. Back in the late 1800s, a Methodist church called Bethany stood at Vanessa's present location. Mills were built nearby, and soon the town grew large enough to have a post office. Unable to choose a name, the residents left the decision to Henry Bartholomew, the local postmaster. In 1876, Bartholomew made his choice and Vanessa came into being. Bartholomew stayed in Vanessa for 57 years, becoming one of Canada's oldest postmasters.

The East Quarter Town Line meets Cty Rd 4 in the middle of a bend; turn [R] and then [L] onto West Quarter Town Line. Enjoy this flat stretch of blacktop as you ride further into the heart of tobacco country and Norfolk County. Along this section of road, ginseng farms have become quite common and today almost outnumber tobacco farms. They can be identified thanks to thousands of posts set about 1.8m apart and covered with a roof of slats. Ginseng is a much-sought-after commodity in East Asian and North American health-food outlets. It is used as a tonic and cure-all.

Riding past 14th St W and over the Canadian National Railway tracks, signal and make a [L] turn when you reach Hwy 3/Queensway St. Simcoe is only a short distance away. At Hwy 24/ Norfolk St turn [R] and ride along the maple-lined streets of downtown Simcoe.

Located at the headwaters of the Lynn River, **Simcoe** was originally known as Bird Town and celebrated its 100th anniversary in 1978. The town quickly became a focal point for railway development in the late 1800s because of its abundance of agricultural products. Called the "People Place," Simcoe is best known for its annual Christmas "Festival of Lights," which features more than 0 colourful displays.

eg 2
Simcoe to Long Point, 56km)

ide south towards Lake Erie on Hwy 24 past South St (hospital n corner), and turn [L] onto Woodhouse St. At Owen St, turn R] and follow it to the Lynn alley Trail in Memorial Park.

Turn [L] onto this former rail line, which was constructed along a pioneer river trail in 1873 and follows the twisting right of ways along the banks of the Lynn River to Port Dover.

Abandoned in 1988, the rail corridor was purchased as a possible route for future water and sewer lines. That same year, the Lynn Valley Trail Association was formed, and soon the greenway was developed into a recreational corridor. The rail line was originally the Port Dover and Lake Huron Railway. It began in Stratford and ran through Tavistock, Hickson, Woodstock, Burgessville, Norwich, Simcoe, Lynn Valley and finally completed its run in Port Dover. Originally a main line, it ultimately became a feeder line to the Wellington, Grey and Bruce, as well as the Grand Trunk lines.

The rail-trail exits into **Port Dover** at the Ivey Flowers Mill, which was founded in 1908 and is one of Canada's oldest and largest growers of roses. Take some time to explore this historic fishing port, which at one time was the largest freshwater fishery in the world. Today, more than 30 tugs still continue to ply their trade from here. Before leaving Port Dover, cycle out onto the pier and then browse the many nearby lakefront boutiques. To continue along the lakeshore, head north cycling back through town on Hwy 24. Turn [L] onto Nelson St, which eventually turns into Radical Rd.

Lake Erie will now be on your left. At Port Ryerse Rd turn [L], and ride past the Hay Creek Conservation area. Continue following the road as it heads for the blue waters of Lake Erie. The road descends into Port Ryerse. To continue along the lake, turn [R] onto Front Rd.

As this leg is not very long, take the time to stop and sample the freshly baked goods at the Port Ryerse General Store. The store is also famous for an event that occurred many years ago and is explained by the interesting postcard article tacked up inside the store. **Port Ryerse** was discovered by Colonel Samuel Ryerse in the fall of 1795. As he was exploring Lake Erie, he came to a place where a beautiful stream flowed into the lake, in front of a steep hill. Upon landing, he climbed the hill and declared; "Here is where I will settle and on this place where I stand, I will be buried." He died in 1812 and was buried on the spot he had designated. Before leaving Port Ryerse, visit the Anglican Memorial Church and cemetery, at the top of the hill, to the left of the general store. Built in 1870, the church is an excellent example of board and batten architecture.

Follow Front Rd as it passes the Norfolk Conservation Park (historic plaque) and a Christian retreat. At the Fisher Glen Rd [T] intersection, signal and make a [L] turn, and enjoy the first of two great downhill rides on this leg. At the bottom of the hill, Fisher Glen Rd swings sharply to the right and then climbs to Normandale Rd. Turn [L] and ride towards **Normandale**. Make sure to stop at the old cemetery where many Lake Erie ship captains have been buried. The road descends as it arrives in Normandale. At the bottom of the hill, turn [R] at the stop sign onto Main St (Lakeshore Rd) and ride uphill to the Turkey Point Golf Club turnoff. Turn [L] at the top of the hill onto Conces-

sion Rd A/Main St and follow it past the golf course and the commemorative stone cairn. This area was originally known as the town of Charlotteville; Fort Norfolk was located here. This former capital of the Western District of Upper Canada is now a ghost town. The thrilling downhill to the lake will leave your brakes smoking at the bottom!

At the lake, turn [R] onto Cedar St and ride past the sandy public beaches of **Turkey Point**. Thousands of people flock here during the summer months, as this beach has one of the safest swimming areas on the shores of Lake Erie. Cycling to Regional Rd 10, turn [R] and ride uphill. At the top of the hill, turn [L] onto Lakeshore Rd/Front Rd/the Talbot Trail. The view from the bluffs is simply stunning. Cycle past the fish hatchery; then upon reaching Cty Rd 16, turn [L] and then [R] and continue riding along Lakeshore Rd/Front Rd towards Port Rowan. While in St. Williams, take a few minutes to ride a short distance north on Cty Rd 16 to see the octagonal bell tower at the United Church. A little further north is the St. Williams Forestry Station.

Front Rd/Haldimand-Norfolk Rd 42 winds its way through the countryside and eventually straightens out before passing through the village of **Port Rowan** (formally Dutcher's Corners). At the T-intersection on Main St, turn [L] and follow Lakeshore Rd to Hwy 59. Turn [L] and ride out onto the spit of **Long Point**. (Or turn right and cycle out to the Backus Mills Conservation Area and cycling trails.) Known as "the ship killer," the spit has claimed more than 200 vessels over the years. You could spend days exploring this wetland. When walking through the marsh, wear a long-sleeved shirt and long pants as deer in the area carry a tick that may cause Lyme disease. Three lighthouses have had to be built over the years because the sand spit is constantly shifting. Today, the area has developed into one of the country's best-run nature preserves thanks to the Long Point Company, which is held in high regard for its conservation practices.

Leg 3
(Long Point to Woodstock, 89km)

Starting at the flashing light at the junction of Hwy 59 and Lakeshore/Haldimand-Norfolk Rd 42, cycle west along the lake through the village of **Port Royal**, which was named after its sister village in Nova Scotia. Cross Big Creek, turn [R] onto Haldimand-Norfolk Rd 23, and ride for 1km on hard-packed gravel. Almost 14km later, after cycling through the village of **Glen Meyer**, ride across Regional Rd 38 onto Regional Rd 28. This road is gravel, and the next section is a fun ride. At the [T] intersection at the bottom of the hill, turn [R] and pedal across Otter Creek. Turn [L] at the next [T] intersection and follow the gravel road as it joins the blacktop once again at the top of the hill. Continue straight and swing right onto the [RB] a short distance ahead.

Be careful as you ride the rail bed, as there will be a number of road crossings before you reach Tillson-burg. Turn [R] at Rokeby Sideroad (the rail bed ahead

still has the ties in) and then turn [L] onto Bell Mill Sideroad and ride to Simcoe St. Turn [L] and follow Simcoe St to the traffic lights at Tillson Ave. Make a [R] turn and cycle uphill, going past Annandale House to North St, several kilometres ahead. Cross North St and follow Cranberry Rd for a short distance. At the wishing well, turn [R] onto the abandoned Brantford-Norfolk & Port Burwell Railway line.

Main street in **Tillsonburg** has an interesting characteristic: Riding straight through the lights at Tillson Ave, you will join the very wide Broadway St. It was designed to accommodate a team of oxen when they made a U-turn.

Continue along the rail bed; as you pass a tract of recently planted pine trees, look for a number of beehives hidden among the trees on the right. Just after riding by Camp Two-moondy, the rail-trail exits into the Springford Ball Park. Cross Cty Rd 19 and Cty Rd 13, and continue riding past some silos to Conc Rd 7. Turn [R] and pedal this gravel road to Middletown Line. Make a [L] turn onto Middletown Line and enjoy a leisurely ride through the town of **Burgessville** and back through the village of Oxford Centre. At the first [T] intersection in Oxford Centre, turn [R] and then bear [L] at the next road. Riding uphill to Patullo Ridge, turn [L] and enjoy the ride past the local fish and game club, to Hwy 59. Turn [R] onto Norwich Ave/Hwy 59, and ride across the Hwy 401 bridge, finishing Leg 3 where you began the first leg of the trip.

Practical Information

Population:
Woodstock: 33,000
Simcoe: 15,500
Port Dover: 5,000
Port Rowan (Long Point area):
800
Tillsonburg: 14,000

 Tourist Information

Woodstock

Oxford County Tourist Association
78 Light St, Woodstock, ON N4S 6H1
☎ *(519) 539-0015 ext 475*
www.tourismoxford.ca

Simcoe

Simcoe and District Chamber of Commerce
76 Kent St S, Simcoe, ON N3Y 2Y1
☎ *(519) 426-5867*
www.country.simcoe.on.ca/tourism

Port Dover

Port Dover Board of Trade
Box 239, 19 Market St W, Port Dover, ON N0A 1N0
☎ *(519) 583-1314*
www.portdover.ca

Port Rowan

Backus Heritage Conservation Area
RR 1, Port Rowan, ON N0E 1M0
☎ *(519) 586-2201 or 877-990-9932*
www.lprca.on.ca

Long Point Country Chamber of Commerce
PO Box 357, Port Rowan, ON N0E 1M0
☎ *866-281-1416*
www.portrowan-longpoint.org

Tillsonburg

Tillsonburg Chamber of Commerce
2 Library Ln, Tillsonburg, ON N4G 4S7
☎ *(519) 842-5571*
www.ocl.net/chamber

 Bicycle Shops

Woodstock

Pedal Power Bikes and Boards
590 Dundas St, Woodstock, ON N4S 1C8
☎ *(519) 539-3681*

Oxford Source for Sports
11 Riddell St, Woodstock, ON N4S 1C8
☎ *(519) 537-7801*

Simcoe

McArthur Source for Sports
25 Sydenham St, Simcoe, ON N3Y 1R6
☎ *(519) 426-5190*

Harrington Sports
31 Norfolk St N, Simcoe, ON N3Y 3N6
☎ *(519) 426-0614*

Independent Bikes & Boards
44 Robinson St, Simcoe, ON N3Y 1W6
☎ *(519) 426-9998*

Port Dover

Stoney's Hardware
320 Main St, Port Dover, ON N0A 1N0
☎ *(519) 583-0730*

Tillsonburg

Oxford Source For Sports
102-B Tillson Ave, Tillsonburg, ON N4G 3A4
☎ *(519) 688-3224*

Special Sights and Events

Woodstock

Ontario Toy Show, Woodstock Wood Show, Canadian Farm Expo, Canterbury Folk Festival Canada Day, Dairy Capital Mountain Bike Race, Embro Highland Games

Simcoe

Norfolk County Fair and Horse Show, Simcoe Friendship Festival, Christmas Panorama

Port Dover

Perch Derby, FishFest, Light- house Festival Theatre, Summer Festival, Dragonboat Festival, ChristmasFest, Friday the Thir- teenth

Port Rowan and Long Point

Bayfest, Nature Hikes and Events, War of 1812 Re-enactment, Rib Fest, Festival by the Bay, fishing derbies

Tillsonburg

Canada Day, Kinsmen Hobby and Recreation Show, Lions Club Car Show, Down Home Coun- try Christmas

 Accommodations

Woodstock

Hotel/Motel/B&B/Camping

Simcoe

Hotel/Motel/B&B

Port Dover

Inns/Cottages/B&B/Camping

Port Rowan

Motel/Cottages/B&B/ Camping

 Off-Road Cycling

Woodstock and Port Rowan

Yes; refer to "Off-Road Cycling" at the end of this chapter.

 Market Days

Woodstock

Saturdays, year-round

Simcoe

Thursdays at fairgrounds, year round

Port Dover

Saturdays, year-round

Tillsonburg

Saturdays, early spring to late fall

4. Shakespeare's Stonetown: Stratford and St. Marys

This ride is an excellent afternoon excursion that leaves you plenty of time to enjoy an evening show at the Stratford Festival. Beginning along the banks of the Avon River, the tour quickly leaves Stratford behind and follows

Harmony Rd through the lush rolling farmlands of Perth County. It passes through the town of St. Marys, with its many architecturally superb stone buildings, before heading out of town on the former Grand Trunk Railway. The return route follows another peaceful country road through the hamlet of Avondale before joining the Stratford riverbank trail on its loop around Lake Victoria.

Return Distance:
65km

No. of recommended legs:
1

Level of Difficulty:

Surface:
Asphalt, some gravel and several kilometres of hard-packed rail bed

Villages/Towns/Cities:
Stratford, Harmony, St. Marys, Avonton

Local Highlights:
Stratford Festival Theatre, Gallery Stratford, Stratford Perth Museum, St. Marys Museum, Canadian Baseball Hall of Fame, St. Marys Quarry, Historic Shakespeare, The Grand Trunk Railway Trail

Bicycle Type:
Touring/Hybrid/Mountain

Tour Suggestion:
Before setting out, ride through the older residential streets near the river and in the downtown core. It's a great way to become familiar with Stratford and its heritage homes. Also, pack a picnic lunch and enjoy it along the

banks of the Thames River when visiting St. Marys.

How to get there:
Stratford can be reached from the west by following
Hwys 402, 81, 19 and 7. From the south, take Hwy 401 to Cty Rd 6, and from the east follow the Queen Elizabeth Way to Hwys 403, 6, 401 and 8. From the north, follow Hwy 19. This tour starts at the William Allman Arena located on Lakeside Dr at Nile St, two blocks north of Ontario St.

Stratford was originally known as Little Thames named after the nearby Thames River. The first hotel was built in 1832 and called the Shakespeare Inn, in honour of the large painting of William Shakespeare that hung inside. In late 1832, the town was renamed Stratford after Shakespeare's birthplace because of the Shakespeare Inn's location, close to the Avon River. It wasn't until 1953 that the townspeople decided to capitalize on the Shakespearian connection. The first Shakespeare festival was held in a tent along the Avon River; Sir Alec Guinness played Richard III, helping to make the event a huge success. Today, the city's theatre draws well over 500,000 patrons to Stratford on the Avon each year.

Itinerary:
Turn [L] out of the parking lot onto Lakeside Dr and ride to the traffic lights at Waterloo St. Turn [L] and cycle past Ontario St, which is Stratford's main thoroughfare. Coast downhill and ride by the Church Restaurant and several other historic buildings. Veer [L] onto Downie St and pedal past the round church, but that way so the devil can't catch

Southwestern Ontario
Tour 4: Shakespeare's Stonetown

0   2.5   5km

ou in the corner! Cross Lorne Ave and begin the ride south, ending up in the village of **Harmony**.

After crossing Perth Rd 26, the road dips and then climbs a short hill before gradually descending to the next turn. At Line 20, one road north of the [T] intersection, turn [R]. Riding a short distance on gravel, cross Perth Rd 6/113 (Embro Rd). On asphalt once again, Line 20 remains fairly level as it travels past Downie School House No. 10 to a stop sign at Hwy 7.

Turn [L] onto Hwy 7 and begin riding towards St. Marys. The cycling lane is fairly wide as you continue past the St. Pauls Station turnoff and over Wildwood Lake via the Wildwood Dam and past the junction of Hwy 19. A couple of kilometres past Hwy 19, look for the remains of the old rail bed between Embro and St. Marys. For the more adventurous, the rail bed makes an interesting ride that eventually ends in downtown St. Marys.

Riding west, follow Hwy 7 over a set of railway tracks. At Perth Rd 123, turn [R] and follow

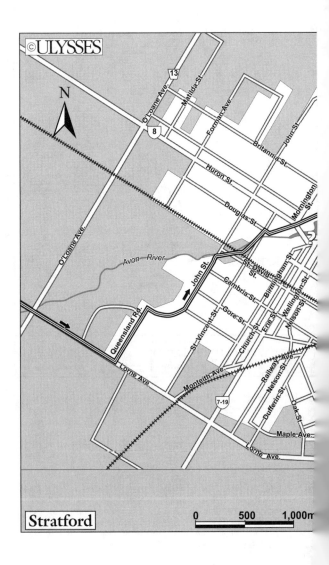

Stratford

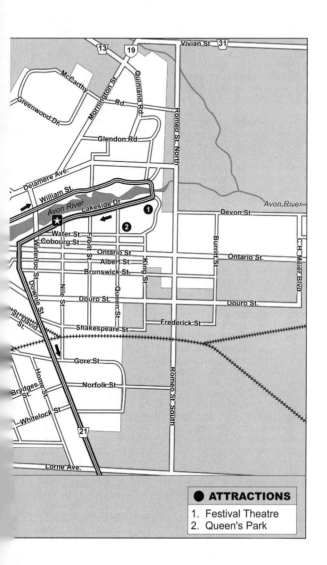

● **ATTRACTIONS**

1. Festival Theatre
2. Queen's Park

Water St as it descends into St. Marys. Turn [L] at the sports complex, just before the quarries swimming hole, Canada's largest natural spring-fed swimming pool, and join the Riverview Walkway. The walkway makes for a nice ride along the river into downtown St. Marys.

Before leaving the trail, stop to admire the view of the Thames River as it flows under one of the town's stone bridges. This is a good place to stop for a rest and a picnic lunch. The trail exits into a parking lot which joins Queen St E; take note of the Mill Wheel by the bridge on the left just before turning [R] onto Queen St.

Laura Secord's brother, Thomas Ingersoll, founded **St. Marys** in 1841. The town was initially called Little Falls after the falls that ran over the rocky ledges in the river. It was later named St. Marys in accordance with the wishes of Mrs. Thomas Mercer Jones, who donated funds to pay for the new stone schoolhouse. Its nickname, "Stonetown," comes from the many limestone buildings built here between 1850 and the early 1900s. Another feature that is unique to the city are the two stone viaducts built in the late 1880s to accommodate the railways. It took 20 double teams of horses and 170 men, both skilled and unskilled, to build the 11 stone pillars that stand more than 213m above the river. Some of Canada's most interesting figures grew up in or around St. Marys, including Sir Arthur Meighen, one of Canada's prime ministers, retailer Timothy Eaton and inventor Thomas Edison, who worked at the local railway station nearby. During Edison's time in St. Marys,

he invented an automatic device that transmitted code by the simple turn of a crank. He pawned off his job turning the crank to a friendly watchman so that he could get some sleep, and all went well until a message came to hold the train: of course, Edison failed to relay the message. Fortunately for him, the trains saw each other and stopped. He slipped away silently during the investigation and became famous for inventing the phonograph and the electric light bulb, along with 1,029 other inventions.

The return route follows Queen St E to the top of the hill. The old water tower on your left was built in 1899; it served the town until 1987. Turn around and make your way back to Church St N. Turn [R] and ride past the enormous town hall. In 1891, it was considered the most impressive municipal building in all of Canada. After crossing the bridge make a [R] turn onto Station St and follow it to the left as it becomes James St N.

An alternative route would be to turn [L] off the Riverwalk trail and cross the Thames River. Ride to Ingersoll St and turn [R], then cycle to the end of the street. Turn [R] again to join the recently completed St. Marys Grand Trunk Recreational Trail. Follow the [RB] over the new Sarnia walkway, go past the Optimist Park, and turn [L] on James St N

As the James St hill crests, you will notice several old Cadillacs on the right side of the road. The name of this county road was recently changed from Cty Rd 19 to Per Rd 130. The landscape is predominantly flat until it descends into **Avonton**. Just before turning

[R] onto Perth Rd. 32, look for the stone cairn on the left side of the road. Erected in 1929, it marks the settlement of Ballantyne, now a ghost town.

Just before passing O'Loane Ave, the road dips and then climbs to Queensland Rd. If you're interested, you can ride the single track trails of the T.J. Dolan Natural Area, which are a short distance down O'Loane Ave on the right, and eventually exit onto John St.

Turn [L] onto Queensland Rd, follow it as it swings right past Hamlet Estates and becomes John St. Just a short distance past the hospital, the street descends to the entrance of the T.J. Dolan Park, which is where you find the O'Loane Ave single track. Turn [R] onto T. J. Dolan Dr, just before the road crosses the Avon River. Cycling along the river bank, ride across St. Vincent St and reach the paved pathway. When the pathway ends, continue along the river and walk through a wooden turnstile into the Shakespearean Gardens. Directly opposite the woolen mill's tall chimney is a magnificent old maple which is now beginning to lean out over the Avon River. The garden pathway exits onto Huron St via a few stairs. Turn [L] onto Huron St and cross the Avon River. Make a [R] turn onto William St. At Waterloo St, turn [R] and, just before crossing back over the river, join the Lake Victoria recreational trail on the left side of the road. The river trail is the perfect end to a day in Perth County. It eventually exits onto Lakeside Dr, where you swing [L] and follow the road back along Lake Victoria to the Stratford Arena.

Practical Information

Population:
Stratford: 29,000
St. Marys: 6,300

 Tourist Information

Stratford

Tourism Stratford
PO Box 818, 47 Downie St, Stratford, ON
N5A 1W7
☎ *(519) 271-5140 or 800-561-7926*
www.city.stratford.on.ca

St. Marys

Town of St. Marys Tourist Bureau
PO Box 218, 5 James St N, St. Marys, ON
N4X 1A9
☎ *(519) 284-3500*
www.townofstmarys.com

 Bicycle Shops

Stratford

Wheel Goods
29 Ontario St, Stratford, ON N5A 3G7
☎ *(519) 273-2001*

St. Marys

Dunnys Source for Sports
154 Queen St E, St. Marys, ON N4X 1B3
☎ *(519) 284-1446*

Stonetown Cycle Shop
199 Tracy St, St. Marys, ON
☎ *(519) 284-9985*

Southwestern Ontario

Special Sights and Events

Stratford

Annual Swan Release and Festival, Under the Covers & Quilt Festival, Startford Book Festival, Stratford Fall Fair, Canada Day, Summer Psychic Fair, Dragon Boat Festival and Races, Harvest Day Tours, Stratford Festival Table Talk, HMS Razzamajazz, Jazz at the Cenotaph, Festival Costume Warehouse Tours, Art in the Park, Winterfest, Shakespearean Gardens, Stratford Festival Theatre, Summer Music Festival, DrumFest, Stratford Jazz Festival, Western Ontario Antique Show and Sale

St. Marys

Walkways and bicycle paths, Riverview Walkway and Grand Trunk Trail, St. Marys Quarry, Victoria Day Open House at Museum, Horticultural Society Plant Fair, Canada Day, Stonetown Heritage Festival, St. Marys Fair, Train Market and Open House, Quilt Show, Crafty Christmas, Santa Claus Parade, Canadian Baseball Hall of Fame

 Accommodations

Stratford

Hotel/Motel/B&B/Camping

St. Marys

Inn/B&B/Camping

 Off-Road Cycling

Stratford and **St. Marys**

Yes; refer to "Off-Road Cycling" at the end of this chapter.

 Market Days

Stratford

Saturday mornings, year-round

St. Marys

Saturday mornings, May to October

5. Two Sunsets, a River and a Trail: Goderich and Scenic Huron County

With a vantage point high above the picturesque Maitland Valley, this tour begins at the Goderich Airport, then quickly joins a multi use rail bed. Cycling east into the heart of Huron County, you will pass through several wetland areas before riding a logging road south along the Maitland River. At Windy Hill, enjoy a thrilling downhill ride to the blue waters of Little Lakes and a historic bridge crossing at Balls Bridge. Following an undulating county road back into Goderich, the tour completes its loop by rejoining the rail trail as it crosses the Menesetung Bridge and descends to the sandy shores of Lake Huron.

Return Distance:
55km

No. of recommended legs:
1

Level of Difficulty:
🚲🚲

Surface:
Reconditioned rail bed, jeep trail, gravel roads, asphalt

Villages/Towns/Cities:
Goderich, Benmiller

Local Highlights:
Goderich Historic Gaol, Governor's House, Unique Town Square, Marine Museum, Huron County Pioneer Museum, Tiger Dunlop's Tomb, Goderich Harbour, Maitland Woods Hiking Trails, St. Christopher Beach and Harbour Boardwalk, Menesetung Bridge, Lighthouse Park, The Laithwaite Legacy and Apple Park, Benmiller Conference Centre, Blyth Festival Summer Theatre, Clinton Railway School on Wheels

Recommended Bicycles:
Mountain/Hybrid

Tour Suggestions:
A good place to park your car is Goderich Airport, located just off Hwy 21 north of the Maitland River. Spend some time cycling the unique downtown core area of Goderich.

How to get there:
East of Kitchener, take Hwy 401 to the Kitchener exit at Hwy 8 and continue to Goderich. From Michigan & Sarnia take Hwy 402 east and Hwy 21 N; from London take Hwy 4 north and Hwy 8 west.

Years ago, visiting royalty called **Goderich** "one of the prettiest towns in Canada," and the same can still be said today. It is a town of tradition, heritage and technology tied together by the expanding rim of its unique hub and spoke-like downtown square. When town founders Dr. William "Tiger" Dunlop and John Galt looked down on Lake Huron from the bluffs in 1827, they were most likely the first new settlers to enjoy a unique Canadian site. Goderich is the only place in Canada where you can see the sun set twice, first from the shores of Lake Huron and then from the bluffs high above the lake. Today, Goderich's deep harbour is a busy port of call where massive ocean vessels can be seen as they are guided to the landing dock for loading by powerful tug boats.

Itinerary:
From the Goderich Airport parking lot turn [L] (east) onto Airport Rd. Turn [R] on Tomb Rd, just before the modern windmill. At the end of the street, the paved road ends. Keep right and follow this gravel road as it curves to the left, access the Tiger Dunlop and Maitland Trail [RB] via the gate at the bend.

Turn [L] onto the hard-packed [RB] that crosses Hwy 21. Now the [RB] is called the Auburn Rail Trail. The riding surface of the two-lane jeep road is very hard, due to extensive use, and can be slippery in spring.

The first road crossing is 2km away: you will notice that you have been cycling up a slight grade. After passing a barn with two large and two small silos, the [RB] enters a marshy area, which is a great place to stop and stretch your legs. If your timing is right, you can load up on the fresh raspberries that line both sides of the trail.

The [RB] continues to climb and turns into single-track just past the third road crossing. As you enter another wetland area, known as the McGaw Ponds, the bush closes in over the trail. Look for a windmill and a dilapidated old bridge on your left. Just before the second bridge crossing, the [RB] reverts to dual track and becomes a much easier ride.

On this portion of the ride you will come across gravel pits, another road crossing, a railroad siding with tracks and bluebird nesting boxes that lead you first along the trail into a cedar grove and then through a patch of sweet-smelling spruce trees. Again, the [RB] changes into a jeep trail just before another road crossing.

At Blind Line you have three options. If you turn [L], it is an uphill climb to Cty Rd 25; if you go straight, the rail trail ends at the Maitland River, which is an excellent spot for a morning break. The third option is to continue the tour. By turning [R] at the Blind Line, you will follow it up and down (mostly up) over some rough terrain and past a marvellous view of the Maitland River Valley, which leads to Windy Hill. Keeping to the left, enjoy the cooling breeze as you swiftly descend this gravel road and turn [L] onto the aptly named Little Lakes Rd. Enjoy the scenery surrounding these two small inland lakes and take some time to look for sunbathing turtles.

Before reaching Hwy 8, enjoy a long gradual descent to the Balls Historic Bridge. Spared from replacement, this iron bridge still

has wooden boards: there is nothing quite like the thudding sound of rubber hitting wood when you cross this beautiful section of the Maitland River.

Turn [R] onto Huron Rd 8 for an uphill climb before turning [R] onto Huron Rd 15. The striking scenery includes some dramatic hills and many other breathtaking highlights that can be enjoyed along this road. Just opposite Boundary Bridge, the entrance to the Maitland Trail will be on your right. Take some time to examine some of the old stones marking the site of the Colborne Evangelical Church and Cemetery. Huron Rd 15 turns into Huron Rd 31 just before reaching the hamlet of **Benmiller**.

Follow Huron Rd 31. Keep to your right, and notice the lovely little walking area along Sharpe's Creek opposite the Benmiller Inn and Conference Centre. Continue along Huron Rd 31 to the Falls Reserves Conservation area, a red barn, a number of cemeteries and Riverside Park. As soon as the Goderich water tower will come into view, just around the next bend, you will be treated to a great view of the Maitland River. The Chippewa originally named the river "Menesetung," meaning "Laughing Water," in reference to the sound of water running over the rocks. From here, it's downhill to Goderich—and what a terrific ride! Cross Hwy 21 to what appears to be a dead-end road, but is actually the Tiger Dunlop Heritage Trail. Follow the trail, with the wetlands of the Maitland on your left and the Tiger Dunlop Tomb above you to your right.

Continue up the hill, following the trail as it turns into single track.

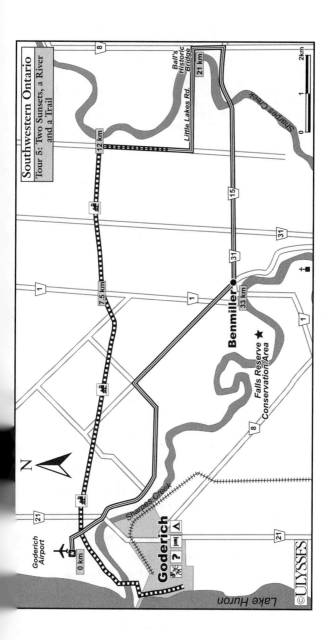

Southwestern Ontario
Tour 5: Two Sunsets, a River and a Trail

Ball's Historic Bridge

Little Lakes Rd.

21 km

Sharpes Creek

12 km

8

7.5 km

1

31

15

31

Benmiller

33 km

Falls Reserve ★
Conservation Area

8

1

21

21

N

Goderich Airport

0 km

Sharpes Creek

Goderich

Lake Huron

© ULYSSES

2km

0   1   2km

Eventually you will have to carry your bicycle up a short flight of wooden stairs. At the top of the stairs, turn [L] onto the [RB] and pass the point where you first entered this [RB], following it to the Menesetung Bridge. Reconditioned by local citizens, the bridge was originally built by the CPR in 1907. It was the longest bridge in Ontario at the time and was in service until 1988. Note the 22-tonne commemorative rock on the far side of the bridge.

Cross the bridge and turn [R] onto North Harbour Rd, taking some time to explore the harbour area before rejoining the [RB]. At the far end of the harbour is the Sifto Salt Mine. Salt was discovered in the area in 1866 by Samuel Platt in what is now referred to as Saltford, just upstream across Hwy 21. The mine shafts at the mouth of the river are presently more than 500m deep, extending westward through a bed of salt that is 30m thick and produces over 3.25-million tonnes of salt per year.

To rejoin the [RB], ride back towards the bridge. Notice a series of cement steps high above you on your left. Carefully cross the railroad track and carry your bike up the stairs, from where you can almost see the top of the grain elevators. Follow the trail to Goderich Harbour, which has been active since 1840. Upon entering the harbour, you will see the CPR Station, which was built in 1907 to link Guelph and Goderich. Cool, refreshing winds off Lake Huron accompany you as you continue to follow the road along the lakeshore. The trail ends at sandy Christopher Beach, where there is clean water and washroom facilities.

Retrace your steps to the Menesetung Bridge. Cross it, and immediately turn [L] onto the Maitland Heritage Tree Trail. At the first fork in the trail, keep to the left, eventually arriving at a magnificent heritage red oak tree, which is 30m high, 3m thick and 218 years old. It is truly a sight to behold! If you turn left here, you will end up at the marina.

There are two different ways to return to the starting point. Either turn [R] at the oak tree and follow the single-track back uphill to the [RB], retracing your steps to the airport, or follow this trail up to the trail access point on your left, which will take you out to Mill Rd. Follow this road to Airport Rd, then turn [R] towards the parking lot.

Practical Information

Population:
Goderich: 7,500

 Tourist Information

The County of Huron Planning and Development Department
Court House Sq, Goderich, ON N7A 1M2
☎(519) 524-2188
www.hurontourism.on.ca

Goderich Tourist Information Centre
91 Hamilton St, Goderich, ON N7A 1M2
☎(519) 524-6600 or 800-280-7637
www.town.goderich.on.ca

 Bicycle Shops

Goderich Cyclery
622 Pentland Ave, Goderich, ON
N7A 3X8
☎(519) 524-4720

Special Sights and Events

Canada Day Celebrations, Summerfest, Celtic Roots Festival, Goderich Festival of Arts and Crafts, Maritime Heritage Weekend, Blue Water Kennel Obedience Trials, Huron Pioneer Threshers Steam Show, museums, beach boardwalks

Accommodations

Hotel/Motel/B&B/Camping

Market Days

Saturdays, May to October

6. Down by the Old Mill Stream: London and Dorchester

Enjoy a ride on the London Bikeway, which originates in downtown London and makes its way along the Thames River to historic Hamilton Rd. Dip your feet in the Dorchester Mill Pond at midday before following the road back into London, then join the northern portion of the recreational trail to cycle along residential streets, paved trails and single track before returning to Greenway Park.

Return Distance:
55km

No. of recommended legs:

Level of Difficulty:

Surface:
Recreational trail, asphalt roads and 200m of single track

Villages/Towns/Cities:
London, Dorchester

Local Highlights:
Banting Museum and Education Centre, Eldon House, Fanshawe Conservation Area and Pioneer Village, London Regional Art Gallery, Middlesex County Building, Royal Canadian Regiment Museum, Imax Theatre, Ska-Nah-Doht Indian Village, Springbank Park, Story Book Gardens, University of Western Ontario, Archival Teaching and Research Museum, Bellamere Country Market, Canadian Medical Hall of Fame, Children's Museum, Grand Theatre, Guy Lombardo Music Centre, Museum of Archaeology, Old Courthouse and Gaol, Victoria Park, Novaks Periscope, Western Fair Raceway

Recommended Bicycles:
Touring/Hybrid/Mountain

Tour Suggestions:
This is a nice, easy ride that will allow you to enjoy a picnic lunch along the banks of the Dorchester Mill Pond.

How to get there:
There are four exits for London from Hwy 401. This tour starts at Greenway Park. To get there, take the Wellington Rd N exit off Hwy 401. At Horton St, turn left and cross Wharncliffe Rd S onto Springbank Dr. Turn right at Greenside Ave and park at the no-charge parking lot on the right.

Colonel John Grave Simcoe founded **London** in 1792 and named it after the great city in England. In 1881, it was the site

Southwestern Ontario

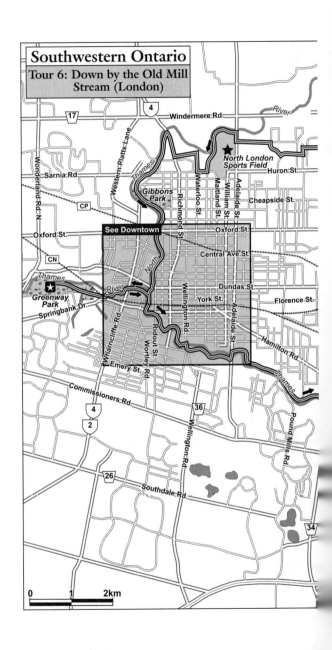

Southwestern Ontario

Tour 6: Down by the Old Mill Stream (London)

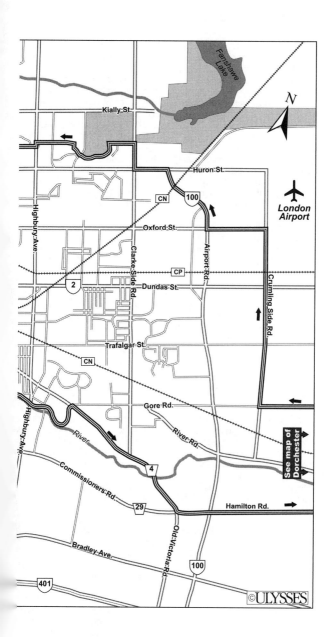

of one of the worst marine disasters in Canada when the steamboat *Victoria* overturned, taking the lives of 200 people. Today, the city is best known as the home of the University of Western Ontario. Nicknamed "Forest City" because of its location at the forks of the Thames River, it has managed to maintain a "green" image thanks to constant conservation efforts and careful urban planning. Currently, the city boasts more than 50,000 trees and over 607 hectares of parks, 405 hectares of which are along the Thames River. London has also kept up with current trends, developing a recreational highway that provides safe cycling routes to almost anywhere in the city.

Itinerary:
Facing the Thames River and the recreational trail, turn [R] onto the trail, keeping the river on your left. Ride through the Greg Curnoe tunnel, which exits onto Evergreen Ave. The tunnel was named for artist and cyclist Greg Curnoe, who was killed by a truck while riding with his local club in 1992. Keep left and turn onto Riverview Ave. At O'Brien St, rejoin the trail and ride past *HMCS London* to the Riverforks Park Bridge. Turn [L] and cross the river; continue along the pathway as it loops left in a clover leaf pattern to join the trail in Ivy Park and the London Peace Gardens below.

Pass under Stanley St and continue along the trail as it merges with the sidewalk at Horton St. Just after the Horton St bridge, swing right and get back onto the recreational pathway. The smell of hops fills the air as you pass the Labatt Brewery. Look for the falls on your right just before crossing

Richmond St to join the South Branch Bikeway.

The trail ends at Nelson St; follow it to the end before joining Wellington St. Turn [R], ride across the bridge, and then quickly turn [L] into the Watson St Park on Front St. The river is again on your left until you reach the Adelaide St loop.

Cross the bridge at Adelaide St and follow the pathway as it passes under Highbury Ave. At Meadowlily Rd N, the trail continues just to the right of where you exited onto the street. Finally, ending at the Pottersburg Creek Pollution Control Plant, bear [L] and follow the driveway up to Hamilton Rd.

Make a [R] turn onto old Hamilton Rd and ride to the traffic lights at Commissioners Rd and Old Victoria Rd. Turn [L] and follow Hamilton Rd through the hamlet of Nilestown, into the village of **Dorchester**. The road begins to descend at the Dorchester Golf and Country Club. At the bottom of the hill, turn [R] before the mill silo. On your left is the old Mill Pond and Dam. The pond itself is a lovely wetland area that takes only 30min to walk around. Remember to lock up your bicycle. If you're lucky, you just might meet the local gaggle of swans or Canada geese.

The town was first settled in 1820 and was called Edwardsburgh, then Dorchester Station, before the name was shortened to Dorchester in 1861 Today, Dorchester is a quiet bedroom community that sits high above the Thames River. In 1925, however, the town was in turmoil. Indeed, Dorchester's Donnybrook Fields was the site

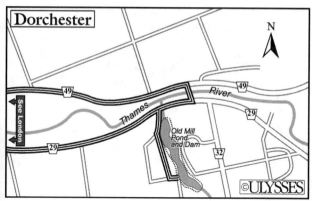

of the Ku Klux Klan's first public recruitment campaign ever held in Canada. Apparently, over 100 residents from nearby London took the oath of the Klan before an altar of flame.

Ride back to Hamilton Rd and turn [R], then cycle uphill and make a [L] turn onto Bridge St. Once across the river, turn [L] onto Catherine St (Middlesex 49). Cycle past two churches and the Dorchester Day Use Conservation Area, and turn [R] onto Middlesex Rd 32, also known as Shaw Rd.

Ride to Knoch Manufacturing and turn [L] onto Gore Rd. The next several kilometres will take you through hydro alley. At Crumlin Side Rd, turn [R] and follow this well-used road past Diamond Aircraft to the four-way stop at the London Airport. Turn [L] onto Oxford St and then turn [R] at the traffic lights onto Airport Rd. Make a [L] turn at the Huron [T] intersection. Follow the road and hang a [R] at Clarke Rd. Look for Ted Earley Park, opposite LaFarge on your left. Ride across the road and join the

northern portion of the London Bikeway.

The trail exits the park onto Cayuga Cr. Bear left and follow the road until you turn [R] onto Oakville Ave. At Chippewa Dr, turn [L] and ride to Idylwood Rd. Make a [L] turn and then swing [R] onto Jensen Rd. At the Highbury Ave [T] intersection, turn [L] and then move into the right-hand lane at the traffic lights. Turn [R] onto Fuller St and ride past the local ambulance station into residential London. At McNay St, turn [L], and then [R] onto Melsandra Ave. Make a [R] turn onto Barker St and cycle to a [L] turn onto Kipps Ln. At the lights, cross Adelaide St and join the recreational trail in the North London Sports Field.

Cycle along a narrow dirt road, and follow it as it bears [R] and joins an asphalt path. Turn [L] onto the path and ride towards a large building that stands majestically high on top of a hill. At an interesting junction where the trail seems to end, keep [L] and cross the large culvert. Ride up the dirt hill that exits to the tennis courts at St. Peters Seminary. Slip up to

Southwestern Ontario

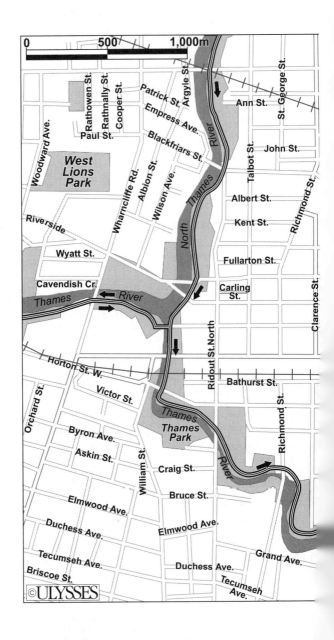

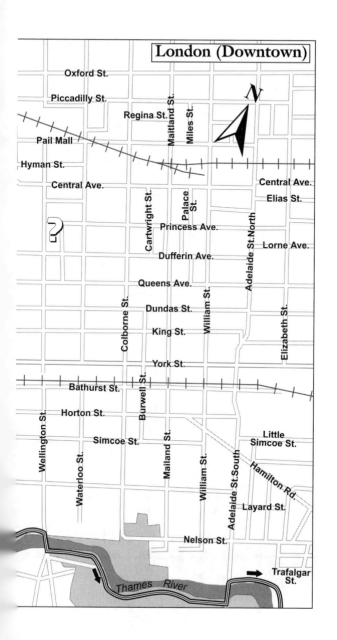

the driveway next to the church and follow it onto Huron St. Turn [R] onto Huron St and then turn [R] once again at Waterloo St, riding past Kings College onto Epworth Ave. At Richmond St, turn [R] and follow the road past the entrance to T.J.F. Roth Park. Just before crossing the river, access the path on your right and follow it under the Richmond St Bridge.

This is perhaps the nicest portion of the recreational trail as it makes its way back towards London's downtown core. As the trail exits onto Parkway St, bear [R] and ride to Victoria St. Enter the gates to Gibbons Park by turning [L] to join the trail and ride across a wide-open field. Keep [R] at the [Y] intersection and continue to follow the river and trail as it crosses Black Friars St, next to the oldest wrought-iron bridge in Ontario, which dates back to 1875.

At Harris Park, cross Riverside Dr and continue to follow the trail along the river. When you get back to the Peace Park/Ivy Park, follow the clover leaf back over the walkway used at the beginning of this leg. Once over the bridge, swing [R] and pedal past the familiar **HMCS London**. Continue to follow the trail as it descends back into Riverforks Park. The trail arcs left, passes the Children's Museum, and then exits onto O'Brien St. Retrace

your route from here to get back onto the Terry Fox Pkwy to reach Greenway Park.

Optional Side Trip:
Once back at Greenway Park, remain on the recreational pathway and ride west, going past the Greenway Park and the Pollution Control plant. Springbank Park has lots of winding pathways from which you can hear the joyful shouts of children visiting the world-famous Story Book Gardens and the musical merry-go-round along the Thames.

Practical Information

Population:
London: 326,000
Dorchester: 9,000

 Tourist Information

London

London Tourist Information Centre
696 Wellington Rd, London, ON
N6C 4R2
☎ *(519) 661-5000 or 800-265-2602*
www.londontourism.ca

Dorchester

North Dorchester Township Offices
PO Box 209, 4305 Hamilton Rd
Dorchester, ON N0L 1G0
☎ *(519) 268-7334*
www.thamescentre.on.ca

Bicycle Shops

London

All Seasons Sports & Cycle
790 Dundas St, ON N5W 2Z7
☎ *(519) 660-6932*

Champion Bicycle Sales & Service
592 Adelaide St N, ON N6B 3J8
☎ *(519) 679-1266*

Cyclepath
737 Richmond St, ON N6A 3H6
☎ *(519) 432-2208*

Cyzzle Cycles
360 Springbank Dr, ON N6J 1G5
☎ *(519) 657-1729*

First Cycleworks
525 First St, ON N5V 1Z5
☎ *(519) 455-9124*

Lloyd's Cycle & Repairs
924 Oxford St E, ON N5Y 3J9
☎ *(519) 452-3881*

Missing Link Cycle & Ski
1283 Commissioners St W
ON N6K 1C9
☎ *(519) 641-5056*

To-Wheels
134 Dundas St, London, ON N6A 1G1
☎ *(519) 663-9447*

Racer Sportif
353 Clarence St, London, ON N6A 3M4
☎ *(519) 434-5652*

South London Cycle
479 McGregor Ave, ON N6J 2S8
☎ *(519) 433-4275*

Herm's Sport Exchange
20 Wharncliffe St S, ON N6J 2N4
☎ *(519) 649-0600*

 Special Sights and Events

London

London International Air Show,
Canada Day, Balloon Festival,
Home County Folk Festival,
Rib Fest, Fanshawe Pioneer Village seasonal events, Western
Fair, Harvest Festival, Snowfest,
Sunfest (world music and dance)
dragon-boat race festival,
Bluesfest International, Covent
Garden Market, London Pride,
International Children's Festival.

 Accommodations

London

Hotel/Motel/B&B/Camping

 Off-Road Cycling

London

Yes; please refer to "Off-Road
Cycling" below.

Off-Road Cycling

Public Trails

Goderich

Tiger Dunlop Heritage Trail and GART
(12km)
Surface:
Jeep Rd/Loose surface
Beginning:
Goderich Airport or Goderich
Harbour

Southwestern Ontario

County of Huron Planning and Development Department
(see p 66)

Sarnia

Howard Watson Nature Trail
(16km)
Surface:
Original rail bed
Beginning:
Exmouth St to outskirts of Camalachie

Tourism Sarnia-Lambton
(see page 46)

Point Edward Waterfront Trail
(1km)
Surface:
Loose/hard-packed
Beginning:
Waterfront Park (Bluewater Bridge) and Canatara Park

Village of Point Edward
36 St. Clair St, Point Edward, ON
N7V 4G8
☎*(519) 337-3021*
www.visitpointedward.com

Simcoe

Lynn Valley Trail
(8km)
Surface: Original rail bed/hard-packed (loose stone at the Port Dover end)
Beginning: Simcoe and Port Dover

Lynn Valley Trail Association
137 Decou Rd, Simcoe, ON N3Y 4K2
☎*(519) 428-3292*

St. Marys

Grand Trunk Trail Committee
PO Box 998, St. Marys, ON N4X 1B6
☎*(519) 284-3556*
www.stonetown.com/gttsm

Windsor

Ganatchio Trail/Little River Corridor
(8.5km)
Surface:
Asphalt/some loose surface
Beginning:
Tecumseh to Isabelle Place

City of Windsor Parks and Recreation
2450 McDougall St, Windsor, ON
N8X 3N6
☎*(519) 253-2300*
www.city.windsor.on.ca/parkrec

Windsor/Leamington Area to Ruthven

Chrysler Canada Greenway
(50km)
Surface:
Original rail bed
Beginning:
Town of Oldcastle, town of Ruthven, town of Harrow, Kingsville train station

Essex Region Conservation Authority
360 Fairview Ave W, Essex, ON N8M 1Y6
☎*(519) 776-5209 or 888-487-4760*
www.erca.org

Woodstock

The Pines
(40km)
Hickson Trail
(14km)
Surface:
Single track, some technical areas
Beginning:
Oxford Rd 4 and Township Rd 4

Woodstock Cycling Club
c/o Pedal Power
590 Dundas St, Woodstock, ON N4S 1B
☎*(519) 539-3681*
woodstockcyclingclub@yahoo.com

Resort and Conservation Trails

Aylmer/ St. Thomas Area

Archie Coulter Conservation Area
(*4km of trails*)

Catfish Creek Conservation Authority
8079 Springwater Rd, RR5, Aylmer, ON N5H 2R4
☎ *(519) 773-9037*

Grand Bend

Pinery Provincial Park
(*10km of trails*)

RR 2, Grand Bend, ON, N0M 1T0
☎ *(519) 243-2220*
www.pinerypark.on.ca

Long Point/ Lake Erie Area

Backus Woods
(*13km of trails*)

Long Point Region Conservation Authority
RR 3, Simcoe, ON N3Y 4K2
☎ *(519) 428-4623*
www.lprca.on.ca

Backus Heritage Conservation Area
RR 1, Port Rowan, ON, N0E 1M0
☎ *(519) 586-2201 or 877-990-9932*
www.lprca.on.ca

London

The London Ski Club at Boler Mountain
689 Griffith St, London, ON N6K 2S5
mailing address:
PO Box 20051, 431 Boler Rd, London, ON N6K 4A6
☎ *(519) 657-8822*
www.bolermountain.com

Chatham Area

Rondeau Provincial Park
(*23km of trails*)

RR 1 (Hwy 15), Morpeth, ON N0P 1X0
☎ *(519) 674-1750*
www.ontarioparks.com/english/rond.html

Exeter Area

Hay Swamp Management Area
(*38km of trails*)

Ausable Bayfield Conservation Authority
7108 Morrison Line, Exeter, ON N0M 1S4
☎ *(519) 235-2610 or 888-286-2610*
www.abca.on.ca

Simcoe/Port Ryerse/ Lake Erie Area

Hay Creek Conservation Area
(3km of trails)

Long Point Region Conservation Authority
(see above)

Southwestern Ontario

Simcoe/
Nanticoke Area

**Haldimand Conservation
Area**
(*3km of trails*)

**Long Point Region
Conservation Authority**
(see page 77)

St. Marys

Wildwood Conservation Area
(*24km of trails*)

**Upper Thames River
Conservation Authority**
1424 Clarke Rd, London, ON N5V 5B9
☎*(519) 284-2292 or 284-2931*
www.thamesriver.org

St. Thomas/
Aylmer Area

**Springwater Conservation
Area**
(*12km of trails*)

Catfish Creek Conservation
(see page 77)

North Bay

Sudbury

QUÉBEC

Ottawa⊛

Parry
Sound

Kingston

Lake Huron

Owen
Sound

Peterborough

Lake Ontario

Toronto⊕

London

•Niagara
Falls

Lake Erie

Sarnia

UNITED
STATES

Windsor

Festival Country

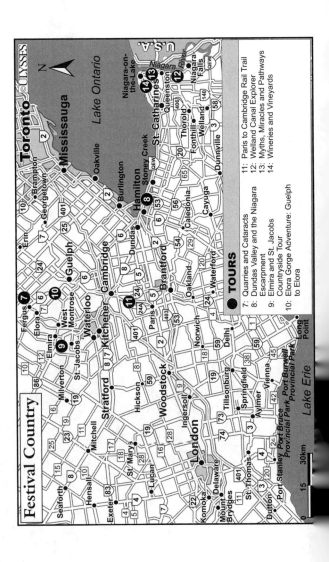

Festival Country

N

Toronto ©ULYSSES

Lake Ontario

Brampton
Georgetown
Mississauga
Oakville
Burlington
Stoney Creek
Hamilton
Dundas
St. Catharines

Niagara-on-the-lake

Niagara-Falls

U.S.A.

Queenston
Thorold
Fonthill
Welland
Dunnville

Erin
Guelph
Cambridge
Brantford
Caledonia
Cayuga
Waterford
Norwich
Delhi

Fergus
Elora
West Montrose
Waterloo
Kitchener
Paris
Oakland

Milverton
St. Jacobs
Elmira
Stratford
Hickson
Woodstock
Ingersoll
Tillsonburg
Springfield
Aylmer
Vienna

Seaforth
Hensall
Exeter
Mitchell
St. Marys
Lucan
London
Delaware
Komoka
Mount Brydges
St. Thomas
Dutton
Port Stanley
Port Bruce
Port Burwell Provincial Park
Port Burwell Provincial Park
Long Point

Lake Erie

0   15   30km

● TOURS

7: Quarries and Cataracts
8: Dundas Valley and the Niagara Escarpment
9: Elmira and St. Jacobs
10: Elora Gorge Adventure: Guelph to Elora
11: Paris to Cambridge Rail Trail
12: Welland Canal Explorer
13: Myths, Miracles and Pathways
14: Wineries and Vineyards

Festival Country

meanders along the north shore of Lake Erie, from Port Rowan to Fort Erie, passing through the fruit- and wine-producing region of Niagara, and finally touching the time-honoured traditions of Ontario's Mennonite community.

7. Quarries and Cataracts: Elora to Cataract Rail Trail Adventure

Like a good story, this ride begins dramatically in Elora and follows an interesting and varied path through the countryside that concludes in a thrilling finale at the thundering falls of Cataract. Try to imagine what it was like to ride the rails in the late 1800s as you cycle along this former branch line of the Credit Valley Railway. In 1879, the railway ran from Elora to Cataract Junction, acting as a primary feeder line for the main line from Toronto to Orangeville.

Return Distance:
96km

No. of recommended legs:
2

Level of Difficulty:
🚲🚲

(slightly rough terrain in some sections)

Surface:
Reconditioned rail bed, slightly loose to hard-packed, some undeveloped portions

Villages/Towns/Cities:
Elora, Fergus, Belwood, Orton, Erin, Cataract

Local Highlights:
Elora Gorge & Quarries, Lake Belwood, Cataract Falls, portions of the Niagara Peninsula

Recommended Bicycles:
Mountain/Hybrid/Touring

Tour Suggestions:
The tour can be completed in one day by experienced riders or by travelling with two vehicles and leaving them at opposite ends of the trail. If you decide to do the tour in two legs, cycle from Elora to Cataract on the first day, overnighting on the way back. Complete the return ride to Elora on the following day, leaving plenty of time to enjoy this unique village.

How to get there:
From Hwy 401, take Hwy 6 N (Exit 295) to the village of Elora. At the traffic lights turn [R] onto Metcalfe St and follow the road, keeping to your left. At the traffic lights, turn [R] onto Mill St and travel approximately 1.5km. After passing the quarries, take the next [L], Gerrie Rd; a 20-vehicle parking lot is located a short distance from the highway on your right.

Elora is a place with some amazing and extreme features that include a dramatically carved gorge, caves, rock ledges, islet rocks and natural waterfalls. Originally called Irvine but better known by its nickname, "City of Rocks," the town was first settled in the winter of 1817 by Roswell Matthew. This pioneer had cleared some 12ha of land by 1832 before selling out to William Gilkison. Renaming the town "Elora" after his brother's ship, itself named after the famous Cave Temples of India, Gilkison made his influence felt across the province when he assisted in the drafting of human rights legislation that included representation by population and the secret ballot.

Itinerary:
The [RB] at Elora has recently been reconditioned and is hard-packed. Three cyclists can ride side by side. Travelling east for half a kilometre from the trail-head, look for a cattle-crossing sign and be prepared to stop if these gentle beasts are encountered. Notice the abundant wooden rail fencing and the gentle aroma of the nearby cedar trees.

When the GSW water tower appears, you are close to **Fergus**. Entering town, the water tower is on your [L] and the [RB] exits onto Hill St. Follow Hill St, turning [L] onto Maiden Ln, and look for the "four-armed" tree next to the stop sign at Garafraxa St. Turn [R] and proceed [E] along Garafraxa St, crossing Hwy 6 (St. David St N).

Initially called Little Falls, Fergus was renamed after a Scottish lawyer. Many of the town's original buildings (circa 1850s) in the downtown area and along the Grand River have survived. Your time will be well spent exploring the village. Fergus is also home to

the oldest curling club in Ontario and to the pauper's grave of drunkard George Celphane, who is best remembered for the gospel song "The Ninety and Nine."

Following Garafraxa St, turn [L] onto Gartshore. Rejoin the [RB] on your right just before the industrial park. Small information centres at various spots along this trail reveal tidbits of information about the area and local wildlife, as well as the Conservation Ontario Motto: "Leave Tracks not Trash."

Over the last 6km, the elevation rises. A great deal of planning has gone into designing this greenway. There are gates at all of the [RB] access points to the road, but it is still recommended to approach these areas with caution, especially when cycling with children.

Those with keen eyes and good hearing will find plenty to see along the way: a triangular corral, dog kennels, broken windmills and, far off in the distance, a castle. Actually, the castle is the 60-year-old Shand Dam. Built in 1942 as Canada's first flood control project, the dam created the Belwood Conservation Area. A beautiful lake is on your left, but on your right is a 75m-drop to the Grand River. Make use of the park's comfortable rest area and washrooms on the far side of the dam.

Continue toward the park's entrance; the [RB] is to the left of the gate booth. Because this section of the trail is multi-use, you will probably encounter hikers and horseback riders on nice days. There is a direction post a short distance past the park entrance. A word of advice: stick

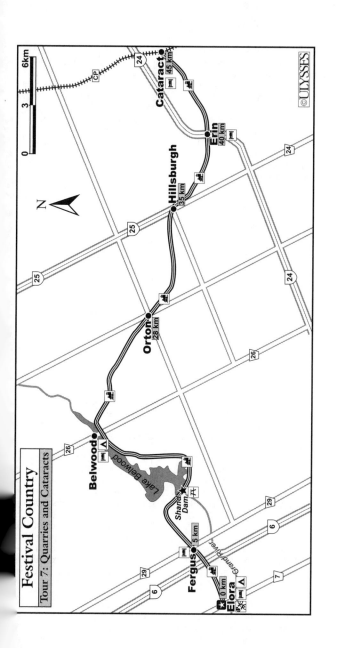

Festival Country

Tour 7: Quarries and Cataracts

0   3   6km

© ULYSSES

N

CP

Cataract
24
45 km

Erin
40 km

Hillsburgh
35 km

24

25

Orton
28 km

25

26

24

Belwood
26

Lake Belwood

Fergus
5 km

29

6

Shand Dam

Elora
0 km

Grand River

6

7

29

to the [RB] because most directions are for snowmobilers and cross private land so they are not recommended for cyclists in the summer months.

Hugging the lake's shoreline, the [RB] passes an old mill at the 18-km trail mark. Cross Cty Rd 26, which emerges just to the south of Belwood. Some bed and breakfasts can be found in this quaint little town.

Now the [RB] dwindles to little more than a cattle trail. Hard-packed, sometimes double track, and often overgrown, it is obvious that it has only recently begun to be used again. This problem will disappear as more and more of the rail bed is reconditioned. Notice the two large homes high above you on your right as the rail bed climbs and then descends to the White Pines of Springhill Farms. Single track draws you forward, and by the time you reach the 20 dead trees on your left, you will have gained 150m in elevation. As you approach Cty Rd 3, take a few minutes to admire a perfect scene for a painter's canvas: an old stone house, a pond and a worn-out, upside-down rowboat. You should also keep an eye out for a rather large, wild potbelly pig that might be wandering the trail. As you approach a blue greystone house standing guard, the [RB] once again becomes double track. The elevation starts to decline, allowing you to coast by a house that looks like a red-roofed barn, into the village of **Orton**. Fresh baked goods and coffee are available at the general store.

In Orton, the [RB] changes back into hard-packed single track that feels as though it's rolling up and down. Arriving in Hillsburgh, you will notice, to your left, a very unique pond that is only a few inches deep, while on your right is Morett's Fine Furniture. Follow the [RB] over a wooden bridge crossing Hwy 25, then cycle through some loose, sandy stretches before crossing Cty Rd 22 onto an improved hard-packed rail bed.

This portion of the trail is an excellent ride that takes you past a sand-and-gravel operation, the ruins of an old stone barn and through a corridor of sweet-smelling cedar. Listen carefully for a babbling brook. The odour of burning steel lets you know that the town of **Erin** is nearby. Spend some time in this interesting little village, poetically named after Ireland. You will pass by some rusty farm implements on your left, a cattle crossing sign and a stagnant pond. Cross Mississauga Rd to enter one of Ontario's best-kept secrets, the Forks of the Credit Provincial Park. The [RB] has been completely resurfaced with hard-packed stone dust and measures some 3m wide from Hillsburgh to the Forks of the Credit Provincial Park.

The [RB] is well used and hard-packed but be careful; as you travel further into the park, the [RB] is beginning to wash away in some spots. You will come across a spectacular view of the valley—try and pick out the fast-flowing Credit River. If you are lucky, you might see a train making its way up towards the [RB]. At the [T] junction, turn [R] down into the valley, then cross a wooden bridge and follow the path to Cataract Falls. It's well worth it to explore this area. Notice the striking and rugged exposed rock of the Niagara

Escarpment and the massive rolling topography created by glacial deposits. Turning [L] at the [T] junction will lead you out of the park and into the village of **Cataract**, where you will find the Cataract Inn, a quaint English-style inn.

Practical Information

Population:
Elora: 4,500
Fergus: 10,000
Erin: 9,900

 Tourist Information

Elora

Elora Information Centre
144 Geddes St, Elora, ON N0B
☎*(519) 846-9841*
www.eic.elora.on.ca

Fergus

Fergus Information Centre
400 Tower St S, Fergus, ON N1M 2P7
☎*(519) 843-5140 or 877-242-6353*
www.ferguselora.com

Erin

Town of Erin
5684 Wellington Rd 24, RR 2, Hillsburg,
ON N0B 1Z0
☎*(519) 855-4407 or 877-818-2888*
www.town.erin.on.ca

 Bicycle Shops

Elora

Salem Cyclery
320 Erb St, Elora, ON N0B 1S0
☎*(519) 846-8446*

Water St Cycleworks
21 Water St W, Elora, ON N0B 1S0
☎*(519) 846-8196*

 Special Sights and Events

Elora

Elora Festival, Elora Antique Car and Truck Show, Elora Antique Warehouse, horse-and-carriage rides, Art in the Park, Elora Gorge Conservation Area, Elora Quarry Conservation Area, Islet Rock, Wellington County Museum and Archives, artist studio tour

Fergus

Scottish Festival, Fergus Fall Fair, Summer Theatre, unique Saturday & Sunday Market, Fergus truck show, classic car show, Templin Gardens, Canada Day celebrations.

Erin

Cruise & Bloomin Fest.

 Accommodations

Elora and Fergus

Camping/B&B/Motel

Erin

B&B/Motels.

Festival Country

8. Dundas Valley and the Niagara Escarpment (including Webster and Tew's Falls)

Find hidden treasures in the heart of industrial Ontario! To the towering heights of the Niagara Escarpment, which surrounds and protects the most impressive Dundas Valley, this area of the province offers cyclists a little bit of everything; awesome single track, reclaimed rail bed and wildly winding roads that descend into a developed, urban transportation system that has been designed to accommodate cyclists' needs. Here, country meets city—and it works!

Return Distance:
40km

No. of recommended legs:
1

Level of Difficulty:
🚲 🚲 🚲

(a few steep hills to climb)

Surface:
Asphalt, hard-packed rail bed

Villages/Towns/Cities:
Dundas, Hamilton, Flamborough

Local Highlights:
Royal Botanical Gardens, Dundurn Castle, Canadian Warplane Heritage Museum, Hamilton Place, Dyment's Pumpkin Patch, Copp's Coliseum, Whitehern, Museum of Steam & Technology, Westfield Heritage Centre, Hess Village, Battlefield House, Art Gallery of Hamilton, Dundas Valley Rail Trail System

Recommended Bicycles:
Hybrid/Mountain/Touring

Tour Suggestions:
Since the tour starts at Webster's Falls in Dundas, pack a lunch and plan to spend some time cycling some of the 40km of trail in the Dundas Valley.

How to get there:
Take Hwy 403 to Main St W/Hwy 2/8, then turn left onto King St/Hwy 8 which turns into Brock Rd. Turn right onto Harvest Rd then right onto Short Rd, following it to the Spencer Gorge parking lot. There may be a small parking fee.

Often referred to as "Valley Town" because of its location, **Dundas** was first settled in 1787 by Anne Morden, a United Empire Loyalist widow, who, along with her family, was granted a large piece of land that now represents the north half of the town. Originally named Coote's Paradise after Capt. Thomas Coote, who often hunted in the area, the town has seen prosperity come and go over the years. In 1837, the opening of the Desjardins Canal encouraged shipping by linking Dundas to Lake Ontario. But, the area's rapid development quickly levelled out with the advent of rail transportation in 1853. Today, the town is tucked away in the shadow of Hamilton and its billowing smoke arid stacks still has a strong sense of community, providing a unique natural playground for the surrounding population.

Itinerary:
To the left of the parking lot entrance are a number of interesting

gravestones and the entrance to the Bruce Trail. Turn [R] and proceed to an opening in the wire fence. Keep right on the trail, and watch the wooden steps as the trail descends to Webster Falls. Exiting onto an open field, cross the stone bridge; to the right is Webster's Falls Rd, while Webster's Falls are to the left. Look for the stairs that invite you to explore the Webster's Falls gorge.

Follow Webster's Falls Rd as it exits out onto Hwy 8, then turn [R] and follow the road north as it turns into Brock Rd, turning [L] onto Crooks Hollow Rd (Old Brock Rd)/Harvest Rd. As it bends to the right and starts to climb, bear [L] and stay near the creek. Enjoy the rolling hills and scenic stops along Crooks Hollow Rd, which include the remains of Canada's first paper mill, the Darney Grist Mill and the huge Christie Reservoir further upstream.

Legs will be burning as this rolling road offers up some short stiff climbs. Turn [R] onto Hwy 8 and [L] onto Weirs Ln. As you pass the Free Reform Church, the road becomes somewhat worn and rough in spots. At Governor's Rd, turn [L], then [R] onto Sulphur Springs Rd. Notice the warning sign for the gravel road ahead. It is twisting and hilly, but the road has been oiled so many times that it rides as though it were asphalt.

The entrance to the Brantford-Hamilton rail bed is located approximately 10km west of this tour's starting point, at the bottom of a hill. Turn [L] onto the rail bed's hard-packed calcium riding surface and cycle to the Dundas Valley Trail Centre. Offi-

cially known as the Toronto, Hamilton & Buffalo Railway, the T, H & B was often called "To Hell and Back" and went into service in 1895. The rail line was abandoned in 1986 and its rails were torn up after Brantford's Colborne St landslide. The Hamilton Region and the Grand River Conservation Authorities purchased the trail in 1988 and are currently working to complete the greenway; the master development plan for the rail bed is on display at the Trail Centre.

An afternoon of great riding can be enjoyed around the Trail Centre. This restored train station, flanked on the north and south by 400-million-year-old rocks, offers weary travellers a place to rest. It is also the starting place for over 40km of hiking and cycling trails that pass over streams and through forests, marshlands and the fields of Dundas Valley.

As you continue east along the [RB], which is almost 100m below the level of Lake Ontario, caution is advised as you cross Ancaster Rd and Lynden Ave. The thudding sounds of wood and rubber will bring pleasure to your ears as you cross the 275m Binkley Hollow ravine. In the fall, the brilliant colours of the ravine's many varieties of trees are invigorating. Look for an information sign pointing out their location.

French explorers who passed through this area in the 17th century knew of the escarpment, as referred to by the Aboriginal description "The Head of the Lake." Following the American Revolution, the British purchased land in the vicinity from the Mississauga First Nation to

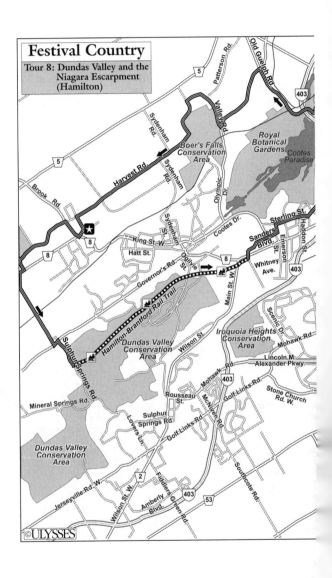

Festival Country

Tour 8: Dundas Valley and the Niagara Escarpment (Hamilton)

5

Patterson Rd.

Old Guelph Rd.

403

Valley Rd.

Sydenham Rd.

Harvest Rd.

Boer's Falls Conservation Area

Royal Botanical Gardens

Cootes Paradise

5

Brook Rd.

Sydenham Rd.

Olympic Dr.

Sterling St.

8

Sanders Blvd.

Haddon St.

Emerson St.

King St. W.

Sydenham St.

Cootes Dr.

8

Hatt St.

Ogilvie St.

8

Main St. W.

Whitney Ave.

403

Governor's Rd.

Hamilton-Brantford Rail Trail

Wilson St.

Iroquoia Heights Conservation Area

Scenic Dr.

Mohawk Rd.

Dundas Valley Conservation Area

Lincoln M. Alexander Pkwy.

Sulphur Springs Rd.

403

Mohawk Rd.

Golf-Links Rd.

Stone Church Rd. W.

Mineral Springs Rd.

Rousseau St.

McNiven Rd.

Sulphur Springs Rd.

Lovers Ln.

Golf Links Rd.

Dundas Valley Conservation Area

Southcote Rd.

Jerseyville Rd. W.

Wilson St. W.

2

Fiddler's Green Rd.

Amberly Blvd.

403

53

©ULYSSES

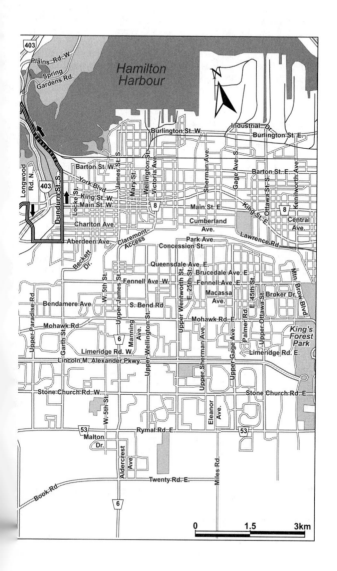

Hamilton Harbour

Plains Rd. W.
403
Spring Gardens Rd.
Longwood Rd. N.
403
Dundurn St. S.
Burlington St. W.
Industrial Dr.
Burlington St. E.
Barton St. W.
York Blvd.
James St. S.
Mary St.
Wellington St.
Victoria Ave.
Sherman Ave.
Gage Ave. S.
Barton St. E.
Kenilworth Ave.
Locke St.
King St. W.
Main St. W.
8
Main St. E.
King St. E.
Ottawa St. S.
8
Central Ave.
Charlton Ave.
Cumberland Ave.
Beckett Dr.
Aberdeen Ave.
Claremont Access
Park Ave.
Lawrence Rd.
Concession St.
Queensdale Ave. E.
Brucedale Ave. E.
W. 5th St.
Fennell Ave. W.
Upper James St.
E. 25th St.
Upper Wentworth St.
Fennell Ave. E.
Macassa Ave.
E. 45th St.
Broker Dr.
Mtn. Brow Blvd.
Bendamere Ave.
S. Bend Rd.
Mohawk Rd. E.
Palmer Rd.
Upper Ottawa St.
King's Forest Park
Mohawk Rd.
Garth St.
6
Manning Ave.
Upper Wellington St.
Upper Gage Ave.
Limeridge Rd. W.
Limeridge Rd. E.
Lincoln M. Alexander Pkwy.
Upper Sherman Ave.
Stone Church Rd. W.
Eleanor Ave.
Stone Church Rd. E.
53
Malton Dr.
W. 5th St.
Rymal Rd. E.
53
Aldercrest Ave.
Book Rd.
Twenty Rd. E.
Miles Rd.
6

0   1.5   3km

provide homes for Loyalists. **Hamilton** was known first as Burlington Bay, then as King's Head, after a local inn. In 1813, it was renamed after George Hamilton. Over the years, it was nicknamed the "Ambitious City" due to its rapid and continued growth.

Cross Main St W and turn [L] onto Ewen Rd. Walter Jakes and Son will be to your right. Turn [R] when rejoining Main St W, then turn [L] onto West Park Ave. Turning [R] onto a very wide Saunders Blvd (the rail trail continues to your left at Cootes Dr), cross Cootes Dr and enter the McMaster University Campus. Following the campus road as it curves to the left, turn [R] onto the next street, Sterling St, and follow it to the traffic lights (this was the first city in Canada to have them) at King St W. Cross King St onto Newton Ave, turning [L] onto Main St W. Take the next [R] onto Longwood Rd S, turning left onto Aberdeen Ave. Continue until you turn [L] onto Lock St. Cross Main St and King St, then turn [L] onto York Blvd. At the entrance to Dundurn Castle, which was home to Canada's first Prime Minister, rejoin the multi-use trail of Dundurn Park.

On your left, enjoy the inspiring view of Hamilton Harbour, the Burlington Skyway and Hamilton's Bayfront and Pier 4 waterfront developments. Cross the York St high-level bridge, which was built in 1931 to replace the first bridge that was built on this site in 1896. A little further down, York St turns into Plains Rd W, where the many original floral displays of the Royal Botanical Gardens are found.

Just after the bridge, turn [L] onto Old Guelph Rd, which rapidly descends to and under Hwy 403. The road begins to climb immediately once clear of the underpass; the Royal Botanical Nature Centre and Arboretum is halfway up the hill on your left.

Turn [L] onto York Rd; when the Valley Rd pumping station comes into view, turn right. Be prepared for a steady climb as you wind your way back up the escarpment to the town of **Flamborough**, where every fire hydrant has its own flag! At Rock Chapel Rd, turn [L], and continue past the Rock Chapel Falls Lookout and Piccioni Mushroom Farm. Keep to your right as Sydenham Rd joins Harvest Rd. From here, it is just a short distance to the railway bridge underpass and Tews Falls. Once you clear the bridge, turn [L] into the parking lot and cycle to an inspiring view of the escarpment and Tews Falls, which are only a few metres shorter than Niagara Falls. Two viewing platforms offer different perspectives, while a walking trail to the left of the falls follows the Bruce Trail to Dundas Peak and other spectacular lookouts.

Rejoin Harvest Rd, pass Greensville School, and turn [L] onto Short Rd, returning to the Spencer Gorge Parking lot on Fallsview Rd.

Practical Information

Population:
City of Hamilton (including Dundas and Flamborough): 467,000

Tourist Information

Hamilton

Tourism and Convention Services
127 King St E, Hamilton, ON L8N 1B1
☎*(905) 546-2666 or 800-263-8590*
www.hamiltonundiscovered.com

Dundas

Dundas Valley Information – Hamilton Conservation Authority
PO Box 7099, 838 Mineral Springs Rd
Ancaster, ON L9G 3L3
☎*(905) 648-4427*
www.conservationhamilton.on.ca

 Bicycle Shops

Hamilton

Main Cycling & Sports Ltd
1461 Main St E, Hamilton, ON L8K 1C5
☎*(905) 544-0338*

Mountain Top Bicycles
525 Mohawk Rd E at Upper Sherman
Hamilton, ON L8V 2J5
☎*(905) 575-8773*

Scattolon Cycle & Sports
1527 Upper Ottawa, Hamilton, ON
L8W 3E2
☎*(905) 574-6778*

Springy's
1048 Barton St E, Hamilton, ON
L8L 3E5
☎*(905) 544-2657*

Central Cycle & Sport
965 King St E, Hamilton, ON L8M 1C3
☎*(905) 522-8445*

Davidson's Sports & Cycle Shop
952 Upper Wellington, Hamilton, ON
L9A 3S2
☎*(905) 383-0435*

Pierik's Cycle Ltd.
840 King W, Hamilton, ON L8S 1K3
☎*(905) 525-8521*

Dundas

Freewheel Cycle
9 King St W, Dundas, ON L9H 1T5
☎*(905) 628-5126*

 Special Sights and Events

Tiger Cats Football, Greater Hamilton Tattoo, Royal Botanical Gardens Floral Festival, Steel City Oktoberfest, Summer Music Festival, Outside In Art Exhibition, Paranormal Summit, Red Hot Jazz & Cool Blues Festival, Provincial Music Festival, Cactus Festival, Winona Peach Festival, Kids Coping Car Rally, Christie Conservation Area, Confederation Park, Devil's Punch Bowl, Felkers Falls, Fifty Point Conservation Area, Spencer Gorge Conservation Area, Devil's Punchbowl Conservation Area, Valens Conservation Area, Tew's Falls, Webster's Falls, Westfield Heritage Village (Rockton), Dundas Valley Conservation Area, Albion Falls, Griffin House (Dundas Valley), The Hermitage Ruins (and museum), Concession Street Festival, Aquafest

Festival Country

 Accommodations

Hotel/Motel/B&B/Hostel/
Camping

9. Elmira and St. Jacob's Countryside Tour

Beginning in the Mennonite town of Elmira, this route includes such sights as a local buggy factory, St. Jacobs blacksmith's forge and a ride through a 60m-long Mennonite buggy bridge.

Return Distance:
60km

Number of recommended legs:
1

Difficulty:

Surface:
Asphalt and gravel, some single track

Villages/Towns/Cities:
Elmira, West Montrose, Winterbourne, Conestogo, St. Jacobs, Hawkesville, Wallenstein

Local Highlights:
Maple Syrup Museum of Canada, The Meeting Place, St. Jacobs Farmers Market & Flea Market, St. Jacobs School House Theatre, Fifties Steam Liner, Horse-Drawn Trolley Tours, St. Jacobs Main St, Elmira Raceway

Recommended Bicycles:
Hybrid/Mountain/Touring

Tour Suggestions:
A full day's ride, but lunch can be prepared ahead from the local farm products available at the St. Jacobs Farmers Market.

How to get there:
From Hwy 401, follow Hwy 6, known as the Hanlon Express-
way. Turn left onto Hwy 7 and then right onto Regional Rd 86, Elmira Rd, on the outskirts of Guelph. Follow Rd 86 into Elmira and at the stop light, turn left onto Arthur St. Go through town to get to the Crossroads Restaurant, located on the left side of Regional Rd 21 and the starting point for the tour. Park your vehicle under the lone maple tree next to the old cemetery.

The town of **Elmira** was settled in the early 1800s and was known first as Bristow's Corners, then as West Woolwich. In 1867, the name was changed to Elmira after the city of the same name in New York State. Many of the area's first settlers were Mennonites from Pennsylvania. Today, Elmira is a subdued little town that has managed to hold on to its traditions of yesteryear. While riding along the main street, notice how it has been designed to accommodate a horse and buggy, the traditional transportation of the local population. Mainly old-order Mennonites live in this area. The order originated under reformer Menno Simons, a Roman Catholic priest who led the Anabaptist movement in the Netherlands and northern Germany in the 1530s. The first Mennonites belonged to a church in Zurich, Switzerland and arrived in the state of Pennsylvania, where William Penn offered them religious liberty, in 1683. The Amish, who follow the teachings of Jacob Ammann, broke away from the Swiss Mennonites in 1690, primarily because of disagreements with church doctrine regarding the practice of shunning. Amish people can be found in 23 U.S. states, as well as in Ontario. The Amish are pacifists, do not swear oaths and will not

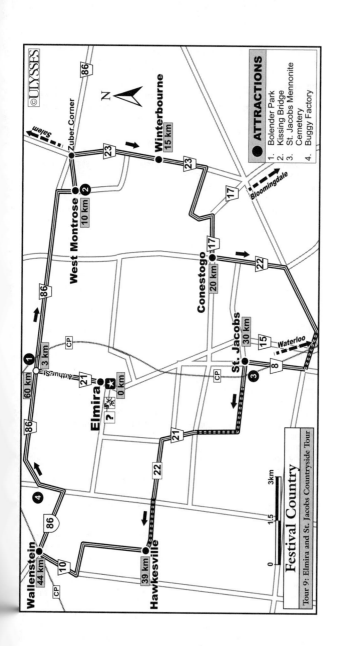

Festival Country
Tour 9: Elmira and St. Jacobs Countryside Tour

ATTRACTIONS
1. Bolender Park
2. Kissing Bridge
3. St. Jacobs Mennonite Cemetery
4. Buggy Factory

N

©ULYSSES

Salem
Zuber Corner
86
Winterbourne 15 km
23
23
17
Bloomingdale
West Montrose 10 km
2
86
Conestogo 20 km
17
22
Waterloo
St. Jacobs 30 km
15
8
3
CP
CP
Arthur St.
21
60 km
1
3 km
86
Elmira
2
0 km
86
4
Wallenstein 44 km
86
CP
10
21
22
Hawkesville 39 km

0   1.5   3km

hold an office that involves the use of force.

Itinerary:

Turning [L] out of the Crossroads parking lot, cycle north along Arthur St into downtown Elmira. Take a few moments to visit the Gore Park bandstand in the downtown core. The bandstand's base was built in 1892 by Henry Zilliax and was located behind his inn (near the present-day Royal Bank). The roof was added in 1912. Continue along Arthur St as it climbs through the town's retail section to the Church St traffic lights. Make a [R] turn and follow Regional Rd 86, past Bolender Park and two local cemeteries.

Enjoy the ride through some of this province's richest agricultural land. Along this road are some very impressive farms. At Waterloo Rd 22 (Salem Rd), a generous cycling lane has been incorporated into the road. A short distance past the **West Montrose** sign, make a [R] turn onto Church St. Coasting downhill, ride by the stone United Church and continue following the road as it passes by the general store and then descends into the Grand River Valley. At the bottom of the hill is the 60m-long West Montrose Buggy Bridge, better known as the Kissing Bridge. The bridge was built in 1881 at a cost of $3,100. Today it is one of the province's last original covered bridges. The name "Kissing Bridge" comes from the early days when it had no windows and was lighted by coal oil lamps. The darkness proved to be the perfect hiding place for young romantic couples. Crossing the Grand River via the bridge, turn [L] and follow the road along the river. Swinging to the right, the

road begins to climb past a restored 1874 home to Wellington Rd 23. Make a [R] turn at the corner and ride past the fluorescent-green school crossing sign and the one-room West Montrose schoolhouse.

Take Wellington Rd 23 into the Scottish settlement of **Winterbourne**. Just past the welcome sign, the road descends and crosses Cox Creek. To the left of the bridge, notice the lovely pond and conservation area, and rushing waters to the right. In the village centre is a very old church. Built in 1870, Chalmers Church continues to serve the needs of the local townsfolk. On this predominately flat road, ride past the Presbyterian Cemetery and Cribit's Seeds. Turn [R] onto Woolwich Rd 45 and enjoy a leisurely ride along one of Ontario's most charming roads.

At the stop sign, turn [L] and cycle past the local golf course. The road swings sharply to the left at the river and joins Waterloo Rd 17. Turn [R] and cross back over Grand River, cycling uphill past a large mill and the Black Forest Inn. Continue along King St, **Conestogo**'s colourful main street, which is lined with many boutiques and craft shops. Make a left turn onto Waterloo Rd 22 (Northfield Dr) and ride south into the southern portion of the Conestogo River Valley.

Cross the Conestoga River and then make a [R] turn onto University Ave, just before the "City of Waterloo" sign. This paved road cuts across the north end of Waterloo and it is here that the country meets the city. At the stop sign facing Priority One Packaging, swing [R] onto Bridge St W. At King St (Waterloo Rd

15), turn [R] and follow this road as it goes over Hwy 86, past a set of lights, the St. Jacobs Farmers Market and the Outlet Mall, into downtown **St. Jacobs**. Here, King St is also called Waterloo Rd 8.

In contrast to Elmira, St. Jacobs has developed commercially, becoming a beehive of activity. First called Jacobstettel by the German and Pennsylvania Dutch settlers who came here in the 1840s, the name was changed to its present one in 1852 to honour two local residents, Jacob Snider and Jacob Eby, who were early millers. Today, St. Jacobs has become one of Ontario's most famous tourist attractions, drawing people from far and wide. Walking along its main street, you can hear the sounds of a blacksmith at work, feel the heat of a glass blower's oven and breathe in the aroma of freshly baked bread.

Note:
Just behind the St. Jacobs Country Mill and the Old Mill Shed is a little bridge that crosses the river and leads to some single track. Follow the Mill Race trail along the creek. It's a lovely ride that exits at Krammer's Buggy Bridge. The bridge was built by a local Mennonite to allow a road crossing at the St. Jacobs Mill Race Pond and Dam.

To finish the ride in Mennonite Country, retrace your path on King St (Waterloo Rd 8) back towards Waterloo. At Henry St, turn [R] and ride past the head office of Home Hardware and the local buggy washing booth and parking lot. Crossing a set of railway tracks, proceed to the [T] intersection at Township Rd 32. Turn [R] and follow the road as it swings to the left. Immediately

after riding over a bridge, the road becomes gravel. As you pass the local Mennonite church and cemetery, notice how the cemetery stone inscriptions all face west. Cross Woolwich Rd 17 and follow Cty Rd 21 north.

Riding past the St. Jacobs Mennonite Cemetery and Three Bridges Public School, look for the home of a local Mennonite who outsmarted the township's building inspector. As the story goes, the local farmer wanted to build a granny flat next to the main part of his home. The township gave him permission to go ahead as long as the new building was attached to the original. Of course, when it was built and wasn't attached, the building inspector became quite upset. The quick-thinking farmer saved the day by taking a beam of wood and attaching it to the two separate buildings. Thus, he complied in a roundabout way with the township's requirement.

At the farm of Elias Martin, notice the windmill that rocks back and forth. Just a few metres ahead, turn [L] onto Woolwich Rd 22. The road immediately descends to Donald Creek and cuts through a dramatically sculpted countryside. Continue along Woolwich Rd 22 into the village of **Hawkesville**.

Turn [R] onto the main street, Geddes St. Enjoy this stimulating ride as you follow the road along the upper banks of the northern portion of the Conestogo River Valley. At Woolwich Rd 10, turn [R] and begin the ride towards the village of **Wallenstein**.

Every so often, look skyward for gliders from the nearby flying club. The groans and squeaks of

Festival Country

several windmills along this road fill the air as you cycle north. The Martins, a local Mennonite clan, own most of the property in the area—as you can see by the names listed on the mailboxes along the road. At the junction of Hwy 86, turn [R] and cycle east toward Elmira.

Riding past the Wallenstein General Store and Wallenstein Brick Company, you will find that Regional Rd 86 is quite busy. When Waterloo 86 begins to arc left, do not take the St. Jacobs/Elmira cutoff (shortcut) on the right. A short distance ahead, a dilapidated silver building will appear on the horizon. Take a few moments to cross the road and visit with the proprietor of this timeless building, which is home to the Elmira Buggy Works.

Now Waterloo 86 swings sharply to the right. On Saturday afternoons, it is quite common to see the black buggies of local Mennonites heading into town for church. Cycling past the Elmira Mennonite Church and its very large cemetery, turn [R] at the traffic lights onto Arthur St. As you make your way back to the Crossroads parking lot, take a few minutes to relax at the Gore Park bandstand... try to imagine how the band would have sounded back in 1892!

Practical Information

Population:
Elmira: 7,300
St. Jacobs: 1,525
Wallenstein: 265

 Tourist Information

Woolwich Visitor Services
5 First St E, Elmira, ON N3B 2E3
☎*(519) 669-2605 or 877-969-0094*
www.elmiramaplesyrupfestival.com

 Bicycle Shops

Central Source For Sports
48 Arthur St S, Elmira, ON NAB 2M6
☎*(519) 669-2706*

 Special Sights and Events

Elmira Maple Syrup Festival, Elmira Quilt Auction, Elmira Country Fair, the Kissing Bridge (West Montrose).

 Market Days

St. Jacobs

Tuesdays, Thursdays, Saturdays, year-round

10. Elora Gorge Adventure (Guelph to Elora)

This tour is ideal for a beginner's first outing. It's great for the first ride of the season and also makes an excellent "fall colours" tour. Cycling north from Guelph, the ride is an easy one, as only a few climbs are encountered on the way to the Elora gorge. The day will quickly slips away as you follow the trail along the gorge past the "Tooth of Time" and into downtown Elora. Enjoy Elora's historic downtown and explore the dramatic gorge before riding

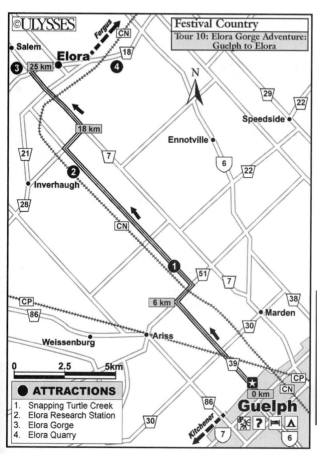

out to the famous cool "Quarry" waters.

Return Distance:
50km

No. of recommended legs:
1

Level of Difficulty:
🚲🚲

Surface:
Asphalt

Villages/Towns/Cities:
Guelph, Elora

Local Highlights:
Elora Gorge Conservation Area, Islet Rock, The Arboretum, Church of Our Lady, Guelph Civic Centre, Guelph Civic Museum, Guelph Lake Conservation Area, Kortright Waterfowl Park,

MacDonald Stewart Art Centre, McCrae House, Riverside Park, town lattice-covered footbridge

Recommended Bicycles:
Touring/Hybrid/Mountain

Tour Suggestions:
Pack a lunch and make a full day of it. Be careful when walking along the gorge; a number of people have actually fallen into it.

How to get there:
From the north and south, Elora can be reached via Hwy 6. From the east, it can be reached by taking Hwys 9 & 24 and from the west, Hwy 86. This tour starts in Guelph. From Hwy 401, take Hwy 6, also called the Hanlan Expressway, north to Hwy 7. Turn right and then immediately turn left onto the Silvercreek Parkway. Begin the tour from the TSC parking lot on your left.

Beginning at Guelph's northern outskirts, just a short distance to the southeast and at the confluence of the Speed and Eramosa rivers, is the city proper. Founded in 1827, the town was named after the British Royal Family by Scottish novelist John Galt, who planned it according to a unique radial street pattern. The town kept its nickname of "The Royal City" over the years because no other city in the entire Commonwealth has the same name. The city was also the home of Colonel John McCrae, the WWI physician who wrote the immortal poem "In Flanders Fields." Today, Guelph is home to the highly regarded Ontario Veterinary College and the Ontario Agriculture College.

Itinerary:
Turn [R] out of the TSC parking lot and cycle north on the Silvercreek Parkway. Riding past School House No.4, you will quickly leave the city behind. Wellington Rd 39 becomes a comfortable and interesting ride after you cross Wellington Rd 30, since at this point motor-vehicle traffic virtually disappears. At the Schuett's Corners [T] intersection, turn [R] onto Wellington Rd 51. Ride past the abandoned rail bed and make a [L] turn at the next road, 2nd Line E. The road climbs, then levels out and passes through a marshy area known as Snapping Turtle Creek. Be careful: in spring, these "hardshells" cross the road in numbers. Just past Side Rd 14 is the Ponsonby Conservation Area and Ball Park.

The road goes uphill past a farm-tractor graveyard before it levels out and reaches the Elora Research Station complex. It then descends through a wetland. Make a [R] turn onto Side Rd 7 and enjoy a short ride through the Elora Highlands before turning [L] onto Wellington Rd 7, which leads into Elora. Continue past the traffic lights and follow the road as it descends to the bridge lookout. Walk out onto the bridge to take in the dramatic view of the gorge's tall walls, rocks, crevices and caves. To the left is the beginning of the Elora Gorge Conservation Area, which offers excellent camping and is a favourite spot for tubing during the summer months. There are trails here, but you must pay the admission fee to enter the park.

Join the single-track trail on the right, just before the bridge, and ride along the top of the gorge towards downtown Elora. There are many side trails to explore, all of which access the river below. If you go down to the river, it is best to dismount and walk to the bottom of the gorge. The path is steep and treacherous, and there are often other trail users on it. As you ride into Elora, the heritage buildings, bridges and the impressive Tooth of Time will come into view. The Tooth of Time, a stone islet in the middle of a waterfall, is Elora's landmark as well as the official end of the gorge. Look for the rope suspended over the rushing waters of the Grand River; it offers adventurers a chance to test their mountain-climbing skills (at their own risk). The trail exits onto the street at some local factories, including Little Folks Furniture Factory. Continue through this area until you come to the wooden footbridge, where you turn [R] to cross the river and visit downtown Elora.

The Elora Gorge was formed by two separate geological events, separated by almost 300-million years. The Elora Gorge begins at the Irvine Creek low-level bridge, west of town, and extends all the way to the Tooth of Time. The gorge also continues up the Irvine Creek to the village of Salem, where it ends at a waterfall under the highway bridge. The village of Elora was not settled until the winter of 1817, when Roswell Matthews walked from Niagara to Elora to begin construction of his log home. The town was named "Elora" after the ship owned by the brother of the town benefactor, Captain Gilkison.

Today, the village of Elora is building on its past, so be sure to spend some riding time exploring old Elora along the Grand River. Here, you will find a town that is blessed with many magnificent old homes and stone churches. After crossing the footbridge, turn [L] and follow Mill St into the Old Mill Restaurant parking lot and to the stable lookout, which is now closed. Retracing your path east back along Mill St, past the traffic lights, leave Elora to reach Elora Quarry. At the old grist mill entrance, follow the road to the right to get to the path along the upper portion of the gorge and a set of stairs that leads into it.

The Elora Quarry is an excellent place to end the day. Although it is possible to walk completely around the top, be extremely careful as the trail is narrow at the back. To return to Guelph, simply retrace the route back to Hwy 7 and the Silvercreek Parkway.

Practical Information

Population:
Guelph: 100,000
Elora: 4,500

 Tourist Information

Guelph

Guelph Visitor and Convention Services
42 Wyndham St N, 1st Floor
Guelph, ON N1H 7T8
☎ *(519) 837-1335 or 800-334-4519*
www.city.guelph.on.ca/visit

Elora

Fergus Information Centre
400 Tower St S, Fergus, ON N1M 2P7
☎ *(519) 843-5140 or 877-242-6353*
www.ferguselora.com

Festival Country

Bicycle Shops

Elora

(See page 85)

Guelph

Bicycles Etc.
9 Elizabeth St
☎(519) 763-3325

Bits & Bikes
17 Gordon St, ON N1H 3V5
☎(519) 824-0866

George Vettor Cycle & Sport
RR 6, ON N1H 6J3
☎(519) 824-5829

Paramount Ski & Sports
4-35 Harvard Rd, ON N1G 3A2
☎(519) 822-1767

Revolutions Bicycles
43 Cork St E, ON N1H 2W7
☎(519) 766-4082

Speed River Bicycle
135 Wyndham St N, ON N1H 4E9
☎(519) 824-9371

 Special Sights and Events

Canada Day, Guelph Jazz Festival, Hillside Festival, Rotary Club Ribfest, Guelph Spring Festival

 Accommodations

Hotel/Motel/B&B/Camping

 Off-Road Cycling

Yes; refer to "Off-Road Cycling" at the end of this chapter.

11. Paris to Cambridge Rail Trail

The bicycle ride from Paris to Cambridge along the abandoned Lake Erie & Northern Railway has to be one of the loveliest single-day outings in the province. It's a leisurely ride that is enhanced by the stunning backdrop of the Grand River Valley.

Return Distance:
38km

No. of recommended legs:
1

Level of Difficulty:
🚲

Surface:
Crushed gravel

Villages/Town/Cities:
Paris, Glen Morris, Cambridge

Local Highlights:
Adelaide Hunter Hoodless Homestead, Bell Homestead, Brant County Museum & Archives, Royal Chapel of the Mohawks, Paris Cobblestone Architecture, Antique Market, Canning Perennials, Churchill Park, African Lion Safari, Cambridge Arts Theatre, Cambridge Galleries, Bi-Annual Can-American Games, Cambridge Riverfest, Fat Tire Festival, Mill Race Festival, Downtown Funfest, Cambridge Fall Fair

Recommended Bicycles:
Hybrid/Mountain/Touring

Tour Suggestions:
This is a great family ride and a great "fall colours" outing. Pack a

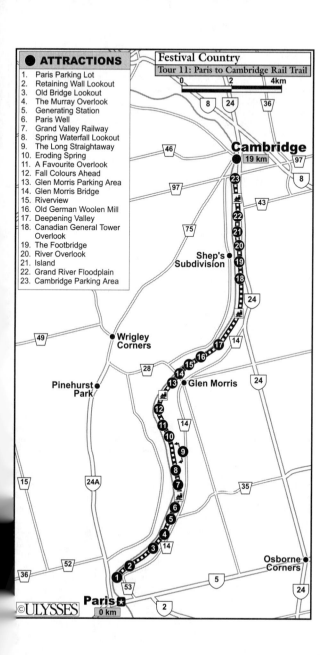

● ATTRACTIONS

1. Paris Parking Lot
2. Retaining Wall Lookout
3. Old Bridge Lookout
4. The Murray Overlook
5. Generating Station
6. Paris Well
7. Grand Valley Railway
8. Spring Waterfall Lookout
9. The Long Straightaway
10. Eroding Spring
11. A Favourite Overlook
12. Fall Colours Ahead
13. Glen Morris Parking Area
14. Glen Morris Bridge
15. Riverview
16. Old German Woolen Mill
17. Deepening Valley
18. Canadian General Tower Overlook
19. The Footbridge
20. River Overlook
21. Island
22. Grand River Floodplain
23. Cambridge Parking Area

Festival Country
Tour 11: Paris to Cambridge Rail Trail

0   2   4km

Cambridge
19 km

Shep's Subdivision

Wrigley Corners

Pinehurst Park

Glen Morris

Osborne Corners

Paris
0 km

©ULYSSES

picnic lunch and spend part of the day in Churchill Park.

How to get there:
Paris can be reached from the east and west by following Hwy 2, and from Hwy 401, via Exit 286 (Cedar Creek Rd/Hwy 97), travelling east to Road 47, where a right turn will take you into town. Start from the Paris Lions Park (free parking) to get a great view of the Grand River. The park is located just off Hwy 2, at the top of the hill before the junction of Hwy 2 and the Grand River Rd. At the cemetery, follow the park road down to the river. Take the wooden walkway across the Nith River to the main street, Grand River Rd. Turn [L] and, upon reaching the traffic lights, turn [R] and cross the Grand River. Turn [L] immediately after the bridge and join the trail that runs along the river. The trail exits onto East River Rd; continue riding north. A short distance ahead, on the right, is the Paris Pavilion and the parking lot for the Grand River Trail. Turn left into the parking lot and join the rail bed.

Paris is probably the second most important town in the County of Brant. Located at the confluence of the Grand and Nith rivers, it is one of Ontario's most picturesque and inviting spots. Settled by immigrants in 1821, it was known as "The Forks of the Grand River." The settlement was officially named Paris after the large plaster-of-paris beds developed by its founder, Vermont native Hiram Capron, in 1828. Paris also played a role in Alexander Graham Bell's first long-distance telephone call, which took place on August 10, 1876. As you ride along the main street, you are surrounded by cobblestone

buildings. Paris has Canada's largest number of cobblestone buildings, 11 homes and two churches.

Itinerary:
There are several lookouts along the rail bed that should not be missed. The Spring Waterfall Lookout is sometimes hard to locate. Approximately 1km past the Paris Well, the falls can be heard and found along the left side of the trail. They are hidden from view by overgrown bushes, so look for the entrance carefully.

Another interesting spot is the old German Woolen Mill, which is a short distance past the **Glen Morris** parking lot. Be careful here as the old stone walls may be unstable. The mill is on private property, so respect the owner's rights. If you are ready for a water refill, line up at the freshwater spring (one of many along the trail) and enjoy a cold, invigorating drink.

The trail passes the Cambridge Water Treatment Plant and exits onto Hwy 24, near a gas station and Churchill Park. Churchill Park is the second largest park in **Cambridge** and features deer, bird pens, washrooms, picnic and limited camping facilities. Churchill Park is a great place to stop for a break before returning to Paris along the river trail.

Optional Side Trip:
The more adventurous can follow Hwy 24 to Concession St. Cross the Grand River and turn [R], joining the Cambridge River Bank System. Follow this network of pathways along the river through numerous parks to the 21m-high Devil's Creek Waterfall and Devil's Cave.

Also note that from Paris, the SC Johnson Trail provides a 10km link to the Hamilton-to-Brantford Rail Trail (32km).

Practical Information

Population:
Paris: 9,000
Cambridge: 111,000

 Tourist Information

Paris

County of Brant
66 Grand River St N, ON N3L 2M2
☎(519) 442-6342
www.brant.ca

Cambridge

Cambridge Tourism
750 Hespeler Rd, ON N3H 5L8
☎(519) 622-2336 or 800-749-7560
www.cambridgetourism.com

 Bicycle Shops

Paris

Paris Sporting Goods
52 Grand River N, Paris, ON N3L 2M2
☎(519) 442-6843

Cambridge

Bikes At Rivers 'n Trails
22 Queen St W, ON N3C 1G1
☎(519) 658-2155

Cycle Cambridge
305 Hespeler Rd, ON N1R 6J2
☎(519) 740-8766

Sears & Grills
10 Hespeler Rd, ON N1R 6J6
☎(519) 624-5814

Ontario Sports Distributors
653 King St E, ON N3H 3N7
☎(519) 653-4651

 Special Sights and Events

Canada Week and Parade, Springtime in Paris, St. James Annual Miniature Show, Paris Country Fair, Annual Steam Show, Christmas in Paris, Cambridge Highland Games, Mill Race Festival of Traditional Folk Music, Cambridge Fall Fair, Oktoberfest, Fall Foliage Hike, Cobblestone Festival, St George Apple Harvest Festival

 Accommodations

Motel/B&B/Camping

 Off-Road Cycling

Yes; refer to "Off-Road Cycling" section at the end of this chapter.

 Market Days

Saturdays, May to late fall

12. Welland Canal Explorer: Port Dalhousie, St. Catharines and Welland

Beginning in Port Dalhousie, the first leg is an adventurous ride along the Merritt Trail as it follows a portion of the original canal and the rushing white waters of Twelve Mile Creek. The route visits Lock 7 in the city of Thorold for a close-up view of large ocean

Festival Country

freighters and ends in the city of Welland. Leg 2 begins by taking in Welland's many large murals before crossing Merritt Island to join the Welland Canal Parkway Trail. The highlight of this much-easier return leg is the Lock 3 Visitor's Centre and the water-front trail from Port Weller to Port Dalhousie.

Return Distance:
108km (58km, 50km)

No. of recommended legs:
2

Level of Difficulty:
🚲 🚲 🚲

Surface:
Asphalt, single track, jeep road, loose gravel

Villages/Towns/Cities:
Port Dalhousie, St. Catharines, Thorold, Port Weller

Local Highlights:
Welland Canal Locks 7 and 3, Brock University, British Methodist Episcopal Church, Happy Rolph Bird Sanctuary, Morningstar Mill and Decew Falls, Rodman Hall Arts Centre, Stokes Seeds, Port Dalhousie Mercantile District, Lakeside Park Carousel, Hernder Estate Wines, Henry of Pelham Family Estate, Battle of Beaverdams Park, Welland Historical Museum, Welland Recreational Canal, The Wine Route, Wiley Brothers Farms

Recommended Bicycles:
Mountain/Hybrid

Tour Suggestions:
The tour can be completed in a day, but staying in Welland overnight makes it much more interesting and relaxing.

How to get there:
From the east or west, take the Queen Elizabeth Way and exit at Ontario St. From the south, follow Hwy 58/ 406 to Ontario St, then turn left onto Lakeport Rd and follow it into Port Dalhousie's Lakeside Park.

As the starting point for the first Welland canals, almost 170 years ago, **Port Dalhousie** has tried to preserved much of its heritage. Here, along the lake shores, are two lighthouses from the early 1800s and an antique hand-carved 1898 indoor carousel, brought here from Rhode Island in 1921. As well, just a short distance from the beach and attracting much attention, are two English-style double-decker buses and some intriguing sailing vessels hailing from many different ports of call.

Itinerary:
Leg 1
(Welland to Port Dalhousie, 58km)

First, take a few moments to ride out on the pier, then exit the parking lot and go past the red double-decker buses onto Hogans Alley. Turn [L] onto Lock St, then make a [R] turn onto Main St. Follow the tree-lined boulevard past the Anne St memorial statue, Martindale Rd and the three-armed tree, then make a [L] turn onto Third St S.

A short distance past the tree nursery, swing [L] onto the Green Ribbon Trail, which is dedicated to missing children. Descending quickly, the trail crosses a class-one wetland before exiting onto Martindale Rd. Cycling past the Martindale Pond and over the Queen Elizabeth Way, prepare for a [L] turn onto the Merritt Trail. As you approac

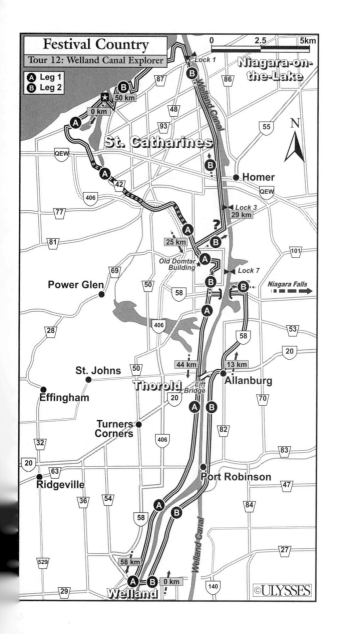

Huntington Square Mall, the trail entrance is on your left, just before Erion Rd.

Descending quickly to the old Welland Canal, also known as Twelve Mile Creek, the trail appears to be below water level, and in the spring and fall, this area may be wet. You can hear plenty of rushing water and noise as the canal exits at Welland Ave on the Niagara College Business Campus. Turn [L], cross the canal and follow Welland Ave/Vale Rd about halfway uphill, and rejoin the trail by going through the gate on your right. The trail is now high above the canal's deep, green waters, which are still noisily churning and frothing. On the right is a unique salmon-coloured firehouse. Exit onto a paved cul-de-sac, continue straight, and rejoin the trail at the far end as it descends to Burgoyne Bridge. Climbing, look for the rocks indicating the trail direction, and go straight as the trail runs parallels to the road. At McGuire St and St. Pauls Cr, turn [R] onto the walkway and cross Hwy 406 on Westchester Cr.

Follow this four-lane road across Hwy 406 (for the second time) to the Captain Scott Misner section of the Merritt Trail. The trail entrance is on the right, just before the traffic lights at Oakdale Ave, at the Knifeworks Historical Site.

Turning [R], the trail immediately descends and quickly arrives at a split in the road; make a [L] turn, cross the wooden bridge, and follow the crushed-gravel surface to Moffatt St, where it crosses Disher St, and rejoin the trail on the left. Both trail and canal are ascending. Pass a bridge on your left and continue to the end of

Moffat St. A paved path starts here and crosses the CN tracks (which are active, so proceed with caution). Ride along between the canal and Glengary Park. As the trail changes into gravel, it exits onto Glendale Ave. Take note of Johansson's Bar on the left, and visit the remains of the old Domtar building across the road, on your left.

As a suggestion, it will be safer and much quicker to walk across Glendale Ave into Mountain Locks Park or onto Mountain St. Once across the road, there are two ways to join the trail: either take the path on the other side of the trees at the park entrance, or go past the historical plaque just a short distance down Mountain St, on the left. This section is a lot of fun to ride as it dips and dives, twists and turns, and finally exits onto Bradley St. Follow Bradley St to the [T] intersection at Town Line Rd W. Turning [L], the road crosses the canal, which disappears underground. At Front St, turn [R] and cycle into downtown **Thorold**. The town was named after Sir John Thorold and was the site of a mighty battle during the War of 1812, at Beaverdams Park. This battle was a major loss for the Americans, who were defeated by a much smaller contingent of Aboriginal soldiers led by Major William Johnson Kerr.

Turn [L] onto Clairmont St, cross Ormond St S, and pass two very impressive churches to the stop sign at the Chapel St [T] intersection. Turn [R] and then [L] onto Flight Locks Rd, which will bring you alongside Lock 7 of the Welland Canal. Here you can almost reach over the fence and touch the ships as they travel through the last lift over the Niagara Escarpment. The canal was built to bypass Niagara Falls, which connect Lake Ontario to Lake Erie. The first canal was built in 1829, and the first leg of this journey began and will end alongside one of the original canals. The present-day canal, near which you are now standing, has seven locks, each with a height gain of 14.2m.

Return to Chapel St, turn [L] and then [R] onto Portland St. When you come to a mosque at Ormond St, turn [L]. Follow Ormond, keeping left, and go past Beaverdams Rd until you reach a set of gates. Proceed through the gates and follow the upper jeep road, keeping the canal on the left. Ahead in the distance are two black towers that cross the canal. They disappear from view as you turn at the small, fenced-in hydro power station located a short distance past the fluorescent-green markings on both sides of the canal. Turn [R] on the jeep trail on the far side of the station and follow it across some abandoned railway tracks to a [T] intersection. Turn [L] and continue to the first trail on the right, which leads down and across the old waterway.

Once across the water, swing [L] and continue following the sandy old jeep roads to a railway bridge. Turn [R], and cross the bridge to join the jeep road on the other side. As the trail approaches a water-control dam, watch for glass—now is not the time for a flat tire! Leave the dam by following the road back to the canal and the twin towers of lift bridge No. 11.

The constant twanging sound of the bridge's guy wires fills the air as the jeep road enters Allanburg Park. Leave the park and turn [R] onto Niagara Regional Rd 20. After crossing a small bridge, turn [L] onto Princess St, cycle uphill and join the trail on your left. Be careful as this is single-track. Keep your wits about you as this section of trail is somewhat difficult. Exiting along the canal, keep right, following the water to a [T] intersection. Swing [R] and follow the jeep road up a slight grade moving away from the canal into a wooded area. The trail exits onto a cul-de-sac and then descends past some large rafts along the canal and around a gate at Fox Rd. Ride through the steelyard and cross the railway tracks. This fourth section of the Welland canal is no longer used for shipping but for recreational purposes.

The trail quickly changes from loose gravel to asphalt and then back into gravel as it enters a green area along the canal. After passing Notre Dame College School, join the single-track path on your left, which leads back to the canal and Main St. At Main St, turn [L], cross the old Welland Canal and make an immediate [L] onto Boardwalk St.

Festival Country

The "Rose City," **Welland** has always been prosperous due to its proximity to the canal. The original settlement was called Aqueduct, and the name changed to Merrittsville in 1842, in honour of William Hamilton Merritt, the financial agent for the Welland Canal. In 1858, upon its incorporation, Lt. Gov. Simcoe renamed the settlement Welland after the river in Lincolnshire, England.

Leg 2
(Welland to Port Dalhousie, 50km)

Take a few minutes to explore Welland's famous murals on the back streets that branch off Main St. Within a four-block radius of your present location, there are over 27 giant outdoor murals painted by some of Canada's finest artists.

A short distance along Boardwalk St at the S-bend, get on the pathway as it passes between some cedars on the left side of the road. Riding along the canal into Merritt Island Park, keep to the left and follow the paved pathway as it goes under one bridge, over another and changes into a crushed gravel trail just before arriving at a set of railway tracks. At the railway tracks, turn [L] and cross the canal. On the far side of the bridge, turn [R] and rejoin the trail you were on earlier.

To get to the best spot along the canal to view ships in motion, cross the train tracks and follow the jeep road to the canal's [Y] junction, located where the road swings sharply to right. Here, the ships heading for Lake Erie can be seen as they send tall plumes of steam into the air.

Follow the trail back to Niagara Regional Rd 20, turn [R] and walk your bicycle across the lift bridge. Turn [L] onto Regional Rd 58/Davis Rd and cycle to the traffic lights at Thorold Stone Rd. Immediately after crossing the lights, turn [L] and join the bicycle path, which goes under the canal into the Thorold Tunnel. This was the first tunnel built under the Welland Canal. After passing through the tunnel, at the top of the hill, turn [R] onto Ormond St and ride to St. David St. Turn [L] and then [R] onto Front St, and cycle back to Mountain Locks Park. At Glendale Ave turn [R] and pedal to the Welland Canal Parkway Trail.

Do not cross the canal. Once on the canal trail, cycling is much easier. The first stop along the Welland Canal Parkway Trail is the visitors centre at Lock 3. The main information centre for the canal (washroom facilities and refreshments available), the visitors centre houses many historical artifacts. There is also an elevated observation deck and the Lacrosse Hall of Fame. Lacrosse is Canada's national sport—it is not hockey, as many people tend to think. The observation deck is an ideal place to stop and see the ocean-going freighters make their way across the Niagara escarpment. For the most part, the trail runs parallel to Government Rd. Ride under Queenston St, past Lock 2 and then Lock 1 at Lakeshore Rd before entering Malcomson Park. At the Port Weller Municipal Beach, the trail swings left and turns into the Waterfront Trail, which runs from Niagara Falls to Gananoque. Follow the Waterfront Trail signs as they guide you along Arthur S into Cherrie Road Park. For the most part, the trail hugs the Lake Ontario shoreline and passes through Spring Garden Park and

Belmont Park before following a few back streets into Westcliffe Park. After the old lighthouse, the trail rounds the harbour and finally returns to the starting point, at Port Dalhousie's Lakeside Park.

Practical Information

Population:
St. Catharines: 140,000
Welland: 48,000

 Tourist Information

St. Catharines

St. Catharines Chamber of Commerce
PO Box 940, 1 St. Paul St, ON L2R 6Z4
☎*(905) 684-2361*
www.scchamberofcommerce.com

Welland

Tourism of Welland Niagara
Seaway Mall
800 Niagara St N, ON L3C 5Z4
☎*(905) 735-8696*
www.tourismwelland.com

 Bicycle Shops

St. Catharines

Liberty Bicycles
40 St. Paul St, ON L2R 3M2
☎*(905) 682-1454*

Ski Pro Shop
278 Geneva St, ON L2N 2E8
☎*(905) 934-2682*

Bikefit
84 Scott St, ON L2N 1H1
☎*(905) 646-9396*

Buckner's Souce for Sports
120 Welland Ave, ON L2R 2N3
☎*(905) 641-0066*

Rapid City Cycle
331 St. Paul St, ON L2R 3N1
☎*(905) 684-9111*

Uptown Sports
13 Queenston St, ON L2R 2Y8
☎*(905) 685-4535*

Cooke's Cycle
9 Lock St, ON L2N 5B6
☎*(905) 937-2859*

Thorold

Clarkson Cycle & Fitness
103-A Pine St S, ON L2V 1P7
☎*(905) 227-0810*

Welland

Thornton's Cycle & Sports
Lincoln Plaza
300 Lincoln St, Welland, ON L3B 4N4
☎*(905) 732-4770*

Buckner's Source for Sports
545 Niagara St, ON L3C 1L7
☎*(905) 734-6422*

Goods Service & Cycle
17 Southworth St N, ON L3B 1X8
☎*(905) 732-5535*

 Special Sights and Events

St. Catharines

Niagara Grape & Wine Festival, Oktoberfest, Ontario Sausage Festival, Royal Canadian Henley Regatta, Salmon Derby, Folks Arts Festival, Strawberry Festival, Summer Solstice Festival

Welland

Canadian Canoeing Championships, Niagara Food Festival,

Festival Country

Niagara Regional Exhibition, Soiree Traditionelle, Welland Heritage Folkfest, Canada Day, Vanely Nights by the Canal, Welland Rose Festival

 Accommodations

St. Catharines

Hotel/Motel/B&B/Camping

 Off-Road Cycling

St. Catharines: Yes; several in the area. Refer to the "Off-Road Cycling" section at the end of this chapter.

 Market Days

St. Catharines

Tuesdays, Thursdays and Saturdays, year round, behind the Old Court House

13. Myths, Miracles and Pathways

This tour begins in Niagara-on-the-Lake, the first capital of Upper Canada, and travels through Queenston Heights, one of the province's oldest towns. Passing under the shadow of Brock's Monument, it follows the Niagara Recreational Trail along the Niagara River. It then climbs high above the rapids at the Niagara Generating Station, and heads to the Seventh Wonder of the World, Niagara Falls.

Return Distance:
55km

No. of recommended legs:
1

Level of Difficulty:

Surface:
Asphalt, very little gravel

Villages/Towns/Cities:
Niagara-on-the-Lake, Queenston Heights, Virgil, Niagara Falls

Local Highlights:
Casino Niagara, Great Gorge Adventures, The Guinness Book of World Records, Journey Behind the Falls, Louis Tussaud's Waxworks, Lundy's Lane Historical Museum, *Maid of the Mist*, Marineland, Minolta Tower, Mount Carmel & St. Therese Shrine, Niagara Falls Art Gallery, Niagara Falls Museum, Niagara helicopter rides, Niagara Parks Butterfly Conservatory and Greenhouses, Queenston Heights Park, Air-Combat Canada, Fort George National Historic Park, Laura Secord Homestead, Mackenzie Heritage Printery, McFarland House, Niagara Historical Society Museum, Niagara Parkway, Shaw Festival, Samuel E. Weir Library, 11 local wineries

Recommended Bicycles:
Touring/Hybrid/Mountain

Tour Suggestions:
Pack a lunch to enjoy on the tour

How to get there:
Get off the Queen Elizabeth Way at the exit for Hwy 55 and follow it to Niagara-on-the-Lake. Start the trip at the Fort George parking lot on the Niagara Parkway. Parking is free and it is safe to park here. As the Niagara River Recreational trail winds its way

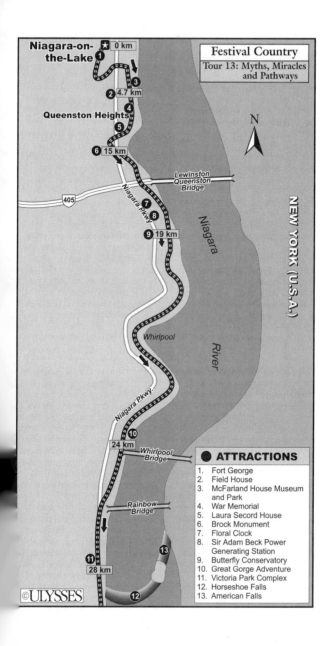

Niagara-on-the-Lake ⭐ 0 km
①

③

② 4.7 km
④

Queenston Heights
⑤

⑥ 15 km

405

Niagara Pkwy.

*Lewinston
Queenston
Bridge*

⑦

⑧

⑨ 19 km

Niagara

NEW YORK (U.S.A.)

Whirlpool

River

Niagara Pkwy.

⑩

24 km

*Whirlpool
Bridge*

*Rainbow
Bridge*

⑬

⑪ 28 km

⑫

©ULYSSES

N

● **ATTRACTIONS**

1. Fort George
2. Field House
3. McFarland House Museum and Park
4. War Memorial
5. Laura Secord House
6. Brock Monument
7. Floral Clock
8. Sir Adam Beck Power Generating Station
9. Butterfly Conservatory
10. Great Gorge Adventure
11. Victoria Park Complex
12. Horseshoe Falls
13. American Falls

through the region's fruit belt, you will see many historical landmarks and enjoy the breathtaking scenery of the Niagara River gorge. The highlight of this ride is the impressive American and Canadian falls. Here, the myths of the past are only surpassed by the falls' stunning beauty and the legendary barrel riders who have braved its thundering water to the bottom of the gorge.

Itinerary:
Facing historic Fort George, built in 1796, turn [R] then [R] again and follow the Niagara Recreational Trail across Queen's Parade, and past modern replicas of period barracks and cannons. After arcing to the left and passing the vine-covered fences along John St, the trail crosses the parkway, follows the Niagara River and soon arrives at the back door of a well-preserved Georgian brick house. This was the home of His Majesty's Boat Builder, James McFarland. A short distance ahead, on the other side of the road, just after Line 2, is the "Field House," now a private residence. Built in the 1800s, it is one of the oldest brick buildings in the province. The trail crosses many wooden bridges and passes several local wineries as it makes its way to the spot where Roger Wood-ward, at age of seven, was the first person to be swept over the falls unprotected and survive!

Just a short distance ahead of the adjacent Inniskillin water tower, the trail enters a residential area. Remember to yield the right of way to cars and other trail users. At the first driveway past the water tower, turn [L] and follow the trail into the woods instead of proceeding along the parkway portion of the trail. This is a lovely ride that offers refreshing shade

on hot days. The trail climbs back up to the parkway, where you are rewarded with a great view of the Niagara River. The river is approximately 56km long and moves along at a respectable 64kph.

After passing some intricate residential stone fences, the trail leaves the parkway and descends into the town of **Queenston**. Coast downhill past a pillared Georgian mansion known as Willowbank. Built for Alexander Hamilton in 1833, it served as the area's first post office. To the left of the mansion is a laneway that leads down to an excellent view of the Niagara River.

At the bottom of the valley, an exhilarating climb begins on Queenston St as you cycle past the Queenston Baptist Church (1842) and Laura Secord's homestead. As the road swings to the right, notice the glass-enclosed bronze statue of Sir Isaac Brock's horse. At the Niagara Parkway, turn [L] and then [R] onto York St and access the trail on your left. Then it's a long climb to the top of the Niagara Escarpment. At the top of the hill, the trail enters Roy Terrace, where the Niagara River Gorge begins. To the right are 260 steps leading to Queenston Heights Park, and to the left is the Niagara Parkway. Take the easier way into the park by following the parkway to the park's entrance. Since one of the most important battles of the War of 1812 took place here, a 64m monument dedicated to the battle's hero, Sir Isaac Brock, dominates the park and the valley below. To the left of the statue, enjoy a fantastic view of the Niagara River as it flows into Lake Ontario. Here, the Bruce Trail begins its 693km long journey across the province to the tip of the Bruce Peninsula.

Rejoin the trail by exiting the parking lot, crossing the parkway, and accessing the trailhead on the left. The trail crosses a parking lot and goes under the Lewiston Queenston Bridge. On the far side of the road is one of the world's largest floral clocks (12m in diameter), built by Ontario Hydro in 1950. The face of the clock is now a landmark, covered with 19,000 plants and maintained by the gardeners and students of the Niagara Parks Commission.

The trail rounds a bend and arrives at the Sir Adam Beck Power Generating Station. Here, it passes under a row of hydro towers and overlooks the rapids on the Niagara River far below. After the ivy-covered Hall of Memory, the trail exits into a large parking lot. Keep left as you ride along the gorge, and follow the trail across the Niagara Parkway. After passing the Butterfly Conservatory and the Niagara Parks School of Horticulture, you will notice the Niagara Glen Picnic and Nature Area on the opposite side of the parkway. Its unique nature shop makes for an interesting stop. The trail crosses back over the parkway just after Niagara Glen, and enters Thompson Point. This is an excellent rest spot where you can watch a cable car cross the gorge that separates Canada and the United States.

The trail enters a grove of gnarled pine trees and follows what used to be the double-track bed of the electric Niagara Falls Park and River Railway. As you ride past the helicopter landing pad, the Minolta Tower is clearly visible in

the distance. The trail ends at the Whirlpool Rapids Lookout and the Spanish Aero Car ride which dangles its riders some 550m above the swirling whirlpools of **Niagara Falls**.

At this point, the trail joins the parkway and the spectacular gorge fades into the distance. We suggest you walk your bicycle along the sidewalk for the next several kilometres, as the view is just too good to miss.

Ahead is the Great Gorge Adventure and the Whirlpool Bridge. As you pass the magnificent stonework of Christ Church, you will feel the mist off the American falls spray your face. The gorge is much wider here, and the water movement has slowed considerably. Just after passing under the Rainbow Bridge, you can see both the 56m-high American Bridal Falls and 54m-high Canadian Horseshoe Falls. The Rainbow Bridge marks the beginning of Queen Victoria Park. One of North America's most prestigious gardens, it encompasses some 62ha of rock and rose gardens, stately trees and over 500,000 daffodils that bloom in the spring. To the right is the new casino and just ahead is the Victoria Park Restaurant and the Maid of the Mist Complex. There are so many people here that it is much easier to get around by walking your bicycle. This recreational trail continues all the way to Fort Erie, but with so much to explore, it is perhaps best to leave that trip for another day.

The return ride to Niagara-on-the-Lake is much safer and quicker if you take the road rejoining the trail at the Spanish Aero Cars. As the trail approaches Thomson Park, look for a single-track trail to the right. Follow this old Aboriginal trail to one of the best lookouts on the river. Be careful: just before it rejoins the recreational trail, it drops dramatically over several tree roots. After passing Vrooman's Battery, continue following the river trail along the parkway to Brown's Point instead of descending along the tree-lined path taken earlier. Finally, keep to the right, following the trail along the gorge through a grove of stately oaks and French thorn trees. On this return leg, the trail you have been following exits onto the parkway behind Fort George. Turn [R] onto the road and follow it as it descends to the Navy hall and the refurbished steamship *SS Pumper*. At Melville St, turn [L] and pedal uphill to a [L] turn onto Byron St. After riding past the front doors of Queens Landing, join the path at the end of the road and return to the Fort George parking lot.

Practical Information

Population:
Niagara-on-the-Lake: 14,000
Niagara Falls: 82,000

 Tourist Information

Niagara-on-the-Lake

Niagara-on-the-Lake Chamber of Commerce
PO Box 1043
26 Queen St, Niagara-on-the-Lake, ON
L0S 1J0
☎ *(905) 468-1950*
www.niagaraonthelake.com

Niagara Falls

Niagara Falls Chamber of Commerce
4056 Dorchester Rd, ON L2M 6M3
☎ *(905) 374-3666*
www.nflschamber.com

Niagara Falls Tourism
5515 Stanley Ave, ON L2G 3X4
☎ *(905) 356-6061 or 800-563-2557*
www.discoverniagara.com

 Bicycle Shops

Niagara-on-the-Lake

The Bike Shop
996 Lakeshore Rd, Niagara-on-the-Lake, ON
☎ *(905) 934-3815*

Niagara Falls

Pedlar Bicycle Shop
4547 Queen St, Niagara Falls, ON
☎ *(905) 357-1273*

Cupolo's Sports Bicycle Rentals
5510 Ferry St
☎ *(905) 356-4850*

Leisure Trails Bike Rentals
4362 Leader Ln, Niagara Falls, ON
☎ *(905) 371-9888*

Steve's Place Bicycles and Repair
181 Niagara Blvd, Fort Erie, ON
☎ *(905) 871-7517*

 Special Sights and Events

Niagara-on-the-Lake

Shaw Festival, Virgil Stampede, Hillebrand's Vineyard, Peach Festival, Canada Day, Cherry Festival, Strawberry Festival, Tou of Homes

Niagara Falls

May Blossom Festival, Police Pipes and Drums Tattoo, Winter Festival of Lights, Flower shows at the Niagara Greenhouses, Fort Erie Friendship Festival, Living History Weekend, Blues in the Park, All Hallow's Eve, Chrysanthemum Show, McFarland Christmas,

Falls Friday Fireworks, Folkarts Festival.

 Accommodations

Niagara-on-the-Lake and Niagara Falls

Hotel/Motel/Inn/B&B/Camping

14. Wineries and Vineyards

The quiet backroads of the picturesque Niagara Escarpment and the surrounding vineyards and countryside provide the picturesque backdrop for this tour. Occasional stops along the route will allow you to experience the traditions and hospitality of a number of world-class wine producers.

Return Distance:
~6km

No. of recommended legs:

Level of Difficulty:

Surface:
asphalt, very little gravel

Villages/Towns/Cities:
Niagara-on-the-Lake, Queenston Heights, Virgil, Niagara Falls

Local Highlights:
Casino Niagara, Great Gorge Adventures, The Guinness Book of World Records, Journey Behind the Falls, Louis Tussaud's Waxworks, Lundy's Lane Historical Museum, *Maid of the Mist*, Marineland, Minolta Tower, Mount Carmel & St. Therese Shrine, Niagara Falls Art Gallery, Niagara Falls Museum, Niagara Helicopters Ride, Niagara Parks Butterfly Conservatory and Greenhouses, Queenston Heights Park, Air-Combat Canada, Fort George National Historic Park, Laura Secord Homestead, Mackenzie Heritage Printery, McFarland House, Niagara Historical Society Museum, Niagara Parkway, Shaw Festival, Samuel E. Weir Library, 11 local wineries

Recommend Bicycles:
Touring/Hybrid/Mountain

Tour Suggestions:
Pack a lunch to enjoy on the tour. The Vineyard Bicycle Tour at Hillebrand Estates is very enjoyable and educational.

How to get there:
Get off the Queen Elizabeth Way at the exit for Hwy 55 and follow it to Niagara-on-the-Lake. Start the trip at the Fort George parking lot on the Niagara Parkway. Parking is free, and it is safe to park here.

Following the wine route along the rolling roads in the Niagara Peninsula is a soothing experience. There are 11 wineries in the immediate area of Niagara-on-the-Lake, three of which will be visited during this tour. These

Festival Country

wineries lie on the same latitude as Florence, Italy and parts of France, and produce excellent Chardonnay, Riesling, Pinot Noir and icewine. It is difficult to choose which winery to tour. Most winery tours include the vineyards, the barrel-aging room and the underground cellar, as well as a sampling of their most popular wines.

Itinerary:
Exit the Fort George parking lot by turning [R] onto Queens Parade, which changes into Picton St just after passing the Shaw Festival at Wellington St. Just before reaching the 1921 clock tower, located right in the middle of the road, turn [L] onto King St. Once past the Prince of Wales Hotel, turn [R] onto Mary St. At the Mississauga St traffic lights, turn [L] and follow Regional Rd 55 out of **Niagara-on-the-Lake**.

Cycling through the heart of the Niagara wine country, you will pass a number of benchtop and estate wineries. Although all of these wineries use similar varieties of grapes, they each produce a wine with a unique taste. Most of the wineries in the area offer tours and are required by law to charge a nominal fee for their wine tasting. Also, wine cannot be served before 11am. Since

most of your riding will take place under the hot afternoon sun, pack plenty of water.

Continue straight through **Virgil**—the town of many names. It was originally known as Four Mile Creek, then as Cross Roads, and then Lawrenceville before the post office established its present name in 1895. Just past the second set of lights, turn [L] into Hillebrand Estates Winery. The region's largest wine producer, it offers many different ways to experience the art of winemaking.

Hillebrand is a good place to start a day of cycling in wine country. Beginning next to their Vineyard Cafe, exit the grounds via their back entrance.

Note: If the area is wet, consider avoiding Line 4 and Concession Rd 4.

Turn [R] out of the parking lot onto Niagara Line 3, and at St. Michael's School turn [L] onto Niagara Concession Rd 6. As you cycle past row upon row of grapevines, you will notice that these rows are planted north to south, allowing for even lighting on both sides of the vines. At Line 4, turn [L], cross Four Mile Creek Rd, and turn [L] onto Concession Rd 2. After passing a

● ATTRACTIONS

1. Fort George
2. Butler's Burial Grounds
3. Hillebrand Estates
4. Candle Factory
5. Château des Charmes Wines
6. St. Davids Church and Cemetery
7. Brocks Monument
8. Laura Secord House
9. Weir Library of Art
10. Willowbank
11. Wayside Chapel
12. Inniskillin Wines
13. Field House
14. Walkers Fruit Market
15. McFarland House
16. Upper Virgil Dam Conservation Area

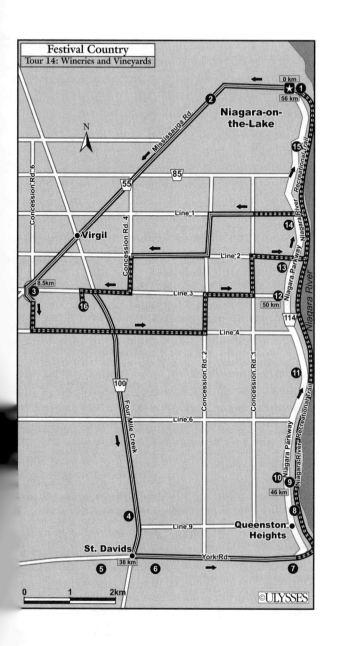

Festival Country
Tour 14: Wineries and Vineyards

Niagara-on-the-Lake

0 km
56 km

Mississauga Rd.

N

Concession Rd. 6

85

55

Virgil

Concession Rd. 4

Line 1

8.5km

16

Line 2

Line 3

Line 4

114

50 km

100

Four Mile Creek

Line 6

Concession Rd. 2

Concession Rd. 1

Niagara Parkway

Niagara River Recreational Trail

Niagara River

Niagara Parkway

Niagara River Recreational Trail

46 km

Queenston Heights

Line 9

St. Davids

36 km

York Rd.

0   1   2km

©ULYSSES

greenhouse complex, make a [R] turn onto Line 3 and follow it to Concession Rd 1. Turn [L], cycle past a field of grapes that has been planted east to west because of poor land drainage. Notice that the type of grapes grown here is quite different from the varieties seen earlier. At Line 2, turn [R].

Upon reaching the Niagara Parkway, turn [L] onto the Niagara River Recreational Trail, and return to the road at Walkers Fruit Market. Turn [L] onto Line 1 and follow this gravel road across Concession Rd 1. At this point, Line 1 is paved once more, and if you are in the right place at the right time, you can enjoy a cooling shower, compliments of the local irrigation pumps. At Concession Rd 2, turn [L], go past a man-made dam and irrigation ditch, and make a [R] turn onto Line 2. Turn [L] onto Concession Rd 4. What begins as a fairly good gravel road quickly becomes quite rough. At the [T] intersection turn [R] onto Line 3 and ride back to Four Mile Creek Rd. If you packed a lunch, continue on Line 3 past Four Mile Creek for about 150m, where you will find an excellent lunch stop at the Upper Virgil Dam and the back entrance to the Hillebrand Estates.

When you are ready to continue, ride out of this rest area and turn [L] onto Line 3 and [R] onto Four Mile Creek. Go past the Niagara Nut Grove, where many types of nut trees, such as American chestnut, black walnut, butternut, Chinese chestnut and European filbert, are grown. A few kilometres further, the road passes the Nabisco factory and a candle factory before climbing into the village of St. Davids. At the stop sign, turn [R] onto York Rd, and

cycle past the old fire hall and the Burning of St. Davids plaque. At the green-roofed mansion, turn [L] into Chateau des Charmes Wines. This winery uses state-of-the-art equipment, but like all wineries, it still ages its wine in oak barrels.

Return to St. Davids, cross Four Mile Creek Rd and go past the large grave stones of St. Davids United Church and cemetery. Major David Secord, St. Davids' namesake and brother-in-law to Laura Secord, is buried here. Cycle downhill on the Niagara Parkway, turn [L], and then [R] and follow Queenston St as it rapidly descends into **Queenston**.

After climbing uphill past the Weir Library, join the Niagara River Recreational Trail and follow it to a split in the river trail. Bear right and follow the trail down and through a wooded area along the Niagara River. The trail eventually returns to the parkway. At this point, instead of joining the recreational trail, ride on the parkway and make a [L] turn at the bridge onto Line 3. You'll easily spot the water tower of the Inniskillin Winery just up the road. This winery offers guided and self-guided tours, and has a unique wine-tasting facility where you step right up to the bar.

Return to the Niagara Parkway and resume your ride on the Niagara River Trail. Cycle past Reif Estate Winery on your left. Follow the river back to Fort George and the Niagara-on-the-Lake tourist information booth.

If time permits, cycle around the delightful Edwardian town of Niagara-on-the-Lake. Originally, this area was the Neutral First Nation village of Onghiara. Whe it was settled by Loyalists, it became known as Newark. It was the first capital of Upper Canada and the site of some important battles during the War of 1812, including one that burned the town to the ground in 1813. Today, Niagara-on-the-Lake is best known for the Shaw summer theatre festival. The plays are staged in an 822-seat proscenium arch theatre, the only one in the world solely devoted to presenting the works of George Bernard Shaw. Other building highlights in town are the St. Vincent de Paul Roman Catholic Church and the St. Andrews Presbyterian Church. One stop that should not be missed is the Niagara Apothecary, the oldest pharmacy still in operation in Canada. The picturesque back streets of this 19th-century community are steeped in history and make for a relaxing ride after a day in the country.

Practical Information

See also Tour 13: Myths, Miracles and Pathways

 Selected Local Wineries

Niagara-on-the-Lake

Hillebrand Estate Wineries
249 Niagara Stone Rd
Niagara-on-the-Lake, ON L0S 1J0
☎*(905) 468-7123 or 800-582-8412*
www.hillebrand.com

Chateau des Charmes Wines
1025 York Rd, Niagara-on-the-Lake, ON
L0S 1J0
☎*(905) 262-5202*
www.chateaudescharmes.com

Inniskillin Wines
Niagara Parkway at Line 3, RR 1
Niagara-on-the-Lake, ON L0S 1J0
☎*(905) 468-2187 or 888-466-4754*
www.inniskillin.com

Stonechurch Vineyards
1242 Irvine Rd, RR 5
Niagara-on-the-Lake, ON L2N 1L1
☎*(905) 935-3535*
www.stonechurch.com

Marynissen Estates
1208 Concession 1, RR 6
Niagara-on-the-Lake, ON L0S 1J0
☎*(905) 468-7270*
www.marynissen.com

Pillitteri Estates Winery
1696 Niagara Stone Rd
Niagara-on-the-Lake, ON L0S 1J0
☎*(905) 468-3147*
www.pillitteri.com

Reif Estate Winery
15608 Niagara Parkway, RR 1
Niagara-on-the-Lake, ON L0S 1J0
☎*(905) 468-7738*
www.reifwinery.com

Sunnybrook Farm Estate Winery
1425 Lakeshore Rd, RR 3
Niagara-on-the-Lake, ON L0S 1J0
☎*(905) 468-1122*
www.sunnybrookfarmwinery.com

Joseph's Estates Wines
1811 Hwy 55, RR 3
Niagara-on-the-Lake, ON L0S 1J0
☎*(905) 468-1259*
www.josephestatewines.com

Konzelmann Estate Winery
1096 Lakeshore Rd
Niagara-on-the-Lake, ON L0S 1J0
☎*(905) 935-2866*
www.konzelmannwines.com

Strewn Winery
1339 Lakeshore Rd
Niagara-on-the-Lake, ON L0S 1J0
☎*(905) 468-1229 or 888-478-7396*
www.strewnwinery.com

Festival Country

Off-Road Cycling

Public Trails

Cambridge

Cambridge Heritage River Trail
(*18km*)
Surface:
Asphalt/loose surface
Beginning:
Churchill Park to Blackridge Rd and Townline Rd

Cambridge Trails Advisory Committee
PO Box 669
73 Water St N, Cambridge, ON N1R 5W8
☎(519) 740-4681, ext. 4229
www.cambridge.galganov.net/ trails.html

Cambridge to Paris Rail Trail
(*18km*)
Surface:
Gravel/hard-packed
Beginning:
Cambridge or Paris

Grand River Conservation Authority
Box 729
400 Clyde Rd, Cambridge, ON N1R 5W6
☎(519) 621-2761
www.grandriver.ca

Elora

Elora Cataract Trailway
(*47km*)
Surface:
Original rail bed/hard-packed (some rough sections)
Beginning:
Elora and Cataract

Grand River Conservation Authority *(see above)*

Fonthill

Stop '19' Trail
(*4.5km*)
Surface:
Original rail bed/hard-packed
Beginning:
City boundary and Welland River

Welland Community Planner, City of Welland
411 E Main St, Welland, ON L3B 3X4
☎(905) 735-1700
www.city.welland.on.ca

Guelph

Guelph Spurline
(*1.6km; part of 20km Royal Recreation Trail*)
Surface:
Loose surface/hard-packed
Beginning:
Dufferin/George St to London Rd

Recreation and Parks Department, City of Guelph
59 Carden St, Guelph, ON N1H 3A1
☎(519) 837-5618
www.city.guelph.on.ca

Hamilton Area

Hamilton to Brantford Rail Trail
(*32km*)
Surface:
Loose surface/hard-packed
Beginning:
Brantford and Hamilton

Grand River Conservation Authority
(see above, under Cambridge)

Waterdown Trails
(*25km*)
Surface:
Technical single track
Beginning:
Waterdown

Halton Region Conservation Authority
PO Box 7099
838 Mineral Springs Rd, Ancaster, ON
L9G 3L3
☎ *(905) 648-4427*
www.conservation.on.ca

Chedoke Radial Trail
(2.7km)
Surface:
Paved/loose surface
Beginning:
West Hamilton to Ancaster

Parks Division, City of Hamilton
71 Main St W, 3ʳᵈ Floor
Hamilton, ON L8P 4Y5
☎ *(905) 546-2489*
www.city.hamilton.on.ca

Escarpment Rail Trail
(7km)
Surface:
Crushed gravel
Beginning:
Hamilton Core to East Mountain

Parks Division, City of Hamilton
(see above)

Cootes Drive Trail
(2.5km)
Surface:
Paved
Beginning:
McMaster University to Dundas

Parks Division, City of Hamilton
(see above)

Niagara-on-the-Lake

Upper Canada Heritage Trail
(14km)
Surface:
Original rail bed/hard-packed
Beginning:
York Rd and John St

Upper Canada Equestrian Association
PO Box 4075, St. Catharine's, ON
L2R 7S3
☎ *(905) 384-2066*
www.ucea-niagara.com

St. Catharines Area

Shoreline Trail
(8km)

Participark Trail
(4km)

Merritt Trail
(11km)

Terry Fox Fitness Trail
(1.5km)

Walker's Creek Trail
(5km)

Burgoyne Woods
(1km)

Welland Canal Parkway Trail
(9km)

Green Ribbon Trail
(0.5km)

Participark Trail
(2km)

Recreation and Community Services, City of St. Catharine's
PO Box 3012
50 Church St, St. Catharines, ON
L2R 7C2
☎ *(905) 688-5601*
www.stcatharines.ca

Festival Country

Resort and Conservation Trails

Alton/Caledon Area

Terra Cotta Conservation Area
(*10km of trails*)

14451 Winston Churchill Blvd
Halton Hills, ON
☎*(905) 877-9650*

Backus Heritage Conservation Area
(*12km of trails*)

RR 42, Port Rowan, ON N0E 1M0
☎*(519) 586-2201*
☎*877-990-9932*
www.lprea.on.ca

Bolton Area

Albion Hills Conservation Area
(*25km of trail*)

Toronto and Region
Conservation Authority
5 Shoreham Dr, Downsview, ON
M3N 1S4
☎*(416) 661-6600*
www.trca.on.ca

Chicopee Ski Club
396 Morrison Rd, Kitchener, ON
N2A 2Z6
☎*(519) 894-5610*
www.skichicopee.com

Guelph/Milton Area

Hilton Falls Conservation Area
(*16km of trails*)

Halton Region Conservation
Authority
2596 Britannia Rd W, RR 2
Milton, ON L9T 2X6
☎*(905) 336-1158 or (905) 847-7430*
www.conservationhalton.com

Hamilton

Dundas Valley Trails
(*41km of trail*)

Hamilton Region Conservation
Authority
PO Box 7099
838 Mineral Springs Rd, Ancaster, ON
L9G 3L3
☎*(905) 525-2181 or 648-4427*
www.conservationhamilton.on.ca

Milton Area

Kelso Conservation Area
(*16km of trails*)

Halton Region Conservation
Authority (see above)

St. Catharines/ Thorold Area

Short Hills Provincial Park
(*13km of trails*)

PO Box 158, Dunville, ON N1A 2X5
☎*(905) 774-6642*
www.ontarioparks.com/english/ shor

Turkey Point Provincial Park
(*6km of trails*)

PO Box 5, Turkey Point, ON N0E 1T0
☎*(519) 426-3239*
www.ontarioparks.com/english/ turk

North Bay

Sudbury

QUÉBEC

Ottawa☆

Parry
Sound

Kingston

Lake Huron

Owen
Sound

Peterborough

Lake Ontario

Toronto

London

Niagara
Falls

Sarnia

Lake Erie

UNITED
STATES

Windsor

The Georgian Lakelands

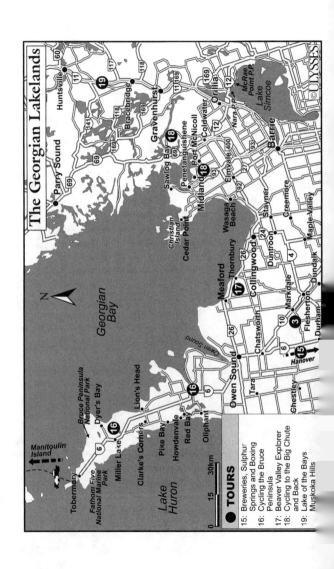

The Georgian Lakelands

● **TOURS**

15: Breweries, Sulphur Springs and Boxing
16: Cycling the Bruce Peninsula
17: Beaver Valley Explorer
18: Cycling to the Big Chute and Back
19: Lake of the Bays Muskoka Hills

© ULYSSES

The Georgian Lakelands

embrace the maple-lined streets of Port Elgin, the inviting waters of Lake Huron and the majestic limestone cliffs of Georgian Bay.

Cycling in this area of the province can take your breath away in more ways than one. Enjoy spectacular scenery, awe-inspiring wildlife and some great single-track. All roads in this part of the province follow the Bruce Trail to Tobermory's famous Fathom Five National Marine Park.

15. Breweries, Sulfur Springs and Boxing: Cycling in the Queen's Bush

If quiet country roads winding through engaging scenery dotted with hamlets of German and Scottish heritage appeal to you, a bicycle adventure in Ontario's Saugeen Country is an experience you won't want to miss.

Return Distance:
8km

No. of recommended legs:

Level of Difficulty:
🚲 🚲 🚲

Surface:
Asphalt and some gravel

Villages/Towns/Cities:
Hanover, Carlsruhe, Neustadt, Mildmay, Walkerton, Formosa

Local Highlights:
John G. Diefenbaker Home, Neustadt Springs Brewery, Mildmay Artesian Spring, Formosa Springs Brewery, Stoneyground Gardens

Recommended Bicycles:
Hybrid/Mountain/Touring

Tour Suggestions:
There are two different routes from Formosa to Walkerton.

How to get there:
From the Kitchener area, take Hwy 401 to Exit 295 and follow Hwy 6 N to Arthur. Make a [L] turn onto Hwy 9, at Walkerton turn [R] and follow Hwy 4 into Hanover. From the London area, take Hwy 401 to Exit 177 and follow Hwy 4 N, make a [R] and then turn [L] onto Hwy 23; at Hwy 9 turn [L], turn [R] at Walkerton on Hwy 4 and follow the road to Hanover.

The Queen's Bush, or the Huron Tract, was one of the last areas in the province to be colonized. Extensive tracts of forest and fertile land waiting to be put to good use could still be found along the Saugeen River in the 1850s. This land was free for the taking for people with strong backs and a lot of determination, and settlers from eastern Ontario and overseas rushed to settle the area. As the Queen's Bush developed, groups of people of common nationality and religious belief settled close together, creating distinct Irish, French and German communities. There is a long tradition of country inns, which continues to play an important role in this corner of the province. Abraham Buck was one of the first settlers in the region, and the predominately German town that grew up around his inn in 1848 became known as Buck's Crossing. It must have been somewhat confusing for map makers at the time, as the town was renamed several times, (Adamstown and Slabtown) before finally being named **Hanover**. Even today, Hanover is known for its furniture production and for the accomplishments of one of its early citizens, Noah Brusso, better known as Tommy Burns. He became the first Canadian Heavyweight Champion in 1906.

Itinerary:
The starting point is the Hanover Town Park, located on Bruce Rd 10, which is north of Bruce Rd 4 (10th St/Hwy 4). Free parking, as well as washroom and picnic facilities, can be found here. Exit the parking lot, turn [R] onto 7th Ave/ Bruce Rd 10 and cross Bruce Rd 4. After passing the Piano Man on your right and the Hanover Convention Centre on your left, keep right following 7th Ave at the [Y] junction. The memorial plaque for Tommy Burns is on your left and further ahead is the Hanover Hospital and Cemetery. As the road curves to the right it becomes Southline Rd, which descends, and once it crosses the Saugeen River, the road becomes Concession Rd 2. Climbing uphill, you will see the Allan Poechman firewood farm on your left. Turn

[L] onto Sideroad 30S, coast down into a pretty valley, then climb to the historic village of **Carlsruhe**. To the right of the main intersection on Concession Rd 14 is the original Carlsruhe Tavern.

Resume your journey along Sideroad 30S, which turns into a gentle gravel downhill. Your swift descent will take you past a wooden rail fence, wild raspberry canes and what appears to be an old stone fort on your right. Caution is recommended as you approach Concession Rd 12. Listen for the forlorn "baas" of sheep grazing amid the marsh on your right and enjoy the cooling shade of an overgrown woodlot before reaching the Haack gravel pit and Bruce Rd 16.

Turn [L] onto the paved Bruce Rd 16 (there is no cycling lane) and travel east towards the birthplace of the 13th Prime Minister of Canada, John George Diefenbaker. Diefenbaker's yellow brick home still stands just northeast of Mill St. It is a quick descent to the main intersection of **Neustadt**. Turn [R] onto Mill St and take some time to appreciate the town's many unique and historic businesses. Along Mill St, the Neustadt Tavern and Restaurant are on your left, the Neustadt Spring Brewery is on your right and the impressive St. Peter's Lutheran Church is at the top of the hill. Tours of the brewery caverns are offered during business hours and bottles of the Neustadt Brewer's unique blend can be purchased here.

Continue along Mill St, past the brewery and the water tower. Turn [R] onto Concession Rd 8 and follow this little-used road as it undulates, dramatically at times

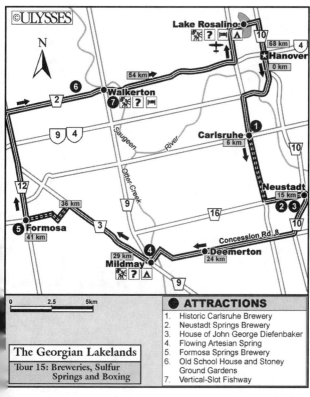

©ULYSSES

N

Lake Rosalino

68 km   4

Hanover

0 km

54 km

Walkerton

Saugeen   River

9   4

Carlsruhe
6 km

10

Otter Creek

Neustadt
15 km

12

36 km

16

Formosa
41 km

3

Concession Rd. 8

Deemerton
24 km

29 km
Mildmay

9

0   2.5   5km

● **ATTRACTIONS**

1. Historic Carlsruhe Brewery
2. Neustadt Springs Brewery
3. House of John George Diefenbaker
4. Flowing Artesian Spring
5. Formosa Springs Brewery
6. Old School House and Stoney
    Ground Gardens
7. Vertical-Slot Fishway

The Georgian Lakelands

Tour 15: Breweries, Sulfur
Springs and Boxing

The Georgian Lakelands

› the hamlet of Deemerton at
ideroad 20. Take some time to
xplore the area on your left
where you will find a magnificent
ld church built in 1872, the pas-
r's home, a stable with a hard-
ood floor and a large, ancient
emetery.

esume your trek along Conces-
n Rd 8. Enter the "Lamplighter
llage," Mildmay, on Absalom St,
you go straight at the lights,
ossing Elora St/Bruce 9. Notice
e old commercial hotel on your
ht, which at one time had
parate men's and women's
trances. The spires you saw in

the distance as you approached
Mildmay are those of the Sacred
Heart Catholic Church, which
you will find if you turn [L] on
Peter St. To continue with the
tour, return to Elora St/Bruce 9
and nead north. On the banks of
Otter Creek, just a short distance
ahead, is the Rotary Spring Park,
which offers a full-service rest
area. Originally named Shield's
Corner after a local innkeeper,
then Mernersville after a well-
known town benefactor, the
town was renamed in 1868 after
Mildmay Park in Scotland. At the
park, look for the naturally flowing
artesian spring from which you

can refill your bottles with fresh, cool water.

Leaving the park, turn [L] onto Bruce Rd 9, towards the downtown core. Turn [R] onto Bruce Rd 3; it has no cycling lane but is reasonably wide. Enjoy this winding road for several kilometres as it passes a gravel pit and the Carrick Township sheds. Once past Bruce Rd 15 and Country Gardens Antiques, look for the "Elora Road Meat" sign, a red-and-white-striped silo lid, a white silo and a radio tower. Just before reaching the top of the hill, turn [L] onto B Line Rd, which is a hard-packed gravel road. Descend to the [T] intersection, turn [R] and then [L] onto Council Rd. Notice the lucky number 13 at the first house on your left. Watch for moose (there is a "beware of moose" sign) as you descend into the village of **Formosa**. Arriving at the [T] intersection of Bruce Rd 12, the Formosa Springs Brewery is to your left.

Turn [R] and follow Bruce Rd 12 up a difficult climb. The magnificent Immaculate Conception Roman Catholic Church is at the top of the hill. Follow Bruce 12 for the next 3km until reaching a [Y] junction of roads on your immediate right (Carrick Brant W and Tower). At this point you have two routing choices to Walkerton: for hybrid or mountain bikes only, turn [R] onto Carrick Brant W Rd, an old jeep road that is very rough in spots. You will join Bruce Rd 3 after riding a wicked downhill stretch of washouts and ruts. Turn [L] onto Bruce Rd 3 and follow it to Bruce Rd 4/Hwy 4/9. Turning [R], cycle to a [T] intersection and

turn [L] following the road past the old jail to downtown Walkerton. Turn [R] onto Durham St/ Bruce Rd 4. The alternative is to continue along Bruce Rd 12, cross Bruce Rd 4/ Hwy 4/9, and follow the road that is now called the Greenock-Brant Rd. Turn [R] onto Durham Rd just before the large silos. Cross Bruce Rd 3 then cycle past an old schoolhouse and Stoneyground Gardens, and take Durham St into the town of **Walkerton**.

Follow Durham St past the local bicycle shop and over the Saugeen River. Walkerton is home to the Traux Dam, which is the only vertical-slot fishway

east of the Rockies, a type of fish ladder that allows rainbow trout to "climb" the dam and swim upstream to their spawning grounds. The newly resurfaced road has a wide cycling lane as you follow this portion of Bruce Rd 4 toward Hanover. A short distance past the truck-inspection station, turn [L] onto Bruce Rd 22, which takes you past the local airport. At the stop sign, turn [R] onto Concession Rd 22 NDR. Follow it east between Rosalind and Marl Lakes. At Bruce Rd 10/7th Ave turn right and make your way back to the starting point at the Hanover Town Park.

Practical Information

Population:
Hanover: 7,000
Mildmay: 1,000
Municipality of Brockton (includes the town of Walkerton): 9,600

 Tourist Information

Hanover

Hanover Library at the Civic Centre
451 10th Ave, Hanover, ON N4N 2P1
☎*(519) 364-1420*

Mildmay

Mildmay Chamber of Commerce
PO Box 549, Mildmay, ON N0G 2J0
☎*(519) 367-5448*
www.town.southbruce.on.ca/mildmay

Walkerton

Walkerton Chamber of Commerce
PO Box 1344, 4 Park St, Walkerton, ON N0G 2V0
☎*(519) 881-3413 or 888-820-9291*
http://town.walkterton.on.ca

 Bicycle Shops

Hanover

Mako Sports
294 10th St, Hanover, ON N4N 1P2
☎*(519) 364-1019*

Mildmay

Liesemer's Home Hardware Cycle
98 Elora St, Mildmay, ON N0G 2J0
☎*(519) 367-5314*

Walkerton

Joy Source for Sports
435 Durham E, Walkerton, ON N0G 2V0
☎*(519) 881-2046*

 Special Sights and Events

Hanover

Ringette Craft Fair, Fall Fair, The Secret Garden, community cycle trail (11.5km)

Mildmay

Mildmay-Carrick Fall Fair, Rotary Park walking trails, artesian spring

Walkerton

Mid-Western Ontario Rotary Music Festival, Saugeen River Trail, Vertical Slot Fishway, Stoney Ground Gardens, Royal Ragtime Renew, Roots of Bruce, Chepstow Lions Club Family Fun Fest, Walkerton Little Royal Fair.

 Accommodations

Hanover

Motel/B&B/Camping

Mildmay

Camping/Motel in Formosa

Walkerton

Hotel/Motel/B&B/Camping

The Georgian Lakelands

Market Days

Walkerton

Fridays, May to October, Agricultural fairgrounds

16. Cycling the Bruce Peninsula: Owen Sound, Tobermory and Sauble Falls

Cycling the Bruce is an exceptional tour. The ride follows the dramatic shores of Georgian Bay northwards and then heads south along the tree-lined roads and sandy beaches of Lake Huron. Begin in the shipping port of Owen Sound and cycle along the quiet country roads into the heart of the Bruce. Since this is a leisurely ride, you will have enough time to stop at many of the area's impressive lookouts and enjoy the view. Hike to the Bruce Caves, visit Wiarton Willy and see the breathtaking beauty of Lion's Head. Other highlights include a walk along the Bruce Trail to the unique cairns at Cypress Lake, and a search for shipwrecks in Fathom Five National Marine Park. The return legs cut through the centre of the peninsula and swing right to join the warmer waters of Lake Huron. After cycling through dense forest, wetlands and the port towns of Pikes Bay and Howdenvale, the highlight of the return trip will be the refreshing rushing waters at Sauble Falls.

Return Distance:
306km (56km, 40km, 54km, 67km, 54km, 35km)

No. of recommended legs:
6

Level of Difficulty:
🚲🚲🚲🚲🚲

Surface:
Asphalt and gravel country roads

Villages/Towns/Cities:
Owen Sound, Big Bay, Wiarton, Hope Bay, Lion's Head, Tobermory, Stokes Bay, Pike Bay, Howdenvale, Sauble Falls, Sauble Beach, Shallow Lake

Local Highlights:
Billy Bishop Heritage Museum, Jones and Indian Falls, County of Grey–Owen Sound Museum, Harrison Park, Hibou Conservation Area, Inglis Falls Conservation Area, Owen Sound Marine & Rail Heritage Centre, The Roxy Theatre, Tom Thomson Memorial Art Gallery, Cape Croker–Chippewa of Nawash First Nations, Bruce's Caves Conservation Area, Spirit Rock Conservation Area, movie set for "Quest for Fire," Bruce Trail in Lion's Head, Big Tub Lighthouse, Larkwhistle Garden–Dyer's Bay, Bruce Peninsula National Park, Fathom Five National Marine Park, Flowerpot Island, St. Edmund's Museum, Glass-Bottom Boat Cruises, Ferry to Manitoulin Island, Sauble Falls, Saugeen Rail Trail

Recommended Bicycles:
Hybrid/Mountain/Touring

Tour Suggestions:
Allow one complete day in the Tobermory area for the Cypress Lake walking trails and a Tobermory glass-bottom boat cruise. While cycling in the upper Bruce Peninsula, watch for black bears and poisonous Eastern

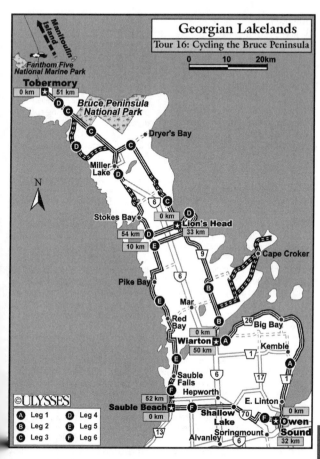

Georgian Lakelands
Tour 16: Cycling the Bruce Peninsula

0   10   20km

Manitoulin Island

Fanthom Five National Marine Park

Tobermory 0 km ★ 51 km

D

C

Bruce Peninsula National Park

C

Dryer's Bay

D

C

Miller Lake

D

N

Stokes Bay

6

C

0 km

D Lion's Head ★ 33 km

54 km **D**

10 km **E**

9

Cape Croker

Pike Bay

6

E

Mar.

B

E

Red Bay

26 Big Bay

B

0 km

A Wiarton ★ A 50 km

Kemble

17

1

E

Sautble Falls

6

Hepworth

A

1

52 km **F**

E. Linton

0 km

Sauble Beach ★ **F**

F ★ Owen Sound

0 km

Shallow Lake

70

32 km

13

Springmount

Alvanley

6

©ULYSSES

A Leg 1	**D** Leg 4
B Leg 2	**E** Leg 5
C Leg 3	**F** Leg 6

Massassauga rattlesnakes which inhabit the area. Inexpensive overnight parking can be arranged at the KOA campground in Owen Sound.

How to get there:
From the north, Owen Sound can be reached by Hwy 6; from the south by Hwys 21, 6 and 10; from the west by Hwy 21 and from the east by Hwy 26.

Because of its location in the Sydenham River Valley, Owen Sound has several good-sized hills to cycle. Owen Sound was a busy shipping centre in the 1800s thanks to its natural harbour. The town is also the birthplace of two of Canada's famous Group of Seven artists, and of WWI flying ace Billy Bishop.

The Georgian Lakelands

Itinerary:
Leg 1
(Owen Sound to Wiarton, 56km)

Begin at the tourist information centre/train station on the banks of the Sydenham River, at the corner of 11th St W and 1st Ave W. Cycle north with the river on your right, cross 9th St and join the road. Cross 10th St and rejoin the trail at Mr. Transmission. Swing [L] onto the river boardwalk and cycle to the bay. On the far side of the river, you can't miss the *Nindawayma*, the sister ship of the *Chi-Cheemaun*. At one time, this ship is said to have provided ferry service from Tobermory to Manitoulin Island, but it never left the docks.

The trail passes numerous information plaques, the Marine Rail Museum, and a large skateboard park. Then it crosses a small parking lot and turns left onto a private roadway that leads to some large grain elevators. Turn [R] and join the trail to the left of the road. Cross a wooden bridge into the lower end of Kelso Park, pass the large outdoor amphitheatre and swimming beach, and ride into the Rusty Gull Marina parking lot. Next, exit the parking lot and turn [R] onto 3rd Ave W (Eddy Sargent Parkway) and follow it north as it changes into Grey Rd 1.

After riding past the historic Royal Orange Lodge, turn [R] onto Grey Rd 26 and descend back towards the water and into Gravelly Bay. At the bottom of the hill, the road arcs to the left and follows the clear waters of Georgian Bay towards Wiarton. It is interesting to read some of the unique, somewhat bizarre cottage names along Island View Dr. Now climbing above the bay,

look for the entrance to Centennial Park on the right. The park is a good spot to rest, and probably the best place in the world for skipping stones. Be careful as it is a very steep ride down into the park. When walking on the stone beach, it sounds like broken pieces of china are being rubbed together.

After Whippoorwill Marsh, Grey Rd 26 descends into the charming community of **Big Bay**. On your right, at the main intersection, is the lake—and a welcoming hello from the local fry shack at the boat launching dock! To the left is the general store and delicatessen, where you can even find spare bicycle parts.

Leaving Big Bay, cycle up the first of three hills. The road levels out after this first hill, and the ditches alongside have been planted with colourful snapdragons. After Cedar Park, Grey Rd 26 swings sharply to the left and then climbs dramatically. Once at the top, take a break, turn around and look back. The view makes the uphill ride well worth the struggle. Now high above the bay, the large parking lot of Skinners Bluff is just ahead. From Colpoys Lookout, the islands of White Cloud, Hay and Griffith are just a small part of the spectacular view that looks across the bay to Colpoys Bluff.

An escarpment will suddenly appear from out of nowhere on your left—this is the last hill to climb before reaching the Bruce Caves Conservation Area. At the top of the hill, make a [L] turn; the caves parking lot is 1km down a gravel road. Because the area cool, damp and covered with moss, it has been nicknamed "Fern Capital of the World."

Many different fern species are found here, including some that are endangered. Walking ferns, slender cliffbrake and holy ferns are native to the area. Lock up your bicycle at the visitor pavilion, then hike another kilometre to the caves, which were created by the erosion of glacial Lake Algonquin almost 8,000 years ago.

Continuing along Cty Rd 26, enter **Wiarton** via Frank St. A right turn will take you into downtown Wiarton and the campground and beaches on Colpoys Bay, whilw a left turn leads to accommodations on the south side of the city. Wiarton's mascot is world famous. Born on the Bruce Peninsula, exactly on the 45th parallel, "Wiarton Willie" is an albino groundhog who has been predicting the coming of spring every February 2nd since 1956. If he sees his shadow, there will be six more weeks of hard winter; no shadow means an early spring. Believe it or not, he has been right about 90% of the time.

Leg 2
(Wiarton to Lion's Head, 40km)

At the corner of Cty Rd 26 and Hwy 6, ride north through downtown Wiarton. Climb a long, steep hill out of town and continue to the turnoff for Cty Rd 9. About 1km out of town, turn [R] into the Spirt Rock Conservation Area. This road leads to the burned-out ruins of the 1882 McNeil Mansion. Look for the spiral staircase that leads down the cliff to the water.

Back on Hwy 6, make a [R] turn onto Cty Rd 9. The road swings left and descends to Colpoys Bay. Notice the "Old Factory" on the shores of the bay. At the Mallory Beach boat launching pier, keep

following the road as it swings left and climbs past the local cemetery. For the next several kilometres, this road passes through some boulder-encrusted farmland that is not in use. At Bruce Rd 18, you can make an optional [R] turn, which will take you to the Cape Croker Campground on the Chippewas of Nawash First Nation Reserve (also known as the Cape Croker Reserve). The return loop around the reserve is approximately 40km.

Cape Croker Side Trip: The Cape Croker Reserve is home to the Chippewas of Nawash First Nation. It was established in the early 1800s after the inhabitants of the Nawash Indian Reserve surrendered their land on the west side of Owen Sound Bay. The reserve's population has travelled from as far as Wisconsin, Michigan, Chicago and Manitoulin Island. Turn [R] onto Bruce Rd 18, ride past Artargan Saw and Lumber Mill and follow the road until it appears to end at a gravel laneway. Stay on the asphalt by turning [L] onto Purple Valley Rd, and cycle through the hamlet of Purple Valley. Ride to the second road and turn [R] onto McIver Rd. A short distance ahead is a spectacular view of McGregor Bay; the Cape Croker Campground is on your left. As the road descends from one of the highest points on the peninsula, it turns into gravel. Cycle along the bay and follow the road past the water tower. It climbs once more before descending into the village of Cape Croker.

Directly across the street from the stop sign is the 1892 United Church. Spend some time exploring the immediate area. It shouldn't take you long to find the only stone house on the reservation which was built in the 1880s for the first Indian Agent. Also look for the 1907 Roman Catholic Church. Nearby is another old church, built in the 1860s, which is the area's oldest landmark. The more adventurous may want to visit the Cape Croker Lighthouse. To get there, continue straight and follow the road as it swings to the left. Turn [R] at Lighthouse Rd and ride through Nayausheeng. Continue along the gravel road until you reach the Cape Croker lighthouse. (On the return route do not make any turns; follow the road back to the United Church.) To complete the Cape Croker loop, keep going past the church and turn [R] at the stop sign. As you leave the village, notice the many wooden homes. You are now travelling through an area known as Cape Croker Prairie. The towering walls of the Niagara Escarpment are on the left and Coveneys Rd climbs for 1km before it ends at Purple Valley Rd. Turn [R] and cycle back to Bruce Rd 9.

Don't blink; you might miss the hamlet of Adamsville! Indeed, it is only discernable by the modern log house on the left. From here, Bruce Rd 9 begins a series of gradual climbs and descents. At the top of the next rise after Adair Quarries, a large stone-block-cutting company, is Hope Bay Rd. Turn [R] here and enjoy a quick descent into **Hope Bay**. Cliffs and blue water dominate the view at the bottom of the hill. It is pleasant to stroll along the bay, whose water is not much higher than the knee. Further up are the caves and potholes of the Hope Bay Forest Provincial Nature Reserve.

Back on Cty Rd 9 at the Hopeness and Jackson's Cove Rd, you can embark on another

enjoyable excursion to the Greig Caves. To get there, turn [R] onto the gravel road and follow it to the first [T] intersection, turn [L] and ride past the CKCO-TV tower to a laneway with a gate. Continue onto the laneway and follow the road to a trail along the escarpment. From here, hike the escarpment to the many caves used in the movie *Quest for Fire*.

Once back on Bruce Rd 9, the road passes the old Barrow Bay mill. Exploring the bridge across the mill reveals a hidden waterfall to the right.

Bruce Rd 9 climbs out of Barrel Bay and passes Cemetery Rd twice before descending into **Lion's Head**. At the bottom of the hill, turn [R] and ride into the municipal park and campgrounds. The frigid, crystal blue waters of Isthmus Bay and the massive cliffs of the lion's mane fill the horizon. To the right of the park entrance, walk up to the bay. When the water is very still, the rotting, wooden ribs of a large ship are visible. Further out, by the floating shallow water marker, another ship can be seen at the bottom of the bay. Lion's Head was known as Point Hangcliffe in the late 1870s. But when ships entered the bay from the lake, sailors noticed that the steep cliffs surrounding it resembled the head of a lion, hence its present name.

While in Lion's Head, take a hike on the Bruce Trail. From the municipal campground, follow Webster St to Helen St. Turn [R] and cycle to Moore St. Turn [L] and follow the road past the hospital and the numerous resort cottages until the road comes to dead end. Lock up your bicycle and follow the trail to the right, then turn [L] onto an old jeep road. As you enter the Lion's Head Provincial Nature Reserve, notice the rusting cars just before the white trail markers of the Bruce Trail. Join the trail and follow it to the top of the Lion's Head escarpment and then down and around to Georgian Bay.

Leg 3
(Lion's Head to Tobermory, 54km)

Starting from the park, follow Webster St to Main St. Turn [R] onto Main St and cycle north out of town. With Isthmus Bay on your right, the road climbs past the rocky 45th Parallel park (the halfway point between the North Pole and equator) and descends to a lovely ride along Whippoorwill Bay.

The waters of Georgian Bay are so clear that flat limestone rocks can be seen metres beneath the surface. When Isthmus Bay Rd swings sharply to the right, it immediately changes into a winding gravel road. Now cycling along 40 hills, this portion of the tour will quickly become one of your more memorable rides. Narrowing, it twists and turns, rises and falls through thick cedar forests and feels like a slow roller-coaster ride! At East Rd, the road changes back to asphalt and continues through open countryside. Upon arriving at Cape Chin, take a few minutes to visit the St. Margaret's Historical Chapel, then cycle to Chin Rd N and turn [L]. From here, it is only a short ride to the local tea room. Continue along East Rd to Brinkman's Corner. Turn [L] and ride past Shouldice Lake Rd to Hwy 6. If you turn right at Brinkman's Corner, an adventurous road lies ahead, which will take you out to the Dyers Bay lighthouse and the world-famous Larkwhistle Gardens.

Turn [R] onto Hwy 6; a short distance ahead is the Crane River Conservation and Rest Area. Hwy 6 can be very busy when the ferries arrive and depart, but with a little planning, riding along on this highway can be a relaxing experience. Cycling past a local Aboriginal artifact dealer, the road descends and goes past a newly renovated gas station with showers. There are no showers in the National Park at the Cypress Lake campgrounds, and the showers at the gas station are 5km away. Continue past Cypress Lake. On the left are the Singing Sands Provincial Park and the shallow waters of Dorcas Bay.

By the time you get to **Tobermory**, the locals will have warned you about black bears and rattlesnakes; if encountered along the route, give these creatures a wide berth. There are another 7km of climbs through cedar forests and several sections of wet, boggy countryside. Upon entering Tobermory, the St. Edmunds Township Museum and the local tourist booth are on the right. Just past the tourist office, turn [R] into the bustling tourist community of Little Tub Harbour. Tobermory is where the Bruce Tail ends its 633km journey from Queenston Heights near Niagara Falls. The town has two harbours, which offer safe anchorage in bad weather. Originally named Big Tub in 1871, it was renamed Tobermory 10 years later, after its twin fishing port on Scotland's Isle of Mull. Today it is a hot spot for divers to explore Canada's first national marine park and its 21 sunken sail and steam vessels. Glass-bottom boats offer excursions to view the ship wrecks, and hikers flock here to explore the Cape Hurd Island system that includes Flower Pot Island.

Leg 4
(Tobermory to Lion's Head, 67km)

Returning to Lion's Head along the shores of Lake Huron is less demanding than the previous route. Follow Hwy 6 south and make a [R] turn onto Dorcas Bay Rd. Ride through a man-made cedar tunnel, past the Singing Sands campground and the beaches of Dorcas Bay. The view over the next 20km can be monotonous at times, but the never-ending green of the cedar trees is occasionally broken by a splash of colour thanks to some of the local cottage signs and the blue waters of Lake Huron. At the Johnson Harbour Rd [T] intersection, swing [R] and have fun riding the next several kilometres on the only winding hills on this return leg.

Finally back on Hwy 6, turn [R], cross the Crane River and ride past Dyers Bay Rd. Continue past the Miller Lake Rd "Drift In" variety store and a colourful artist's fence. As the road begins to arc

left at Lindsay Rd 30, keep right and take the Ira Lake Rd cutoff. This gravel road has little traffic and rides through a wetland area before zigzagging its way around Lake Ira. At Clarks Corners, cycle past the Colonel Clarke Tavern onto a smooth asphalt surface. Stokes Bay Rd swings sharply to the right as it enters Stokes Bay. Just before the turn, look for a forgotten stone address marker leaning up against an old cedar tree. Just before turning [L] at the Copper Kettle Restaurant, ride to the end of the street and look at the baby rattlers next to the telephone booth.

Cycle past the cheering at the Celtic Sports Camp and the tantalizing aroma of the local bakery just up the road. At Bruce Rd 9, turn [L], cross Hwy 6 at Ferndale and return to Lion's Head.

Leg 5
(Lion's Head to Sauble Beach, 54km)

Following Bruce 9 south out of Lion's Head, retracing a portion of the route taken on Leg 2. Turn [R] onto Cemetery Rd, cycle across the peninsula to the village of Spry and make a [L] turn onto West Rd. Once you cross Little Pike Bay Rd, the next several kilometres will be gravel. At Pikes Bay Rd (Harbour Rd), turn [R] and then [L] and follow Sunset Rd as it goes left, passing a little store. Enjoy the water views, the Pike Bay community area and follow the Lake Huron shoreline, riding into **Howdenvale**.

At the next intersection, turn [R] onto Huron Rd. At Spry Lake Rd turn [R] and, as you approach the lake, swing [L] onto Shoreline Rd. Now on gravel, ride past a boardwalk crossing a marsh before entering the village of **Oliphant**. At Mary St, continue straight and follow Bay St along the lakeshore. Once at S Oliphant Rd, turn [L] and turn [R] at the Sauble Falls Parkway/Bruce Rd 21. Cycle a few kilometres past the "Welcome to Sauble Beach" sign into **Sauble Falls**. Years ago along the falls, there was a saw mill and a hydroelectric power station. The ruins of these two buildings can still be found on the north side of the river. Today, the falls are a great place to have fun, so take off your shoes and try to walk across the rushing water. A short distance past the falls, turn [R] onto Lakeshore Rd and follow the dunes and hundreds of colourful bathing suits into **Sauble Beach**.

Leg 6
(Sauble Beach to Owen Sound, 35km)

This final leg is a short one, leaving plenty of time to enjoy the warm waters of Lake Huron. The last leg begins at the corner of Bruce Rd 8 and the Sauble Falls Parkway. Ride south as Sauble Falls Parkway changes into the Southhampton Parkway. At Silver Lake Rd, turn [L]; the road immediately begins to climb and passes the local "adopt-a-toad" sign. This is a peaceful ride through cottage country. Crossing Bruce Rd 10 onto Shouldice Rd, turn [R] at Hwy 6 and cycle through downtown **Shallow Lake**, past the Harley Davidson dealership and the Wayside Chapel.

This portion of Hwy 6 is busy but it has a wide cycling lane, so the trip is a reasonably comfortable cycling experience. Further down the road, look for the Red Cardinal Bird Seed sign and prepare for a left turn. A short distance past

Ledgerock Rd and the Log Cabin Guest House, about halfway down the hill, turn [L] onto Wilcox Rd and follow it to Girl Guide Rd. Turn [R] and cycle to another [T] intersection at West St. From here, the city of Owen Sound dominates the skyline. Turn [L] and enjoy a long downhill ride on 24th St. Bending to the right, 24th St becomes 4th Ave W. At 23rd St W, turn [L] and cycle along the Eddie Sargent Pkwy. Turn [R] and ride until the Kelso Beach traffic lights. Make a [L] turn into the park and follow the trail back to the beginning of Leg 1.

Practical Information

Population:
Owen Sound: 21,700
Wiarton: 2,300
Lion's Head: 550
Tobermory: 1,000
Sauble Beach: 3,500

Tourist Information

Owen Sound

Owen Sound Visitor Information Centre
1155 First St Ave W, Owen Sound, ON N4K 4K8
☎*(519) 371-9833 or 888-675-5555*
www.city.owen-sound.on.ca

Wiarton

Town of South Bruce Peninsula
PO Box 310, 315 George St, Wiarton, ON N0H 2T0
☎*(519) 534-1400 or 877-534-1400*
www.southbrucepeninsula.org

The Georgian Lakelands

Lion's Head

Bruce Peninsula Tourism
PO Box 269, ON N0H 2T0
☎*(519) 793-4734*
www.brucepeninsula.org

Tobermory

Tobermory Chamber of Commerce
PO Box 250, Tobermory, ON N0H 2R0
☎*(519) 596-2452*
www.tobermory.org

Sauble Beach

Chamber of Commerce Sauble Falls
General Delivery, Sauble Beach, ON
N0H 2G0
☎*(519) 422-1262*
www.saublebeach.com

 Bicycle Shops

Owen Sound

Todd's Sporting Goods
80 9th St E, Owen Sound, ON N4K 1N4
☎*(519) 376-0575*

 Special Sights and Events

Owen Sound

All Breed Champion Dog Show, Artist Studio Tour, Celtic Festival, Summerfolk, Canada Day, Roxy Theatre, Spoke and Bustle, Harbour Heat Wave, Owen Sound Fall Fair, Festival of Northern Lights, Eddie Sargent Memorial "Cross the Bay Swim"

Wiarton

Wiarton Willie Festival, Canada Day, fall fair.

Lion's Head

Escarpment Climbing, glass-bottom boat cruise, winter carnival, Canada Day, Bluegrass and Country Music Festival.

Tobermory

Glass-bottom boats, Chi-Cheemaun Spring Cruise, Annual Chi-Cheemaun Festival Weekend, Canada Day, Fathom Five National Marine Park, Flower Pot Island, National Parks Day Celebrations of Flowerpot Island Light Station, Celtic Ceiledh, winter carnival

Sauble Beach

Chantry Chinook Classic Fishing Derby, Sauble Rock, Sandfest and Sandcastle Building Competition, Sauble Open Football Tournament, Oktoberfest, winterfest, summerfest, Canada Day.

 Accommodations

Owen Sound

Hotel/Motel/Resort/B&B/Camping

Wiarton

Cottages/Motel/B&B/Camping

Lion's Head

Motel/Inn/B&B/Camping

Tobermory

Hotel/Motel/Inn/B&B/Camping

Sauble Beach

Cottages/Motel/B&B/Camping

Off-Road Cycling

Owen Sound

Yes; refer to the "Off-Road Cycling" section at the end of this chapter.

 Market Days

Lion's Head

Saturday mornings

Owen Sound

Saturday mornings, year-round

17. Beaver Valley Explorer: Thornbury, Meaford and Markdale

Beginning in the southern reaches of the Georgian Triangle, this ride climbs up to the top of the Niagara Escarpment, travels to the rushing waters of Eugenia Falls and descends into the Beaver Valley. Riding north along the valley through the villages of Kimberly and Heathcote, the first leg joins the recreational trail in Thornbury and follows it along the shoreline of Georgian Bay to the village of Meaford. The second leg has many difficult climbs that are always followed by thrilling downhills. It starts with a climb and then follows the escarpment's upper rim, then descends back into the heart of the valley. Passing through the city of Markdale, this stretch is completed by following the Old Durham Rd back into the Saugeen Valley.

Return Distance:
180km (84km, 75km)

No. of recommended legs:
2

Level of Difficulty:
🚲🚲🚲🚲🚲

Surface:
Asphalt roads

Villages/Towns/Cities:
Durham, Flesherton, Eugenia, Kimberly, Heathcote, Thornbury, Meaford, Markdale

Local Highlights:
Durham Art Gallery, Welbeck Sawmill, Eugenia Falls, South Grey Museum, The Georgian Theatre Festival, Georgian Bay, Georgian Trail bike path, Meaford Tank Training Centre, Walters Falls, Old Baldy Lookout, Epping Lookout, Paul's Hotel Mural, Meaford Museum, Thornbury Dam and Fish Lock

Recommended Bicycles:
Touring/Hybrid/Mountain

Tour Suggestions:
Some are quite steep, but with a little effort, each of these hills can be conquered. Pack extra water as there are only a few places to refill en route.

How to get there:
Durham can be reached from the north and south by following Hwy 6 and from the east and west by travelling along Hwy 4. A good location to begin the trip is the Saugeen Valley Conservation Area. Follow Hwy 6 N and turn right onto Old Durham. There is

The Georgian Lakelands

a small fee for parking a car overnight.

Back in 1842, a group of settlers followed Archibald Hunter as he travelled north from Arthur on the Garafraxa Colonization Rd (Hwy 6). They built a log cabin and founded a settlement that became known as Bentinck. The name was changed to **Durham** 12 years later, after land agent George Jackson's hometown in England. In recent years, Durham has become known for its annual Wood Show and the growing number of murals painted on its storefronts.

Itinerary:
Leg 1
(Durham to Meaford, 84km)

Turn [R] out of the Saugeen Valley Conservation Area onto Old Durham Rd. In the mid-1850s, this road made it possible to clear much of the land between Kincardine and Walkerton. At the [T] intersection of Concession 2, turn [R] and then [L] and join Hwy 4 in the middle of a bend. For the next several kilometres, this undulating road begins a series of climbs and dips. Each time the top of the next hill is reached, the overall altitude will have increased by a few metres. Riding past a large gravel-pit operation and a small art studio in a wooden barn, you may notice that the ditches running along the road are all full of water. This is due to runoff from the nearby escarpment. At the white barn, look for the old 1889 McKenzie Cemetery. A short distance ahead, the road enters the village of **Priceville**. Apart from a few homes, the most striking buildings are the general store and the 1888 Presbyterian Church. Behind the church is a little park and

cenotaph with a German field-machine gun. Upon closer inspection, you will notice that the church has been used by many different denominations.

Hwy 4 descends as it enters **Flesherton**, passing a small pond and a park on the right. Continue straight through town, crossing Hwy 10. Now, the cycling lane disappears and the road is several inches above the shoulder. Originally settled in 1851, the town was given the pretty name of Artemesia. By 1853, however it had become known as Flesher's Corners, named after the owner of the local saw and grist mills. In 1867, the name was changed to Flesherton.

Optional Side Trip:
Just a short distance from Flesherton is a little-known waterfall called Hogg Falls. It is a worthwhile side trip that adds about 6km to the ride. To get there, ride east for 1.5km from the stop light in Flesherton. Turn [L] onto Lower Valley Rd and cycle north, making a [R] turn at the next road. Continue riding for approximately 1km to an unmarked but easily recognizable parking lot. Park your bike and travel on foot, following the path to the falls.

At the red-roofed house on Hwy 4, turn [L] onto Grey Rd 13. Ride uphill until you reach the village of **Eugenia**. Turn [L] onto Tellisier St at the dilapidated old brick house, and ride down a steep, short hill. The village was named after Empress Eugenia, the wife of Napoleon III. Lock your bicycle on one of the many nearby trees (not a pine tree) and walk down to the falls. Be careful as the rocks and exposed roots

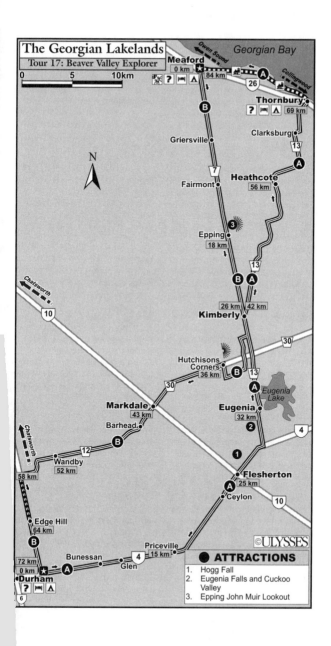

The Georgian Lakelands
Tour 17: Beaver Valley Explorer

0   5   10km

Georgian Bay

Owen Sound

Collingwood

Meaford
0 km

26   84 km

Thornbury
69 km

Clarksburg

13

Heathcote
56 km

Griersville

7

Fairmont

3

Epping
18 km

13

B   A

26 km   42 km

Kimberly

30

Hutchisons
Corners   36 km

B   13

A   Eugenia
Lake

30

Markdale
43 km   Eugenia
32 km

Barhead   2

B   1

Chatsworth

10

12

Wandby
52 km

Flesherton
25 km

A

Ceylon

Chatsworth

58 km   10

Edge Hill
64 km

72 km
0 km

Durham

6

Bunessan   Priceville
15 km

4

Glen

©ULYSSES

● ATTRACTIONS

1. Hogg Fall
2. Eugenia Falls and Cuckoo Valley
3. Epping John Muir Lookout

can be quite slippery. The view of the 23m Eugenia Falls and Cuckoo Valley is simply breathtaking. Be sure to explore the area around the Eugenia Falls lookout. If there is no water flowing over the falls, Ontario Hydro is probably diverting it to two hydro generators further up the valley.

Continue riding north on Grey Rd 13 as it climbs to the top of the Niagara Escarpment. As you ride past what looks like two booster rockets off the space shuttle and a local deer farm, the hill crests and then immediately descends into Beaver Valley. At the bottom of the hill, brakes smoking, ride into the ski village of **Kimberly**. Not much is open during the summer months, but in the winter there is plenty of excitement.

Cycle past the Grist Mill Winery and, under a bridge, bear left at the [Y] junction of Grey Rd 7 and continue along Grey Rd 13 into the widest part of the Beaver Valley. As you ride past an exposed portion of the escarpment known as "Old Baldy," the road remains fairly flat up to the farm and its many long-eared donkeys. Here, the road begins to meander and, just before arriving in **Heathcote**, passes several beehives. You are now cycling through the Georgian Triangle apple belt. Notice how the trees are trimmed and tied to wire fences. The road twists and turns as it enters Clarksburg, passing a unique-looking library-lighthouse and the Ministry of Food Inspection station. Continue along Bruce St, past the traffic lights at Arthur St (Hwy 26). In the village of **Thornbury**, make a [L] turn onto the recreational trail. The trail entrance is located just be-

fore the road bends and begins its descent into the harbour. Take a few moments to relax in town at the little café near the rail-trail entrance. There is a very pleasant view of the harbour.

Thornbury is located at the mouth of the Beaver River on the shores of Lake Huron's Nottawasaga Bay. It was named by the town's surveyor in 1833 after his hometown in Somersetshire, England. While in Thornbury, visit the 8m dam and fish lock and, in spawning season, watch the rainbow and chinook salmon leap high in the air as they swim upstream toward their spawning grounds.

Riding is quite easy along this crushed-gravel rail trail, which runs parallel to Hwy 26 all the way into **Meaford**. At the "Georgian Trail 1989" sign, the trail enters a grove of cedars and crosses two wooden bridges. After passing a lumber company and a school, the rail trail ends at Meaford Harbour. Turn [R] onto Bridge St and pedal into downtown Meaford.

Named Pegg's Landing after the first settler's wife, the town's name was later changed to St. Vincent, but was called Meaford by 1858. Nicknamed the "Golden Town," Meaford is always bustling with activity during the warm summer months. It is perhaps best known for the book *Beautiful Joe*, about the rescue of a badly treated mongrel. Meaford was also briefly the home of Sierra Club founder John Muir, and it is thought that this is where he developed many of his ideas for the environmental movement. The town's history is revealed through its many fine heritage buildings. You can learn about fly casting by watching enthusiastic fly-fishers on Big Head River. And you'll learn why this area is known as "apple country" by simply taking a bite of a local apple.

Leg 2
(Meaford to Durham, 74km)

Beginning at the traffic light at the corner of Sykes St and Trowbridge St, ride east on Sykes St (Hwy 26) to Grey Rd 7. Turn [L] in front of the car dealership onto Beaver Valley Rd. Many of the climbs and descents on this road are steep and the hill in front of you is one of the steepest.

When exposed limestone rock appears on the left and right of the road, about 8km into the leg, look for the historic Griersville Rock plaque on the left, hidden among some bushes at the top of the rise. As you ride past the St. James Anglican Church and Cemetery in the village of Fairmont, Grey Rd 7 (Eric Winkler Parkway) has levelled out and riding is less strenuous. It actually feels as if the road is descending but it is in fact at the same altitude. Several kilometres past the local transformer station, look for the entrance into the Epping/John Muir Lookout. On a clear day you can see right into the heart of the valley, and "Old Baldy" stands out like a sore thumb. After riding through the small hamlet of Epping, the road begins a long, gradual descent, going past some wild-looking trees and the Talisman Ski Resort. At Grey Rd 13, make a [R] turn and head into downtown Kimberly.

Just before cycling uphill on Grey Rd 13, turn [R] onto Grey Rd 30. Descend into the valley and enjoy the ride past the local ski club and

a large home with an airplane sitting in the front yard. Notice the rocket boosters high on top of the escarpment as the road swings to the right and crosses a bridge. The ride out of the valley on Bowles Hill is a difficult one; stop often to catch your breath. In fact, walking your bike will help loosen up those cramped leg muscles. Just imagine what it would be like to ride this hill in a rain storm—it would be more like surfing! At the top of the escarpment, turn [R] at the [T] intersection and continue following Grey Rd 30 as it bears left at Hutchinsons Corners towards **Markdale**.

To add an optional side trip of only a few kilometres, continue straight at Hutchinsons Corners. A short distance ahead is the Beaver Valley Lookout.

Cycling west, the hills quickly disappear in the distance. At Grey Rd 12, turn [L] and ride into Markdale, home of Chapman's Ice Cream. Markdale is another interesting older town whose name was changed from Cornabus as part of a contractual agreement with the Toronto, Grey and Bruce Railway. Take note of the clock tower just before riding across Hwy 10.

As you leave Markdale, the road is very exciting as it winds its way downhill past a little waterfall. The first half of the ride from Markdale to Wandby is perhaps one of the most charming autumn rides in the entire province. Grey Rd 12 levels out and passes a little quarry at the village of Wandby. After the local stock yard and a small conservation area, Grey Rd 12 descends and then climbs to Baseline Rd (Concession

The Georgian Lakelands

Rd 2), the third road past Wandby.

Turn [L] onto Baseline Rd (Concession Rd 2) and follow this gravel road for the next several kilometres. It changes back into asphalt at the Edge Hill Side Rd. Just a wee bit past the Edge Hill Side Rd, look for a herd of black Angus cattle, a rare sight these days. The leg is almost complete upon reaching the familiar stop sign at Old Durham Rd. Hwy 4 is right in front of you. Turn [R] and cycle back uphill on Old Durham Rd to the Saugeen Valley Conservation Area.

Practical Information

Population:
Durham: 2,500
Thornbury: 1,800
Meaford: 4,400

 Tourist Information

Durham

Township of West Grey
PO Box 639
137 Garafraxa St N, Durham, ON
N0G 1R0
☎*(519) 369-2200 or 800-538-9647*
www.township.westgrey.on.ca

Thornbury

Georgian Triangle Tourist Association
30 Mountain Rd , Collingwood, ON
L9Y 4L2
☎*(705) 445-7722*
www.georgiantriangle.org
www.thornbury.net

Meaford

Georgian Triangle Tourist Association *(see above)*
www.meaford.net

 Bicycle Shops

Owen Sound

Jolley's Alternative Wheels
939 2ⁿᵈ Ave E, Owen Sound, ON
N4K 2H5
☎*(519) 371-1812*

 Special Sights and Events

Durham

Herb Fair, Antique Car Show, Durham Wood Show

Thornbury

Blessing of the Boats, Georgian Bay Sailing Regatta, Thanksgiving Apple Festival

Meaford

Summer Concert Series, Meaford Salmon Derby, Great Scarecrow Invasion, Apple Harvest, Georgian Theatre Festival

 Accommodations

Durham

B&B/Camping

Thornbury

Inns/Cottages/B&B/Camping

Meaford

Motel/Cottages/B&B/Camping

18. Cycling to the Big Chute and Back: Midland, Port Severn and Severn Falls

There is quite a difference between cycling the eastern and western shores of Georgian Bay. In the Midland area, rock formations are more rugged and much more colourful, leaving you with the feeling that much of the land on this side of the lake is still untamed. The first leg begins in the city of Midland and follows the Georgian Bay shoreline. Highlights include the lock at Port Severn and seeing the Marine Railway in action at the Big Chute. The second leg follows an ideal cycling road back into the village of Waubaushene before returning to Severn Sound.

Return Distance:
120km (72km, 48km)

No. of recommended legs:
2

Level of Difficulty:
🚲 🚲 🚲

Surface:
Asphalt

Villages/Towns/Cities:
Midland, Port McNicoll, Victoria Harbour, Waubaushene, Port Severn, South Bay, Big Chute, Severn Falls

Local Highlights:
Wye Marsh, Castle Village and Dracula's Museum, Huronia Museum, Huron Indian Village, Martyrs Shrine, Sainte-Ignace II, Sainte-Marie Among the Hurons, 30,000 Island Cruises, Discovery Harbour, Penetanguishene Centennial Museum, St. Ann's Roman Catholic Church, St. James Garrison Church-On-The-Lines, Octopus Craft Gallery, The Glass Attic, The Historic Murals of Midland, Georgian Bay Islands National Park, Beausoleil Island

Bicycle Types:
Touring/Hybrid/Mountain

Tour Suggestions:
Pack extra water as this tour travels through some unpopulated areas.

How to get there:
To reach Midland from the south, follow Hwys 400, 93 or 12. From the north, take Hwy 400 or 12. From the east follow Hwy 12, and from the west take Hwy 92 or 93. The tour begins at Midland Harbour on the shores of Severn Sound. The harbour parking lot is free and can be reached by turning right off Hwy 93 onto Young St and following it to a left turn onto King St.

Over 500 years ago, the present location of **Midland** and Penetanguishene was the centre of the Huron nation and home to several Huron villages. In 1639, French Jesuits established the Sainte-Marie Among the Hurons mission and opened the first hospital and church in Ontario. When the post office opened, John Smith, one of the town fathers, named the town Midland because of its location between Penetanguishene and Victoria Harbour.

The Georgian
Lakelands

Itinerary:
Leg 1
(Midland to Severn Falls, 72km)

Exit the Midland Harbour parking lot by turning [L] onto Bayshore Dr. Enjoy a great view of the bay before the road bends to the right, away from the bay. At this point, the road changes names and becomes William St. There is a long grade before William St crests at a set of traffic lights, then descends quickly to Hwy 12.

At the bottom of the hill, turn [L] onto Hwy 12 and pedal uphill past the Martyrs Shrine and the historic village of Sainte-Marie Among the Hurons. At the top of the hill, turn [L] onto Ogden's Beach Rd and follow it as it turns [R] onto Bayview Ave, passing along Severn Sound and through the village of **Port McNicoll**. Severn Sound has had many different names, including Christendom and Gloucester. In 1872, it was named Munday's Bay after the first settlers off the Midland Railway. The road out of Port McNicoll becomes quite steep and requires a lot of hard pedalling. At Triple Bay Rd, turn [R] and cycle across Talbot St back to Hwy 12.

Turn [L] onto Hwy 12; Hog Bay should be peeking through the trees on the left side of the road. A short distance ahead is a little rest area. Stop for a few minutes to find out why a wooden train-trestle bridge was so important to the area. Ride across Hog Creek to the **Victoria Harbour** welcome sign, then make a [L] turn onto William St and ride into downtown Victoria Harbour. Originally known as Hog's Bay, the town was soon nicknamed "Canary Town" because most of the houses were painted canary

yellow by the town's major employer, the Victoria Harbour Lumber Company. With the arrival of the Midland Railway in 1871, the town was renamed Victoria Harbour in honour of Queen Victoria. At the stop sign, turn [R] onto Albert St and follow it around the bay. Make a [L] turn onto Richard St and pedal past Sunset Park and the Tay township offices.

Riding uphill to Hwy 12, turn [L] and follow the highway over the Sturgeon River and past the Waubaushene cemetery. Turn [L] onto Sturgeon Rd and ride into the village of **Waubaushene**, whose name means "meeting of the rocks" or "place of narrows." There is a heritage bed and breakfast directly ahead at the Pine St [T] intersection. At the stop sign, turn [R], cross Pine St and then swing quickly [L] onto Coldwater Rd and enjoy the downhill ride. Cycling past the local grocery store, turn [R] onto Duck Bay Rd. Wait for the green light before riding across the narrow bridge at the mouth of Matchedash Bay.

When you reach Quarry Rd, turn [R] and cycle a short distance to a [L] turn onto W Service Rd, just before Hwy 69/400. The main highway is on your right as you ride past an old abandoned hotel. By now you may have noticed the red colour of the uncovered escarpment rock next to the road. At the Port Severn Rd [T] intersection, turn [R] and cross over Hwy 69/400 into **Port Severn**. At the stop sign, turn [L] in front of Rawley Lodge and cycle across another narrow bridge to the Lock 45 Visitor's Centre. The centre is the northern gateway on the Trent-Severn Waterway Canal and one of the

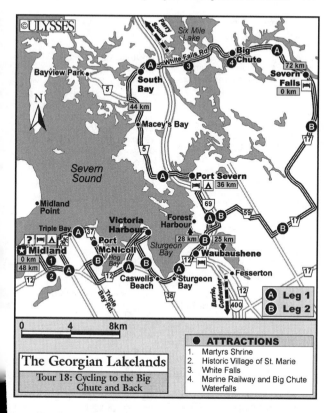

©ULYSSES

Parry Sound

Six Mile Lake

White Falls Rd

Big Chute

A

72 km

Bayview Park

South Bay

3

4

Severn Falls

0 km

5

N

44 km

Macey's Bay

B

17

5

Severn Sound

Midland Point

Port Severn

36 km

B

17

Victoria Harbour

Forest Harbour

A B

59

Triple Bay

137

28 km

B   25 km

B

17

? Midland

Port McNicoll

Hog Bay

Sturgeon Bay

Waubaushene

0 km
48 km

1

A

A   B

A

12

Fesserton

17

2

12

Caswells Beach

Sturgeon Bay

36

Barrie, Coldwater

12

400

A   Leg 1

B   Leg 2

Triple Bay Rd.

12

0   4   8km

The Georgian Lakelands

Tour 18: Cycling to the Big Chute and Back

● **ATTRACTIONS**
1. Martyrs Shrine
2. Historic Village of St. Marie
3. White Falls
4. Marine Railway and Big Chute Waterfalls

most developed service stops on the canal.

Continuing past the lock, rejoin Muskoka Rd 5 (Honey Harbour Rd) and ride up and over Hwy 69. Several kilometres down the road, look for a vacant building that at one time sold all types of watercraft. At South Bay Rd, turn [R] and get ready for an enjoyable ride along a very narrow, meandering road. At the village of **South Bay**, notice the colour of the water in the pond next to the road—it's almost royal blue.

After the recycling depot, the road begins quite a climb at Service Rd 6. The next several kilometres will be spent riding the rolling blacktop of the South Bay Rd as it zigzags through fairly dense bush. Crossing Hwy 69 once again, turn [L] onto Muskoka Rd 34 (E Service Rd).

The landscape here is spectacular, as huge red chunks of granite dominate the skyline. Continue to follow Muskoka Rd 34 by turning [R] off the service road onto White Falls Rd. After crossing the White Falls bridge, stop for a moment and enjoy the view while listening to the relaxing sound of rushing water as it empties into the Severn River from Six Mile Lake. Have your camera ready as there will be a number of great photo opportunities on the road ahead.

When the road swings sharply to the right, North America's only marine railway and the 18m waterfalls of **Big Chute** will come into view. Spend some time looking around the marine railway complex in Big Chute, then walk across the canal bridge and watch the water as it rushes into the river far below. During the summer months, boats are transported via the Marine Railway on a regular basis, and it's quite a sight to see it in operation. As Muskoka Rd 34 crosses the canal, it becomes Simcoe Rd 17 (Upper Chute Rd) and an easy ride towards the village of **Severn Falls**.

Leg 2
(Severn Falls to Midland, 48km)

The countryside opens up as Simcoe Rd 17 arcs south through the Matchedash Valley. Make a [R] turn at the flashing light and ride past the North River General Store to a left-hand bend in the road. Continue straight through at the bend, past the Severn Fire Station Number 3, onto North River Dr. At the [T] intersection, turn [R] onto Quarry Rd (Cty Rd 59). Enjoy the peacefulness of Quarry Rd as you ride past the Lafarge Quarries, then up and over Hwy 69 to the Duck Bay Rd [T] intersection. Turn [L] and retrace your steps, riding back across the bay, then get to Hwy 12 via Waubaushene.

Cycling west along Hwy 12, turn [R] upon reaching William St and

return to the marina parking lot on the shores of Severn Sound.

Optional Side Trip:
Only 10km away, the village of Penetanguishene is known for its carved, stone angels and the tall ship *Tecumseth*, which is docked for most of the summer at Kings Wharf. From the marina parking lot on Severn Sound, travel north along Harbourview Dr and turn [L] onto Fuller Ave. Upon arriving in Penetanguishene, simply follow the signs to Discovery Harbour.

Practical Information

Population:
Midland: 16,430
Port Severn: 2,250
Penetanguishene: 8,000

 Tourist Information

Midland

Southern Georgian Bay Chamber of Commerce
208 King St, Midland, ON L4R 3L9
☎*(705) 526-7884*
www.town.midland.on.ca
www.southerngeorgianbay.on.ca

Penetanguishene

Penetanguishene Tourist Information Centre
2 Main St, Penetanguishene, ON
L9M 1T1
☎*(705) 549-2232*
www.southerngeorgianbay.on.ca

Bicycle Shops

Midland

Total Sports
542 Bay St, Midland, ON L4R 1L3
☎(705) 528-0957

 Special Sights and Events

Midland

Georgian Bay Bass Masters, Wye Marsh Festival, Sweetwater Harvest, Thanksgiving Art and Craft Show, Winterfest, Waterfest, Shriner's Home Show, Ouendat Festival

Port Severn

Christmas on the Bay, Port Severn–Big Chute Cruises

Penetanguishene

Sailor's Sunset Evening Cruises, Winterama, Georgian Bay Poker Run, Halloween Spirit Walk, Library Garden Tour, Huronia Open Step Dance and Fiddle Competition, Fall Colour Cruise

 Accommodations

Midland

Hotel/Motel/B&B/Camping

Port Severn

Lodge/Camping/Resorts

Severn Falls

Motel/B&B/Camping/Resorts

Penetanguishene

B&B/Camping/Inn

---

19. Lake of the Bays and Muskoka Hills

Inspiring and challenging is perhaps the best way to describe this outing into the heart of the Muskokas. Beautiful inland lakes, dense forest and continuous rolling hills coalesce, making this a cycling adventure to remember.

Return Distance:
120km

No. of recommended legs:
2

Level of Difficulty:
🚲🚲🚲🚲

Surface:
Asphalt

Village/Towns/Cities:
Huntsville, Portage North, Baysville, Bracebridge, Port Sydney

Local Highlights:
Bird Mill Mews Gallery, Bracebridge Bay Park, Lady Muskoka Boat Cruise, Lakes of Muskoka Cottage Brewery, Muskoka Art and Crafts Gallery, Santa's Village and Rudolph's Fun Land, Woodchester Villa, Arrowhead Provincial Park, Dyer Memorial, Madill Church, Muskoka Pioneer Village

Recommended Bicycles:
Touring/Hybrid/Mountain

The Georgian Lakelands

Tour Suggestions:
Pack extra water and plan to complete the tour in two days as the ride is physically demanding and there is a lot to see. Remember to book accommodations in advance as cycling season is also tourist season in the Muskokas.

How to get there:
To reach Huntsville from the south, take Hwy 400 to Hwy 11 N; from the north, take Hwy 11 S. From the east, take Hwy 60 W and from the west, take Hwy 141 to Hwy 11 N.

The town of **Huntsville** is the last major community before entering Algonquin Park from the west; it's also an exciting town. Huntsville may have also been one of the province's first "dry" communities. When the area was surveyed in 1869, teetotaller Capt. George Hunt, the town's namesake, settled in the area, then known as Fairy Lake Junction. Hunt divided his land into lots and sold each lot with a "no drinking" clause written into the deeds. As a result, the town first developed on the hilly west side of the Muskoka River rather than on Hunt's flat lots on the river's east side.

Itinerary:
Leg 1
(Huntsville to Bracebridge)

Starting from the Canadian Tire parking lot, east of downtown Huntsville on Main/King William St (Muskoka Rd 3), turn [R] onto Muskoka Rd 3 and [R] again onto Hwy 60 (Muskoka Rd 60). Be careful, as Hwy 60 can be very busy and picturesque Fairy Lake on your right is sure to be somewhat distracting.

Turn [R] onto Muskoka Rd 23, following it through the country-

side. When the Deerhurst golf course comes into view, the road will begin to bend to the left and the Deerhurst Inn will be directly ahead. To remain on Muskoka Rd 23, turn [R] and follow Foot and Bay Rd (the local name for Muskoka Rd 23) to the village of **Portage**. Ever wondered who plans what direction a road will take? Well, when cycling along these Muskoka backroads, that question will come to mind many times throughout the day! A ride through the Lake of the Bays region is like being on a roller coaster—the only difference is that you have to do all the work to get to the top of the next exhilarating drop.

As you enter the town of Portage, the Portage Inn is directly in front and the road bends sharply to the right. Continue along Muskoka Rd 23 and turn [R] at the [T] intersection of Muskoka Rd 9. Not quite as hilly, Muskoka Rd 9 can be quite entertaining. With a sharp eye, you may catch a glimpse of local deer or watch the comical antics of the area's wild grouse. Upon reaching Britannia Rd, the turnoff for Bracebridge is only 18km further down the road.

After arriving at the [T] intersection at the end of Muskoka Rd 9, turn [L] onto Muskoka Rd 2. Take a break and check out the local store or enjoy a brief rest at the Parry Falls Park just ahead, on your left. At the Baysville [T] intersection of Muskoka Rd 2 and 117, turn [R]. Though there is no cycling lane on this extremely wide road, you should not have a problem riding it. Leaving Baysville behind, the road climbs past a beautiful rock garden on your right before levelling out. At Bonnie Lake Rd, the Bracebridge

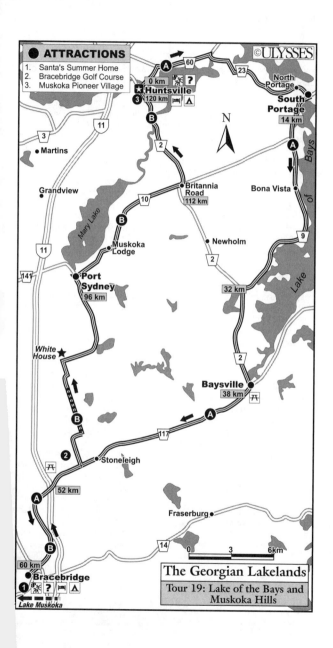

ATTRACTIONS

1. Santa's Summer Home
2. Bracebridge Golf Course
3. Muskoka Pioneer Village

©ULYSSES

The Georgian Lakelands

Tour 19: Lake of the Bays and Muskoka Hills

Golf Course will be on the right. Remember this landmark as it will be your turnoff to Huntsville during Leg 2 of this tour.

Cross Hwy 11 via the Baysville Bridge and do not turn onto Hwy 11. Just over the bridge, the Baysville Rd is now called Cedar Lane, and on your right is a small but comfortable rest area. A narrow road, Cedar Lane has little traffic and is almost void of hills all the way to Bracebridge. After passing the Cedar Lane Fish Farm Pits and the local public school, turn [R] at Muskoka Rd 42 and cycle into downtown **Bracebridge**.

An interesting town, Bracebridge is distinctive for a number of reasons, the most famous being that Bracebridge serves as Santa Claus's summer home. The town also abounds in natural wonders: throughout the city, the relaxing tenor of 22 waterfalls can be heard. Thanks to these falls, Bracebridge became the first municipality in Ontario to own its own hydroelectric station. At night, downtown Bracebridge is lit up thanks to colourful displays, and during the day, a visit to the Bird's Mill and Woodchester Villa is not to be missed.

Leg 2
(Bracebridge to Huntsville)

This leg begins by retracing your steps along Cedar Ln, crossing Hwy 11 and cycling to the Bracebridge Golf Club. Upon reaching the golf course, turn [L] onto Muskoka Rd 46 (Bonnie Lake Rd). Twisting its way through the countryside, Muskoka Rd 46 is a most delightful ride. As you approach a [T] intersection on

Stephenson Rd, a white house will be directly in front; turn [R] and continue following Muskoka Rd 46.

If you're up for a little exploring, turn left at the [T] intersection and cycle a short distance to the little wooden bridge that crosses Sage Creek, which makes a great place to stop for a short break.

Muskoka Rd 46 is a funny little road that seems as if it is heading in the wrong direction. Hang on; eventually, it begins to head north, passing Faun Lake and Clear Lake Roads and arriving at the Muskoka Rd 10 [T] intersection.

Note: turning left will take you into the village of **Port Sydney**, on the picturesque shores of Mary Lake.

Turn [R] at the [T] intersection and follow the delightfully hilly Muskoka 10 along the south shore of Mary Lake. Passing some interesting side-roads, like Candy Town Ln and West Point Sands Rd, a rest stop will be in order when arriving at the Muskoka Baptist Conference Centre.

At the junction of Muskoka 2, turn [L] and make your way into Huntsville. Once past the Treble Clef and the Muskoka Pioneer Village, downtown Huntsville is only a short distance away. At the [T] intersection, turn [R] and return to where this unforgettable ride began.

Practical Information

Population:
Huntsville: 20,000
Bracebridge: 13,200

 Tourist Information

Huntsville

**Huntsville/Lake of Bays
Chamber of Commerce**
8 West St N, Unit 1, Huntsville, ON
P1H 2B6
☎*(705) 789-4771*
www.huntsvillelakeofbays.on.ca

Muskoka Tourism
1342 Hwy 11 N, RR 2, Kilworthy, ON
P0E 1G0
☎*(705) 689-0660 or 800-267-9700*
www.discovermuskoka.ca

Bracebridge

**Bracebridge Chamber of
Commerce**
1-1 Manitoba St, Bracebridge, ON
P1L 2A8
☎*(705) 645-8121*
www.bracebridgechamber.com

Muskoka Tourism
(see above)

 Bicycle Shops

Huntsville

Algonquin Outfitters
86 Main St E, Huntsville, ON P1H 2C7
☎*(705) 787-0262*

Muskoka Bicycle Pro Shop
63 Main St E, Huntsville, ON P1H 2B8
☎*(705)789-8344*

Bracebridge

Ecclestone Cycle Co.
230 Ecclestone Dr, Bracebridge, ON
P1L 1G4
☎*(705) 645-1166*

Nielsen's Bikes
310 Taylor Rd, Bracebridge, ON
P1L 1A1
☎*(705) 645-8534*

 Special Sights and Events

Huntsville

Muskoka River Bathtub Derby,
Huntsville Farmers Market,
Muskoka Heritage Place,
Huntsville Festival of the Arts

Bracebridge

Muskoka Arts and Crafts Show,
Festival of Falls, Santa's Village
Seasonal Grand Opening, Canada
Day, Muskoka Pioneer Power
Association Annual Show, Music
of the Lakes Festival, Bracebridge
Fall Fair, Festival of Lights, The Big
Art Thing

 Accommodations

Huntsville and Bracebridge

Motel/B&B/Cottages/
Resort/Camping

 Off-Road Cycling

Huntsville and Bracebridge

Yes; several in the area. Refer to
"Off-Road Cycling" below.

The Georgian
Lakelands

Off-Road Cycling

Public Trails

Barrie Area

Floss Corridor/
North Simcoe Rail Trail
(14.5km)
Surface:
Original rail bed
Beginning:
Cty Rd 22 Horseshoe Valley Rd
to Essa Transformer Station near
Hwy 90

**City of Barrie Leisure, Transit &
Works**
70 Collier St, PO Box 400, Barrie, ON
L4M 4T5
☎ *(705) 739-4223*
www.city.barrie.on.ca

Georgian Trail
(32km)
Surface:
Loose/hard-packed
Beginning:
Collingwood and Meaford

Georgian Triangle Tourism
(see p 144)

Bracebridge Area

South Monck Trail
(7.5km)
Surface:
Hard-packed
Beginning:
Ball's Dr at Bracebridge Shopping
Centre

Town of Bracebridge
23 Dominion St, Bracebridge, ON
P1L 1R6
☎ *(705) 645-5264*
www.town.bracebridge.on.ca

Midland Area

Tiny Trail
(22km)
Surface:
Original rail bed/sandy sections
Beginning:
Cty Rd 26 to Hwy 27

Township of Tiny
130 Balm Beach Rd W, RR 1,
Perkinsfield, ON L0L 2J0
☎ *(705) 526-4204*
www.township.tiny.on.ca

Orillia

Lightfoot Trail
(6.5km)
Surface:
Asphalt/loose surface
Beginning:
Wilsons Point to Forest Ave

**Orillia and District Chamber of
Commerce**
150 Front St S, Orillia, ON L3V 4S7
☎ *(705) 326-4424*
www.orillia.com

Uhthoff Trail
(11km)
Surface:
Loose surface/hard-packed
Beginning:
North River (no access) to Wilson
Point Rd

**Orillia and District Chamber of
Commerce** *(see above)*

Port Elgin

Saugeen Rail Trail
(14km)
Surface:
Original rail bed/hard-packed
Beginning:
Port Elgin and Southampton

The Saugeen Rail Trail Association
PO Box 2313, Port Elgin, ON N0H 2C0
☎*(519)797-2215*

Resort and Conservation Trails

Blue Mountain Resort
RR 3, Collingwood, ON L9Y 3Z2
☎*(705) 445-0231*
www.bluemountain.ca

Talisman Mountain Resort & Convention Centre
150 Talisman Dr, Kimberley, ON N0C 1G0
☎*(519) 599-2520 or 800-265-3769*
www.talisman.ca

Hardwood Hills
(36km downhill ski trails, 45km single track)
RR 1, Oro Station, ON L0L 2E0
☎*(705) 487-3775*
⇌*800-387-3775*
www.hardwoodhills.on.ca

Horseshoe Resort
PO Box 10, Horseshoe Valley, RR 1, Barrie, ON L4M 4Y8
☎*(705) 835-2790 or 800-461-5627*
www.horseshoeresort.com

Kalapore Trails
(trail maps available at the general store in Ravenna)

Georgian Triangle Tourist Association
(see page 144)

Mansfield Outdoor Centre
(30km single- and double-track trails)
PO Box 95, Mansfield, ON L0N 1M0
☎*(705) 435-4479*
www.mansfieldoutdoorcentre.ca

Port Elgin Area

MacGregor Point Provincial Park
(24km of trail)

Ontario Parks
1450 Seventh Ave E, Owen Sound, ON N4K 2Z1
☎*(519) 376-3860 or (519) 389-9056*
www.ontarioparks.com/english/macg.html

Wingham Area

Wawanosh Valley Conservation Area *(4km of trail)*

Maitland Valley Conservation Authority
1093 Marietta St, PO Box 127, Wroxeter, ON N0G 2X0
☎*(519) 335-3557*
www.mvca.on.ca

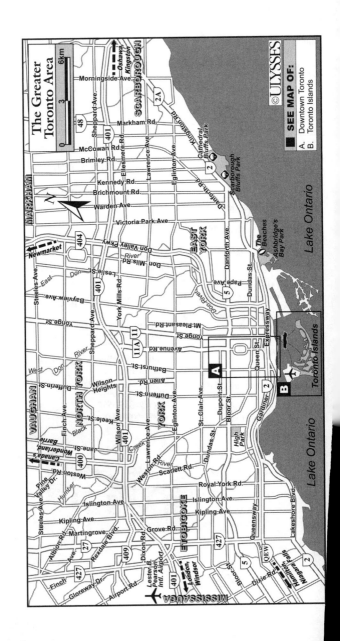

North Bay

Sudbury •

QUÉBEC

Ottawa ⊛

Parry
Sound

Lake Huron

Kingston

Owen
Sound

Peterborough

Toronto ⊙

Lake Ontario

London

Niagara
Falls

Sarnia

Lake Erie

UNITED
STATES

Windsor

The Greater Toronto Area

The Greater Toronto Area

has something for everyone: excellent off-road cycling, a well-developed waterfront and world-class entertainment.

When combined with its renowned intercity cycling network, it is no wonder Toronto happens to be one of the most bicycle-friendly cities in the world.

20. Toronto Islands, Lakeshore and Beaches

Don't be intimidated by the fact that it is Canada's largest city: **Toronto** is a wonderful place to visit by bicycle. The Waterfront Trail along Lake Ontario, a ferry ride to the picturesque Toronto Islands and the beautiful East Beach are only a few of the highlights that make this trip a wonderful experience!

Return Distance:
60km

No. of recommended legs:
1

Level of Difficulty:

Surface:
Waterfront Trail and city streets

Villages/Towns/Cities:
Toronto

Local Highlights:
Allan Botanical Gardens, Art Gallery of Ontario, The Grange, Bay of Spirits Gallery, Campbell House, CN Tower, Canadian Sports Hall of Fame, Casa Loma, Centreville Amusement Park, Fort York, Harbourfront Centre, Colborne Lodge, Hockey Hall of Fame, Mackenzie House, Market Gallery, Ontario Parliament Buildings, Osgoode Hall, SkyDome, Toronto's first post office, Toronto Stock Exchange, Upper Canada Brewing Company, Bata Shoe Museum, Canadian Broadcast Centre and Museum, George R. Gardiner Museum of Ceramic Art, HMCS Haida Naval Museum, Marine Museum of Upper Canada, Police Museum, Museum for Textiles, Redpath Sugar Museum, Royal Ontario Museum, Spadina House and Gardens, Theatre District

Cycling pathways within the city:
The Waterfront Trail, Rosedale Valley and Don River Trail, Willet Creek Trail, Humber River Valley, Mimico Creek, Cedarvale Ravine, High Park, Warden Woods and Taylor Creek, Highland Creek, Leslie Street Spit

Recommended Bicycles:
Touring/Hybrid/Mountain

Tour Suggestions:
This trip can be combined with the tour of Olde Town Toronto (Tour 21).

How to get there:
From the east and west, take Hwy 401; from the north, follow Hwy 400 south; from the south, take Queen Elizabeth Way

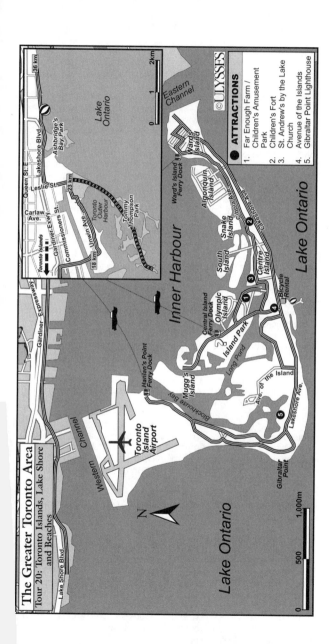

The Greater Toronto Area
Tour 20: Toronto Islands, Lake Shore and Beaches

ATTRACTIONS

1. Far Enough Farm /
   Children's Amusement
   Park
2. Children's Fort
3. St. Andrew's by the Lake
   Church
4. Avenue of the Islands
5. Gibraltar Point Lighthouse

© ULYSSES

Lake Ontario

Inner Harbour

Lake Ontario

Lake Ontario

Eastern Channel

Western Channel

Toronto Island Airport

Hanlan's Point Ferry Dock

Mugg's Island

Blockhouse Bay

Gibraltar Point

Olympic Island

Central Island Ferry Dock

Island Park

Long Pond

Ave. of the Island

Lakeshore Ave.

Bicycle Rental

Centre Island

South Island

Snake Island

Algonquin Island

Ward's Island Ferry Dock

Ward's Island

Cibola Ave.

Lakeshore Ave.

N

Queen St. E.
Lakeshore Blvd
Leslie St.
Carlaw Ave.
Commissioners St.
Unwin Ave.
Gardiner Expressway
Ashbridge's Bay Park
Toronto Outer Harbour
Tommy Thompson Park
36 km
23 km
18 km
Toronto Islands
Gardiner Exwy.
Lake Ontario
Eastern Channel

Lake Shore Blvd

2km
0   1   2km

500   1,000m

(QEW) to Hwy 403. Begin Tour 26 at Ontario Place, where parking fees are very reasonable. Ontario Place is located on Toronto's lakefront between Dufferin and Strachan Aves. Leave the Gardiner Expressway at the Spadina exit and keep right, driving west along Lake Shore Blvd, then turn left at Strachan Ave.

Over 300 years ago, the Huron referred to this area as "Toronto," which means "meeting place." In the late 1790s, the English called it York, but when the town became a city, it reverted back to its Aboriginal name. As Ontario's capital city, Toronto has developed into a true multiethnic community where you can experience the "old world" neighbourhoods of Little Italy, Chinatown and Danforth (Greektown). Toronto has also worked hard to accommodate the needs of cyclists, creating extensive public transportation networks that reduce the amount of traffic and make the city a reasonably safe and enjoyable place to ride a bicycle.

Itinerary:
Starting from the Molson Amphitheater at Ontario Place, ride east past the *HMCS Haida* warship towards the CN Tower. Once you join the Waterfront Trail, you will see hundreds of sailboats bobbing up and down at the Alexandra and National Yacht Club, a short distance ahead. The trail takes you through Coronation Park, where the pathway is divided by green and blue lines. The colours indicate the general direction of the path: west is green and east is blue. Keep riding as the trail swings to the right and around the HMCS York Department of National Defence build-

ing. Back along the lake, the trail crosses Stadium Rd to join Queens Quay W.

Stay on this road for the next couple of kilometres, which take you past the CN Tower, the world-famous SkyDome and the Spadina Gardens. Just before the Harbour Weston Hotel and Conference Centre, turn [R] at the Bay St traffic lights. Join the pathway immediately to your right and ride across the hotel's underground parking lot to the Toronto Island Ferry Docks. For a small fee, board the ferry to Hanlon's Point and enjoy the 15min ride across Toronto Harbour to Gibraltar Point.

Once on the island, follow the road as it arcs left around the harbour. Take a few minutes to look around the old haunted lighthouse across from the Natural Science school, which was built in 1808. A short distance ahead is an old crane boat, next to the Metro Works Marine Yard. Upon reaching Centre Island, there is a path through the gardens on your left, which leads across the bridge to Centre Island Amusement Park and the Centre Island Ferry. On the right is the Dock Inn and pier, where four-passenger bicycles can be rented.

Continue along the main road, keeping right, and join the wooden boardwalk along the lake. Just before the trail ends (it turns into gravel), turn [L] onto First St. Spend some time cycling around the enchanting, narrow cottage-lined streets of Ward Island. The pathway eventually emerges to reveal a striking view of Toronto's skyline. Board the Ward Island ferry and return to the mainland.

Once off the ferry, turn [R] onto Queens Quay E and ride past the Harbour Castle, Captain John's Seafood Ship and the Redpath Sugar Museum. Join the trail a short distance ahead to the right, which runs parallel to the Queens Quay, and later Lake Shore Blvd. Swing [R] and follow the trail over the Cherry Street Bridge. Cross the intersection of Commissioner and Cherry St, at the Toronto Hydro-Electric building, to join the trail on the left side of the road. The trail passes Clarke Beach and the docks of the Toronto Windsurfing Club as it meanders eastward. Exit onto Unwin Ave; at the ship-building facility, keep right and cross the bridge to a [T] intersection at Leslie St. Turn [L] and continue following the trail.

Optional Side Trip:
A [R] turn at Leslie St takes you to Tommy Thompson Park and the Leslie Street Spit. The spit is a man-made landmass that makes for an interesting ride. The road into the park ends at the Tommy Thompson lighthouse. Be careful when riding around the lighthouse as the road crosses an old dump and the rate of tire punctures is rather high in this area!

Watch out for in-line skaters coming around a sharp right-hand bend in the trail at Lake Shore Blvd. At the traffic lights, swing [R] and then turn [L] into Ashbridge Park. You will have to ride past a number of food concessions and an outdoor theatre before arriving at Beaches Park and the Woodbine Bathing Station. The trail ends 1 km ahead at Fernwood Park Ave. If time and weather permit, don your bathing suit and enjoy a refreshing dip in Lake Ontario before returning to Ontario Place.

Practical Information

Population:
Toronto: 4.8 million

 Tourist Information

Tourism Toronto
PO Box 126, 207 Queens Quay W, Suite 90, Toronto, ON M5J 1A7
☎*(416) 203-2600 or 800-499-2514*
www.torontotourism.com

Metro Parks and Recreation
Metro Hall, 55 John St, 24th Floor, Toronto, ON M5V 3C6
☎*(416) 392-8186*
www.city.toronto.on.ca/parks

 Bicycle Shops

Hogtown Skateboard & Snowboard Shop
401 King St W, Toronto, ON M5V 1K1
☎*(416) 598-4192*

Trail Blazer Cycles
1282 Danforth Ave, ON M4J 1M6
☎*(416) 463-0431*

Broadway Cycle
1222 Bloor St W, ON M6H 1N3
☎*(416) 531-1028*

Curbside Cycle and Inline Skate Centre
412 Bloor St W, ON M5S 1X5
☎*(416) 920-4933*

Bathurst Cycle
913 Bathurst St, ON M5R 3G4
☎*(416) 533-7510*

Bicycles at St. Clair Inc.
625 St. Clair W, ON M6C 1A7
☎*(416) 654-6187*

The Greater Toronto Area

The Bike Place
3096 Dundas St W, ON M6P 1Z8
☎ *(416) 766-1085*

Bikes On Wheels Inc.
309 Augusta Ave, ON M5T 2M2
☎ *(416) 966-2453*

Brown's Sports and Cycle Co. Ltd.
2447 Bloor St W, ON M6S 1P7
☎ *(416) 763-4176*

City Cycle
1041 Gerrard St E, ON M4M 1Z6
☎ *(416) 466-1225*

The Cycle Shoppe
630-A Queen St W, ON M6J 1E4
☎ *(416) 703-9990*

Cycle Solutions
615 Kingston Rd, ON M4L 1V3
☎ *(416) 691-0019*

Cyclemania
281 Danforth Ave, ON M4K 1N2
☎ *(416) 466-0330*
863 Bloor St W, ON M6G 1M4
☎ *(416) 533-0080*

Cyclepath
1204 Bloor St W, ON M6H 1N2
☎ *(416) 533-4481*
1510 Danforth Ave, ON M4J 1N4
☎ *(416) 463-5346*

Dave Fix My Bike
130 Harbord St, ON M5S 1G8
☎ *(416) 944-2453*

D'Ornellas Cycle Inc
1882 Queen St E, ON M4L 1H2
☎ *(416) 699-1461*

Downtown Cycle
368 College St, ON M5T 1S6
☎ *(416) 923-8189*

Duke's Cycle
625 Queen St W, ON M5V 2B7
☎ *(416) 504-6138*

Grove Cycle & Sports
335 College St, ON M5T 1S2
☎ *(416) 923-9633*

Ideal Bicycle
1178 Queen St E, ON M4M 1L4
☎ *(416) 463-2453*

L & J Cycle
1144 Davenport Rd, ON M6G 2C6
☎ *(416) 656-5293*

La Bicicletta
2109 Bloor St W, ON M6S 1M5
☎ *(416) 762-2679*

McBride Cycle
2797 Dundas St W, ON M6P 1Y6
☎ *(416) 763-5651*

Peddlar Cycles Ltd.
152 Avenue Rd, ON M5R 2H8
☎ *(416) 968-7100*

Polly's Re Cycle
1256 Queen St E, ON M4L 1C3
☎ *(416) 461-4312*

Racer Sportif
2214 Bloor St W, ON M6S 4Y7
☎ *(416) 769-5731*

Set Me Free - Recycle Bike Co.
653 College St, ON M6G 1B7
☎ *(416) 516-6493*
Roncesvalles Ave, ON M6R 2M8
☎ *(416) 532-4147*
Queen St E, ON M4E 1E3
☎ *(416) 698-3756*

Sport Swap
2063 Yonge St, ON M4S 2A2
☎ *(416) 481-0249*

Sporting Life Bikes and Boards
2454 Yonge St, ON M4P 2H5
☎ *(416) 485-4440*

Velotique
1592 Queen St E, ON M4L 1G1
☎ *(416) 466-3171*

Warren Cycle Works
890 Queen St E, ON M4M 1J3
☎*(416) 466-6958*

 Special Sights and Events

Sunday Market, Toronto Home
Show, Canadian International
Auto Show, Toronto Bicycle
Show, Sportsman Show, Cana-
dian National Exhibition, Dragon
Boat Race, Symphony of Fire
Fireworks Display, Downtown
Jazz Festival, Renaissance Festival,
Molson Indy, Caribana, Interna-
tional Film Festival, Canadian
Open, International Marathon,
Festival of Authors, Toronto Blue
Jays Baseball, Toronto Maple
Leafs Hockey, Toronto Raptors
Basketball, Royal Winter Agricul-
tural Fair

 Accommodations

Hotel/Motel/B&B/Camping

 Off-Road Cycling

Yes, refer to "Off-Road Cycling"
at the end of this chapter.

21. Olde Town Toronto

Toronto is one of North America's most exciting cities, and this
ride takes you along the bustling
streets of its old downtown area.
This urban adventure will take
you across electric streetcar
tracks and past the city's most
important historic and modern
landmarks. The sights include the
unique flat iron building called
Casa Loma, the University of

Toronto, the CN Tower and
Fort York.

Return Distance:
26km

No. of recommended legs:
1

Level of Difficulty:

Surface:
Asphalt and paved recreational
trail

Villages/Towns/Cities:
Toronto

Local Highlights:
Allan Botanical Gardens, Art Gal-
lery of Ontario, The Grange, Bay
of Spirits Gallery, Campbell
House, CN Tower, Canadian
Sports Hall of Fame, Casa Loma,
Centreville Amusement Park,
Fort York, Harbourfront Centre,
Colborne Lodge, Hockey Hall of
Fame, Mackenzie House, Market
Gallery, Ontario Parliament Build-
ings, Osgoode Hall, SkyDome,
Toronto's first post office, To-
ronto Stock Exchange, Upper
Canada Brewing Company, Bata
Shoe Museum, Canadian Broad-
cast Centre and Museum,
George R. Gardiner Museum of
Ceramic Art, HMCS Haida Naval
Museum, Marine Museum of
Upper Canada, Police Museum,
Museum for Textiles, Redpath
Sugar Museum, Royal Ontario
Museum, Spadina House and
Gardens, Theatre District

Cycling pathways within the city:
The Waterfront Trail, Rosedale
Valley and Don River Trail, Willet
Creek Trail, Humber River Val-
ley, Mimico Creek, Cedarvale
Ravine, High Park, Warden

Woods and Taylor Creek, Highland Creek, Leslie Street Spit

Recommended Bicycles:
Touring/Hybrid/Mountain

Tour Suggestions:
Saturday seems to attract fewer people to the Big Smoke (Toronto), so this is the best day to enjoy both of these tours along the shores of Lake Ontario. This trip can be combined with the tour of Toronto's Islands (Tour 20). Caution should always be exercised when crossing electric streetcar tracks.

How to get there:
From the east and west, take Hwy 401; from the north, follow Hwy 400 south; from the south, take Queen Elizabeth Way (QEW) to Hwy 403. Begin Tour 26 at Ontario Place, where parking fees are very reasonable. Ontario Place is located on Toronto's lakefront between Dufferin and Strachan Ave. Leave the Gardiner Expressway at the Spadina exit and keep right, driving west along Lake Shore Blvd, then turn left at Strachan Ave.

Itinerary:
Begin in front of the SkyDome, at the corner of Queens Quay W and Rees St, at Harbourfront Park. Cycle up Rees St and turn [L] on Bremner Blvd, then turn [R] onto Blue Jays Way. Ride down Blue Jays Way and turn [R] onto Front St. The SkyDome has the world's first retractable roof—it opens in under 20 minutes. You can see the CN Tower over your right shoulder; it is the world's tallest freestanding structure, reaching a height of 553m. Riding past the CBC Radio Broadcasting Building and the Metro Convention Centre, you will see the uniquely shaped Roy

Thomson Hall in the distance, on your left. Cross York St and go past Union Station. (Further down York St, the new Air Canada Centre, home to the Toronto Maple Leafs, is on the right.) At Bay St, the Royal York Hotel will be on the left while the Hummingbird Centre, formerly known as the O'Keefe Centre for the Performing Arts, is on the right. As you ride through the intersection at Victoria St, look to your left for the Hockey Hall of Fame. Built in 1885, it was originally the Bank of Montreal and is a fine example of rococo architecture. Further down on Front St W, you will notice a long wedge-shaped building. This striking building known as the "Flat Iron" was owned by Toronto's Godderham family, who was big in the beer industry. On the bottom floor is a local bar called "Down Under" from where you can take an elevator ride to the top of the "Flat Iron" (by request).

At Church St, signal and turn [L]. As you cycle north, you will quickly discover how the street got its name. The first church you will come across is the historic St. James Cathedral. Built in 1853, it was the fourth Anglican church built on this site. Further up the street, at Queen St E, is the Metropolitan United Church of Canada. Today, many of Toronto's homeless have taken to camping on its grounds.

Turn [L] at Shuter St and ride past St. Michaels Catholic Cathedral and Hospital. Directly ahead is the world-famous four-level Toronto Eaton Centre. Cycle past Massey Hall, cross Victoria S and make a [L] turn onto Yonge St. Before turning, look for the Canon Theatre (formerly the

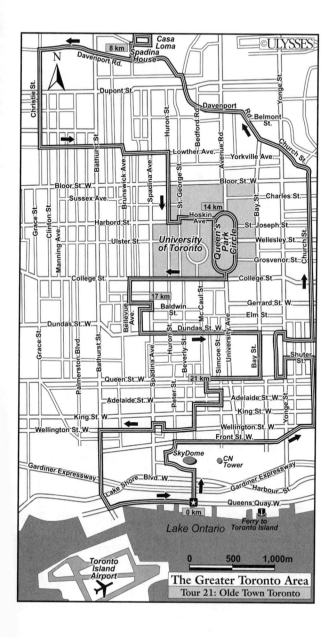

The Greater Toronto Area
Tour 21: Olde Town Toronto

©ULYSSES

N

Casa Loma
Spadina House

8 km
Davenport Rd.

Christie St.
Dupont St.
Davenport Rd.
Belmont St.
Church St.
Lowther Ave.
Yorkville Ave.
Bathurst St.
Brunswick Ave.
Spadina Ave.
Huron St.
St. George St.
Bedford Rd.
Avenue Rd.
Bay St.
Bloor St. W.
Bloor St. W.
Charles St.
Sussex Ave.
14 km
Hoskin Ave.
St. Joseph St.
Grace St.
Clinton St.
Manning Ave.
Harbord St.
University of Toronto
Queen's Park Circle
Wellesley St.
Ulster St.
Grosvenor St.
Church St.
College St.
College St.
17 km
Gerrard St. W.
Baldwin St.
Elm St.
Bellevue Ave.
McCaul St.
Dundas St. W.
Dundas St. W.
Grace St.
Bathurst St.
Palmerston Blvd.
Spadina Ave.
Huron St.
Beverly St.
Peter St.
Simcoe St.
University Ave.
Bay St.
Shuter St.
Queen St. W.
21 km
Adelaide St. W.
Adelaide St. W.
Yonge St.
King St. W.
King St. W.
Wellington St. W.
Wellington St. W.
Front St. W.
SkyDome
CN Tower
Gardiner Expressway
Gardiner Expressway
Lake Shore Blvd. W.
Harbour St.
Queens Quay W.
0 km
Ferry to Toronto Island
Lake Ontario

Toronto Island Airport

0   500   1,000m

Pantages, home of the Phantom of the Opera for a decade), which is just a few metres down the street on the right. Ride past the Elgin Theatre, turn [R] onto Queen St and then make another [R] onto James St.

Follow James St past the historic offices of the Salvation Army. Continue straight through the elbow in the road and follow the cobblestone walkway into an open-air courtyard. Here, tucked away in the shadow of the towering Eaton Centre, is the church of the Holy Trinity, built in 1847.

Swing [L] towards the clock tower, then bear [R] and exit onto Dundas St W via the Marriott Hotel walkway. Turn [R] but be careful as you cross a number of streetcar tracks. Once you have crossed Yonge St, continue cycling to Church St. Turn [L] and ride past Ryerson University to the big blue leaf at Maple Leaf Gardens. Cross Carlton St and continue to follow Church St across Bloor St. Church St swings left, crossing Yonge St and becoming Davenport Rd; it even picks up a cycling lane in the process. Several kilometres along the road, cycle across Dupont St and get into the left-hand-turn lane. About halfway up the hill, turn [L] and continue riding along Davenport Rd.

Past Spadina Rd and the staircase that leads up into the gardens at Casa Loma, turn [R] onto Walmer Rd, which becomes Austin Terrace. It is an uphill ride to the front doors of Casa Loma. At the top of the hill on your right is a castle that dates back to 1866 and is the former home of banker James Austin. Directly ahead is the historic Spadina House. Casa Loma perfectly exemplifies the elegance and opulence of the Edwardian era. This mansion is a great place to explore; its secret passages and underground tunnels are only a small part of its overall appeal.

As Austin Terrace swings to the left past Casa Loma and Spadina House, it turns into upper Spadina Ave. At the next street, turn [L] and ride to the [T] intersection. Turn [L] once more and follow Walmer St past the Casa Loma stables; here, make a [R] turn. Riding downhill, turn [R] at the Davenport Rd traffic lights and coast past George Brown City College. Continue to follow the road as it crosses Bathurst St and goes past a Toronto Transit Commission (TTC) building. Three streets later, turn [L] at the Christie St traffic lights.

Upon reaching Christie Pits Park, make a [L] turn onto Barton Ave and ride through this very quiet residential area. There are a number of four-way stops along Barton Ave, so remember to yield the right of way. Crossing Bathurst St, proceed to the [T] intersection at Brunswick St. Turn [R] and then [L], riding around a small park to join Lowther Ave. Cycling along the annex, ride past the Walmer Road Baptist Church and cross Spadina Rd, turning [R] onto Huron St. This area is highlighted by some very striking architecture, including the St. Thomas Anglican Church, the John P. Robarts Library and Varsity Stadium. As you ride across Bloor St, further down to the left is Canada's largest museum of fine arts and archaeology. The Royal Ontario Museum is also world-famous for its large collection of dinosaurs and Egyptian mummies.

Turn [L] at Harbord St, where a cycling lane will appear as you ride past the Catholic mission. Continue along the road, which is now called Hoskin Ave and is lined with the majestic buildings of the University of Toronto. At Queen's Park, swing [R] and then immediately get into the left-hand lane. Ride one complete loop of the Queens Park promenade. As you pass the Parliament Buildings, immediately after Hoskins Ave, move into the right-hand lane. Bear [R] to get onto University Ave. At the College St traffic lights, turn [R] and pedal across Spadina Ave. Notice the interesting clock tower at fire station No. 8 as you prepare for a [L] turn. Crossing several streetcar tracks, turn [L] and follow Bellevue Ave to a [L] turn onto Nassau St. Riding towards Spadina Ave once again, the lively sounds of Kensington Market will fill the air. Turn [R] onto Spadina Ave and make another [R] onto St. Andrews St, which takes you into the heart of the market. Fresh produce is always available here and Kensington Market is a good place to find all the essentials for a wonderful picnic lunch. Turning [L] onto Kensington St, ride through the rest of this European-style bazaar to Dundas St W.

Turn [L] and cross Spadina Ave into Chinatown, which is one of the largest communities of its kind in North America. Past the Art Gallery of Ontario, the 1817 Georgian-style residence known as The Grange will be on your right, and at McCaul St, St. Patrick's Chinese Church is on your left. Known as the Grange Shopping District, this area offers many unique shopping opportunities. Continue riding east, cycle across University Ave and then turn [R] onto Bay St.

At Queen St, turn [R] and travel west past Toronto's City Hall, Nathan Phillips Square and Osgoode Hall. A short distance ahead, high above the ground, is the CityTV truck, spinning its wheels. At John St, turn [L] and cycle to a [L] turn onto Nelson St, which takes you into the heart of the Toronto Insurance District. Turn [R] onto Simcoe St and cycle to another [R] turn onto Pearl St. Following this quiet little back alley, pass the interesting mural on Old Eds Warehouse before turning [L] onto John St. Glance to the left as you cross King St W and look for the Princess of Wales Theatre.

At Wellington St turn [R]; the SkyDome and CN Tower are now quite near. Ride across Blue Jays Way and bear right at Clarence Square. Make a [L] turn at Spadina Ave and then quickly turn [R] onto the continuation of Wellington St. Spadina can be very busy and it might be easier to walk your bicycle across the road.

At Bathurst St, signal a [L] turn and ride over the Front St bridge to Fort York. The first fort, built in 1783, was destroyed by American soldiers in 1813. It was quickly rebuilt but saw little use after the War of 1812. At the Fleet St traffic lights, continue straight along Bathurst and swing [L] onto the Queens Quay at Canada Malting. Joining a cycling lane, ride to the traffic lights at lower Spadina Ave. Turn [R] and pedal towards and under the Gardiner Expressway, cycling up a slight grade to a [R] turn onto Brimner Ave. At the next street, Navy Court, turn [L] and ride back to the Toronto SkyDome.

Off-Road Cycling

Public Trails

Caledon

Caledon Rail Trail
(36km)
Surface:
Original rail bed/hard-packed
Beginning:
Terra Cotta and Palgrave (Mt. Wolfe Rd)

Infrastructure Department, Town of Caledon
PO Box 1000, 6311 Old Church St, Caledon E, ON L0N 1E0
☎ *(905) 584-2272 or 800-303-2546*
www.town.caledon.on.ca

Newmarket Area

Beaver River Wetland Trail
(17km)
Surface:
Original rail bed
Beginning:
Blackwater and Cannington

Lake Simcoe Region Conservation Authority
PO Box 282, 120 Bayview Parkway, Newmarket, ON L3Y 4X1
☎ *(905) 895-1281*
www.lsrca.on.ca

Richmond Hill/ Markham Area

Sutton Zephyr Rail Trail
(14km)
Surface:
Original rail bed
Beginning:
East of Guillimbury, east of Hwy 48 and Holburn Rd goes to Catering Rd in Sutton

Lands Administrator, Ministry of Natural Resources
10401 Dufferin St, Maple, ON L4A 7X4
☎ *(905) 473-2160*
www.mnr.gov.on.ca

Waterfront Trail
Stoney Creek to Quinte W (350km along Lake Ontario currently completed; projected length: 700km)

Lake Ontario Waterfront Trail
372 Richmond St W, Suite 308, Toronto, ON M5V 1X6
☎ *(416) 943-8080*
www.waterfronttrail.org

Resort and Conservation Trails

Newmarket/Bradford Area

Scanlon Creek Conservation Area
(13km of trails)

Lake Simcoe Region Conservation Authority
(see above)

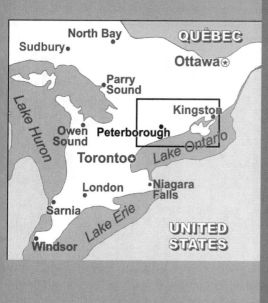

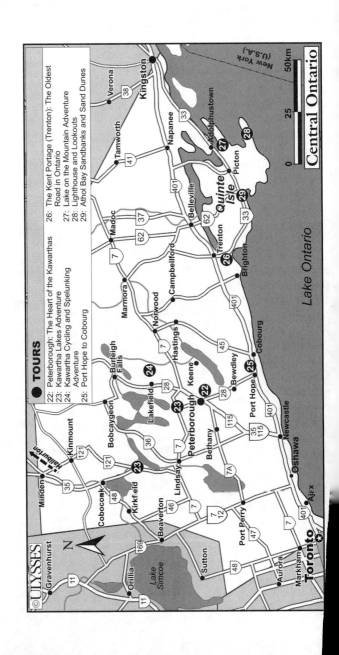

● TOURS

22: Peterborough: The Heart of the Kawarthas
23: Kawartha Lakes Adventure
24: Kawartha Cycling and Spelunking
      Adventure
25: Port Hope to Cobourg

26: The Kent Portage (Trenton): The Oldest
      Road in Ontario
27: Lake on the Mountain Adventure
28: Lighthouse and Lookouts
29: Athol Bay Sandbanks and Sand Dunes

Central Ontario

New York (U.S.A.)

0   25   50km

Lake Ontario

Toronto

Markham
Aurora
Ajax
Oshawa
Newcastle
Port Hope
Cobourg
Brighton
Trenton
Belleville
Napanee
Kingston
Verona

Gravenhurst
Orillia
Lake Simcoe
Sutton
Beaverton
Port Perry
Lindsay
Bethany
Peterborough
Keene
Bewdley
Campbellford
Madoc
Tamworth

Minden
Haliburton
Kinmount
Coboconk
Kirkfield
Bobcaygeon
Lakefield
Burleigh Falls
Hastings
Norwood
Marmora

Picton
Adolphustown
Quinte Isle

11
169
48
47
7
12
7A
115
35
115
401
45
28
28
36
121
7
121
35
48
46
7
7
28
62
37
62
7
41
38
33
33
62
401
N

Central Ontario

is the province's heartland. Beginning along the north shore of busy Lake Ontario, it follows the Trent-Severn Waterway to the Kawartha Lakes, including the highlands of Victoria and the unique liftlocks of the city of Peterborough.

As you continue north, you will learn that there are over 600 beautiful little lakes scattered through the hills, cliffs and forests where the resort town and cycling trails of Haliburton are also found.

22. Peterborough: The Heart of the Kawarthas

With the youthful attitude of a university town and an ideal location near the Kawartha Lakes, Peterborough is the hub for a variety of exciting activities. The highlights of this tour include a very special zoo along the Otonabee River, the world's highest hydraulic lift lock and several recreational greenways within city limits.

Return Distance:
32km

No. of recommended legs:
1

Level of Difficulty:

Surface:
Asphalt and some reconditioned rail bed

Villages/Towns/Cities:
Peterborough

Local Highlights:
Hutchison House, Hydraulic Lift Lock, Trans Canada Trail, Art Gallery of Peterborough, Centennial Fountain, Kawartha Downs, Otonabee Region Conservation Authority, Peterborough Centennial Museum and Archives, Peterborough Petes Hockey, Riverview Park and Zoo, Showplace Peterborough, Trent University, The Canadian Canoe Museum, Lang Pioneer Village, 4th Line Theatre, Whetung Ojibwa Centre, Petroglyphs Provincial Park, Stony Lake Cruises, Warsaw Caves, Indian River Reptile Zoo, Serpent Mounds Park

Recommended Bicycles:
Hybrid/Mountain/Touring

Tour Suggestions:
Because some of this tour runs along multi-use recreational pathways, remember to yield to pedestrians. It's also a good ride for children because of the off-road pathways and the Rivervew Zoo.

How to get there:
A number of highways go to Peterborough: Hwy 7 from the east, Hwys 115 and 28 from the south, Hwy 7 from the west and Hwy 28 from the north. To reach this tour's starting point at

James Stevenson Park, go east on Hunter St, crossing the Otonabee River and turning [R] on Burnham St. Go past the Lions Club building and make a [R] turn onto Dale St, then follow the road into the park. To the left is the parking lot and to the right are the Quaker Oats Tennis Courts. This is a quiet little park, tucked out of the way, making it an ideal location to safely park a vehicle.

In the 1800s, the local First Nations called present-day **Peterborough** "Nogojiwanong," meaning "the place at the end of the rapids." After Adam Scott, the area's first European settler, arrived in 1821 to build a mill, it wasn't long before a settlement grew. The area was known as Indian Plains, then Scott's Plains, Scott Mills and Scott's Landing. For a time, it was even called Robinson Settlement, when the British government settled 2,000 starving Irishmen in the area. When the post office opened in 1829, it was renamed Peterborough in honour of Peter Robinson.

Itinerary:
Cycle to the corner of Burnham and Hunter St, turn [R] onto Hunter St and ride into downtown East City Ashburnham. Riding through a fairly dense commercial core, cross Mark St and pass the Mark St United Church. Just past the church on the left are two cement cairns that mark the entrance to the Rotary Greenway.

Signal and turn [L] onto this re-conditioned Canadian National spur line which was originally 15km long and ran along the banks of the Otonabee River from Sherbrooke St to the hamlet of Lakefield.

As you cycle through a residential section of town, the trail comes out into a large open area. Once the site of the former railway yard, this space is now called Rotary Park. On your right are a hill and Nicholl's Oval Park. Take some time to explore the many paths leading down to the river to your left. Along the river is a series of dams that tame the rushing waters of the Otonabee as it drops more than 300m in less than 16km, creating a local supply of hydroelectric power. Just before crossing Parkhill Rd and rejoining the trail, to your left on the other side of the river is Inverlea Park, which is the site of the city's first house.

Several kilometres into the ride, the pathway passes a group of condominiums. It was here, in 1862, that the four-storey Auburn Woollen Mills were built. Using the power of the Dickson and Ashburnham lumber raceways and the finest wool, the mill created a world-renowned tweed. At the condominiums, look for the paths that lead to an old railway footbridge linking the east and west shores of the Otonabee River. A little farther upstream is a good spot to view Hilliard's Dam. After crossing Armour Rd and Television Rd, the pathway comes to a [T] intersection at Nassau Mills Rd.

Turn [R] on Nassau Mills Rd, then up and over the Trent Canal. Here the canal joins the Otonabee River. As the road bends back towards the canal, look to the left to see the railway swing bridge. You can get a closer look at the 1890s bridge and bridge master's house across the canal by turning [L] at the green rowing-club building and

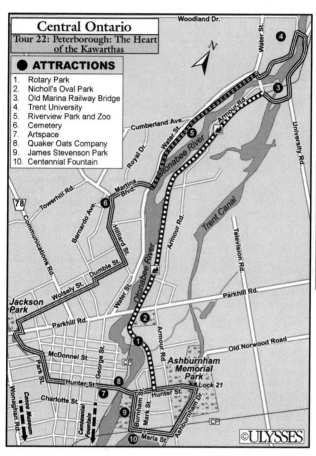

Central Ontario

Tour 22: Peterborough: The Heart
of the Kawarthas

● **ATTRACTIONS**

1. Rotary Park
2. Nicholl's Oval Park
3. Old Marina Railway Bridge
4. Trent University
5. Riverview Park and Zoo
6. Cemetery
7. Artspace
8. Quaker Oats Company
9. James Stevenson Park
10. Centennial Fountain

Central Ontario

©ULYSSES

following the canal back to the bridge.

Cycling towards the Trent University science building, just before going under the walkway, look to the right for a set of stairs and an elevator. Make use of this access point to the walkway. Riding over the river, follow the cement pathway as it weaves its way through the campus, finally exiting onto West Bank Dr. Most people picture a university as an age-old institution, but this is not the case with Trent University: indeed, it was not granted university status until 1963. Leaving the campus grounds, turn [R] at Nassau Mills Rd and [L] onto the pathway at Water St.

Pedalling for approximately 1 km, go past the local golf course and turn [L] into the Riverview Park and Zoo. This well-planned community zoo is great place to explore. Particularly interesting is the old pump house at the far end of the zoo. Known as the Monkey house, for obvious reasons, it was built in 1893 as Peterborough's second pump house, assisting Pump House No. 1 in providing water to a rapidly expanding population. At that same end of the park, the trail resumes and passes the Riverview Railway and an old Sabre jet fighter. The trail gradually narrows and finally ends at the Marina Blvd streetlights. Cross Water St to join Marina Blvd, then pass the Northcrest Arena and Community Centre. At the [T] intersection of Hilliard St, turn [L] and enjoy a wide bicycle lane until making a [R] turn onto Dumble Ave. Cycling to Barnardo Ave, make a [L] turn followed by a [R] turn at the flower triangle onto Wolseley St. You are now in an older residential area of town. Cross Chemong Rd and turn [L] onto Fairbairn St. At Parkhill Ave, the entrance to Jackson Park will be on your right. Upon entering the park, the trail immediately descends to a picturesque little pond with a covered bridge at one end. With tires now rolling over crushed gravel, follow the pathway until it reaches a [T] intersection and the park's trail map. Turning [R] will allow you to follow Jackson Creek Kiwanis Rail Trail, which is part of the Trans Canada Trail. This is a beautiful ride that goes on for several kilometres. Equally pleasant are some of the park's off-road trails.

To continue the ride, turn [L] at the trail junction and follow the rail bed as the map directs, bearing gradually to the right under Parkhill Rd, past a red-brick house and across Bonaccord St. The

trail exits onto McDonnell St and Park St N. Turn [R] onto Park St N by following a unique little cutoff and then make a [L] turn onto Hunter St.

These next few directions can be confusing: simply put, follow the box around. At the Reid and Hunter stop sign, turn [R] and then [L], passing St. Peter in Chains Church. Change to the left-hand lane, turn [L] and then [R], rejoining Hunter St. Cycle back towards the Otonabee River, to the George Street Royal Bank. It is impossible not to notice the murals painted on nearby buildings. Immediately after passing the Quaker Oats building, Hunter St crosses the river via the world's longest unreinforced concrete bridge, going past Burnham St. Cycling back through downtown East Ashburnham, the road begins to climb before descending to the Peterborough lift-lock tower and visitor's centre.

The impressive-looking Lock 21 of the Trent-Severn Waterway is said to be the world's highest hydraulic lift. It is used to carry pleasure craft and water 20m straight up, as demonstrated by a working model in the visitor centre: better yet, wait to see the real thing! The waterway meanders across central Ontario for nearly 386km. Beginning at the Bay of Quinte, a boater would have to travel through a combination of 36 conventional locks, pass through two flight locks, ride up two hydraulic lift locks and be carried along by a marine railway before reaching Georgian Bay.

Cycle under the lift locks and turn [R] onto Ashburnham Dr, following the Trent Canal over a set of railway tracks, past an abandone railway swing bridge, to a [R] turn onto Maria St. (There is a trail that begins at the Lock 21 Visitor's Centre. The trail follows the canal's north bank to Maria St.) To the left of a grated swing bridge is a set of conventional locks allowing access to Little Lake. At Rogers Cove, turn into the parking lot and head for the water. The Centennial Fountain, the highest jet fountain in Canada, spurts water 76m into the air. Cycling along Maria St can be a technical ride, especially when crossing over a set of very rough railway tracks before turning [R] onto Burnham St. To complete this figure eight, turn [L] onto Dale Ave and return to James Stevenson Park.

Practical Information

Population:
Peterborough: 70,000

 Tourist Information

Peterborough and the Kawarthas Tourism
175 George St N, Peterborough, ON
K9J 3G6
☎ *705-742-2201 or 800-461-6424*
www.thekawarthas.net

 Bicycle Shops

Ride On
175 Simcoe St, ON K9H 2H6
☎ *(705) 749-3364*

The Cyclepath
182 Charlotte St, ON K9J 2T7
☎ *(705) 742-7720*

Fontaine Sport and Cycle
84 Queen St, ON K9H 3J6
☎ *(705) 742-0511*

Manfred's Bike and Hike
248 Wolseley, ON K9H 4Z6
☎ *(705) 745-8210*

Spokes n' Pedals
464 Aylmer St N, ON K9H 3W2
☎ *(705) 745-7343*

 Special Sights and Events

Peterborough Summer Festival of Lights, Havelock Country Jamboree, Snofest, Festival of Trees, Hogmanay, Maplefest, Lakefield Larry, Summer Theatre, Canada Day

 Accommodations

Hotel/Motel/B&B/Camping

 Off-Road Cycling

Yes; there are several in the area. Refer to "Off-Road Cycling" at the end of this chapter.

 Market Days

Saturday mornings, Morrow Park; Wednesdays, Charlotte and George Sts, downtown.

23. Kawartha Lakes Adventure: Peterborough, Fenelon Falls and Lindsay

Starting in Peterborough, follow a portion of the Trans Canada Trail onto the rural roads of Kawartha Lakes. The first leg of the journey zigzags through the Kawartha hills, visits the oldest lock on the

Trent-Severn Waterway and concludes at Fenelon Falls, the "Jewel of the Kawarthas." The second leg begins along a former CN rail line and leads into the lovely community of Lindsay. Here, it joins some exhilarating country roads, climbing to several spectacular views of the countryside before returning to the city of Peterborough.

Return Distance:
155km (76km, 79km)

No. of recommended legs:
2

Level of Difficulty:
🚲 🚲 🚲

Surface:
Asphalt, crushed-gravel rail trail, some jeep road

Villages/Towns/Cities:
Peterborough, Fee's Landing, Bobcaygeon, Fenelon Falls, Cameron, Lindsay, Fox's Corners, Downeyville, Fowlers Corners

Local Highlights:
The oldest lock on the Trent-Severn Waterway, Fenelon Falls Historic Rail Station, Kawartha Settlers Village, Maryboro Lodge, Victoria County Museum, Boyd Heritage Museum, Rhymes and Times Doll Museum, Highlands Cinemas and Museum, Emily Provincial Park, The Academy Theatre, Fenelon Falls and Lock 34

Recommended Bicycles:
Hybrid/Mountain/Touring

Tour Suggestions:
The first day covers more distance than the second, but will prove to be an easier ride as it does not encounter as many long climbs.

How to get there:
There are a number of ways to reach Peterborough: Hwy 7 from the east, Hwys 115 and 28 from the south, Hwy 7 from the west and Hwy 28 from the north.

Begin the tour at Jackson Park, which is located at the junction of Parkhill Rd and Fairbairn St.

On any cycling trip, time always seems to fly by. Perhaps we can blame (or thank) one-time Peterborough resident Sir Sandford Fleming for this, as he invented Standard Time in 1884. It also seems appropriate that this trip begins in a recreational corridor: the city of Peterborough has always been involved in the recreational pursuits of its community, in particular the game of hockey. Many famous National Hockey League stars, such as Steve Yzerman, Steve Larmer and Bob Gainey, played for the Peterborough Petes hockey team, one of the Ontario Hockey League's most successful franchises.

Itinerary:
Leg 1
(Peterborough to Fenelon Falls, 76km)

Cycling past the shoreline of the Jackson Park Pond, follow the crushed-gravel trail to a [T] intersection. Here, a number of paths branch off in different directions to destinations outlined on the trail map. Swing [R] and follow the Jackson Creek Kiwanis Trail through forest, open meadows and wetland. After crossing Ackison Rd, the rail trail has not been reconditioned and the ride is somewhat rough. The trail

0   5   10km

Central Ontario
Tour 23: Kawartha Lakes Adventure

Ⓐ Leg 1
Ⓑ Leg 2

passes a transformer station and a radio broadcast tower, then exits onto Lilly Lake Rd, 2nd Line. At this point, turn [L] onto the road and follow it across Hwy 7A.

If you don't mind heights, it is possible to continue along the rail bed joining our intended route at Emily Park Rd (Rd 10), just after it crosses Hwy 7.

Cross Hwy 7A and go past a unique-looking, fenced-in stone home. The road starts to rise and fall after crossing Orange Corners Rd. For the next 2km, this roller-coaster road changes from as-

phalt to a well-oiled gravel surface. Notice the gravel pit and sand hill in the distance on the right. Upon reaching the blacktop of Emily Park Rd (Rd 10), turn [R] and begin a long, gradual climb past Doughty Aggregates and a trio of communication towers, coasting to the lights at Hwy 7.

After Hwy 7, the rail bed joins Emily Park Rd (Rd 10). Prepare for and make a [L] turn onto Peace Rd 14/10, just after passing Emily Provincial Park. Once past Pigeon Lake, ride through the marina town of **Fee's Landing** and turn [R], leaving Peace Rd

(Rd 14) for Centreline Rd (Rd 10). Cycling along a fairly level road at Pigeon Lake Rd (Rd 17), turn [R] and enjoy the ride along this winding road as it makes its way back to the lake. Just after running through a large wetland area, the road ends at Kawartha Lakes Rd 36. Keep right and cycle into the community of Bobcaygeon, crossing Little Bob and Big Bob Channels. At Kawartha Lakes Rd 8, turn [L] and continue toward Fenelon Falls.

At this point in the trip, **Bobcaygeon** makes for an excellent midday stop. Once on Kawartha Lakes Rd 8, take the next street left at the fire hall and cycle into downtown Bobcaygeon. The town's name comes from the Algonquin word Bob-ca-je-won-unk, meaning "shallow rapids." The area around the oldest lock of the Trent-Severn Waterway, built in 1833, makes an ideal spot to stretch your tired muscles.

Rejoining Kawartha Lakes Rd 8, which has recently been widened, the road snakes through the countryside, passing several notable buildings, including Twin Bears Farms and Providence Church. At the junction of Kawartha Lakes Roads 8 and 121, swing [L] onto Kawartha Lakes Rd 121. Cycle past the Westwood Hockey Stick Company into Fenelon Falls.

Fenelon Falls is an exciting little place to visit. Heading into town from the north, make a right turn onto Francis St at the lights and go past the Bank of Montreal. At the end of the street are Garnet Graham Park and a nice swimming area on the shores of Cameron Lake. To the left of the park is a trail that leads past an old

railway swing bridge and the historic Maryboro Lodge Museum, the former home of James Wallis, the founder of the village. The community was originally named Cameron's Falls, but when the post office opened in 1838 it was changed to honour a respected Sulpician missionary. Follow the canal through the downtown core and to the spectacular 7m falls and Lock 34.

Leg 2
(Fenelon Falls to Peterborough, 79km)

A short distance after the falls on Kawartha Lakes Rd 121, look for the renovated red train station on the left. The Victoria Rail Trail can be joined just behind the train station. Heading south out of town, it passes by a senior's centre, through a light industrial area and finally leaves the town at the Fenelon Water Treatment Plant. The trail is in reasonably good condition and cyclists can easily ride two abreast for most of the way. For most of the ride, Kawartha Lakes Rd 121 and 35 can be seen to the right. Some caution is recommended, even though all road crossings are signed and/or have orange gates. Two wetland areas make the ride very special. At the first wetland the trail narrows as bulrushes tower high above, and the grass completely covers the rail bed, silencing all tire noise and allowing the natural sounds of the marsh to be appreciated.

The Victoria Rail Trail crosses Long Beach Rd at **Cameron**, passing two old houses built during the early stages of the railroad. Though it's hard to imagine, Cameron once had a busy two-storey train station that was home to the section foreman, a cattle yard and a siding for additional cars.

Look for Osprey nests as the rail trail travels through the Ken Reid Conservation Area on the west shore of Sturgeon Lake. If you look under the bridge, you can see its original piers. When looking skyward, the large white-winged "birds" circling high above are actually gliders from a nearby airport. As you near Lindsay, the surface condition of the rail trail improves. Caution is recommended when crossing a small wooden bridge over a drainage ditch just before the first trailer park. The rail trail passes between the remains of a 1911-built train trestle as it enters **Lindsay**. After crossing William St N and Eglinton St, the trail exits onto Victoria Ave N near the Calvary Pentecostal Church. Turn [L] and follow Victoria Ave N, past the Victoria Park Armoury, turning [L] onto Kent St and into downtown Lindsay.

Lindsay, with its wide main street, was named in memory of the town's first surveyor's assistant, who was accidentally shot in the leg in 1825 and subsequently died from his wounds. Lindsay has had its fair share of colourful people and interesting events. Character actress Marie Dressler made her debut at the Lindsay Opera House at the age of five, and Ernest Thompson Seton, who grew up nearby, went on to produce 40 books on North American wildlife. In 1958, the first bullfight in Canada was staged here, with matadors armed only with wooden swords. Back in 1872, Pearl Hart, the only woman ever to rob a stagecoach, was born in Lindsay. A ride round the downtown core will reveal much about its heritage

through its architecture. Visit the Chamber of Commerce, located across from the armory, and pick up a walking-tour brochure to make the ride around Lindsay even more satisfying.

Following Kent St to the [T] intersection at the old Academy Theatre, turn [L] onto Lindsay St S, Hwy 7B/35B and follow the road as it descends over Lock 33, turning [R] onto Queen St, Kawartha Lakes Rd 36B. Cross over Rd 36 and continue along Pigeon Lake Rd past the blue Lindsay water tower and the old Century Drive-In. At the stop sign, turn [R] onto Sturgeon Rd 7, ride through the hamlet of **Downeyville**, then make a [L] turn onto Kawartha Lakes Rd 14, also called Peace Rd. This is an appealing, undulating road that winds its way through the countryside, past a green-shingled house at McBrian Farms and the municipal forest.

Travelling this familiar road, cross Pigeon Lake and turn [R] onto Emily Park Rd (Kawartha Lakes Rd 10). Ride past Emily Provincial Park and turn [L] at the next road, Valley. The next 6km will require some effort as the climbs are numerous and the road surface is now mostly hard-packed gravel. The ride is fairly easy and you will get a view of a picturesque valley with wood and stone fences at the top of each hill. Cross Bethel Rd and continue cycling to another stop sign at Frank Hill Rd (Kawartha Lakes Rd 26). Across the road are the St. James Emily Anglican Church and a commemorative cairn. Turn [R] onto Frank Hill Rd (Kawartha Lakes Rd 26) and ride over the southern end of Chemong Lake, crossing Hwy 7 onto Hwy 7A at **Fowlers Corners**. Turn [L] onto the next road, Stockdale, and follow it around a sharp right-hand bend. At this point the road narrows and its surface is hard-packed gravel that is somewhat rutted. Enjoy the spectacular view before the road descends into a valley and exits onto Lily Lake Rd. Turning [R] onto the paved surface of Lily Lake Rd, follow it to another [R] turn onto Ackinson Rd. Turn [L] onto the rail bed and return to Jackson Park. You might want to rejoin the rail bed at Lily Lake Rd. Even though it's a little rough, it does eliminate the hills.

Practical Information

For Peterborough information, see Tour 22: Peterborough

Population:
City of Kawartha Lakes: 72,000 (Lindsay: 17,000, Bobcaygeon: 2,500, Fenelon Falls: 1,800)

 Tourist Information

City of Kawartha Lakes

City of Kawartha Lakes Tourism Office
PO Box 9000, 26 Francis St, Lindsay, ON K9V 5R8
☎*(705) 324-9411, ext. 233*
www.city.kawarthalakes.on.ca

Bobcaygeon

Bobcaygeon and Area Chamber of Commerce
21 Canal St E, Bobcaygeon, ON K0M 1A0
☎*(705) 738-2202 or 800-318-6173*
www.kawarthalakes.net

Fenelon Falls

Fenelon Falls & District Chamber of Commerce
15 Oak St, Fenelon Falls, ON K0M 1N0
☎*(705) 887-3409*
www.fenelonfallschamber.com
www.kawarthalakes.net

Lindsay

Lindsay and District Chamber of Commerce
4 Victoria Ave N, Lindsay, ON K9V 4E5
☎*(705) 324-2393*
www.lindsaychamber.com
www.kawarthalakes.net

 Bicycle Shops

Lindsay

Midtown Sports
351 Kent St W, Lindsay, ON K9V 1A3
☎*(705) 324-2791*

Down to Earth Adventure Outfitters
82 Kent St W, Lindsay, ON K9V 2Y4
☎*(705) 328-0230*

 Special Sights and Events

Bobcaygeon

Kawartha Settlers' Village Settlers' Days, Annual Fiddle & Step Dance Contest, Pigeon Lake Yacht Club Regatta, Fall Fair, Canada Day, Arts and Crafts Show, US/Canada Walleye Tournament, Cruisefest, Boyd Heritage Museum, Trent-Severn Waterway Lock 32

Fenelon Falls

Kawartha Highland Games, Kawartha Arts Festival, Fenelon Agricultural Fair, Lions Club Annual Car and Truck Show,

Canada Day Lobsterfest, Steam Show, Festival of Lights, Old Fashioned Winter Games, Maryboro Lodge Museum, Fenelon Falls Historical Cemetery, Fenelon Falls and Gorge, Trent-Severn Waterway Lock 34

Lindsay

The Museum Garden Party and Ice Cream Social, River Festival, Wine Tasting Event, Candlelight Christmas House Tour, Oktoberfest, Kawartha Summer Playhouse, Skylark VIII – Lindsay's Riverboat Cruises, Lindsay Central Exhibition, Trent-Severn Waterway Lock 33

 Accommodations

Peterborough

Hotel/Motel/B&B/Camping

Bobcaygeon

Inns/Cottages/Motels/
Camping

Fenelon Falls

Motel/Inns/Cottages/
Camping

Lindsay

Motel/Inns/Camping

 Off-Road Cycling

Peterborough and Lindsay

Yes; several in the area. Refer to "Off-Road Cycling" at the end of this chapter.

 Market Days

Lindsay

Saturdays, May to October, Victoria Park

24. Kawartha Cycling and Spelunking Adventure: Peterborough, Lakefield and the Otonabee River

Just a short ride east of Peterborough, in the Indian River Valley, are the interesting little hamlet of Warsaw and a unique geological formation. A day in the area will pass quickly when hiking 13km of trail and exploring the dark nooks and crannies of the Warsaw Caves. The highlight of the outing is cycling along the shores of the Otonabee River and back into the city of Peterborough.

Return Distance:
65km

No. of recommended legs:
1

Level of Difficulty:

Surface:
Asphalt

Villages/Towns/Cities:
Peterborough

Local Highlights:
Hutchison House, Hydraulic Lift Lock, Trans Canada Trail, Art

Gallery of Peterborough, Centennial Fountain, Kawartha Downs, Otonabee Region Conservation Authority, Peterborough Centennial Museum and Archives, Peterborough Petes Hockey, Riverview Park and Zoo, Showplace Peterborough, Trent University, The Canadian Canoe Museum, Lang Pioneer Village, 4th Line Theatre, Whetung Ojibwa Centre, Petroglyphs Provincial Park, Stony Lake Cruises, Warsaw Caves, Indian River Reptile Zoo, Serpent Mounds Park

Recommended Bicycles:
Touring/Hybrid/Mountain

Tour Suggestions:
Bring an extra change of clothing if you plan on going spelunking at the Warsaw Caves; the rocks are not kind to Lycra.

How to get there:
There are a number of routes to Peterborough: Hwy 7 from the east, Hwys 115 and 28 from the south, Hwy 7 from the west and Hwy 28 from the north.

Cycling the backroads of Douro County can be a thrilling experience, especially in the early morning or the twilight hours. This is when the area's abundant wildlife makes its presence known. Don't be surprised if a coyote lopes swiftly alongside you or a deer suddenly jumps out of a ditch.

Itinerary:
To get to this tour's starting point at James Stevenson Park, head east on Hunter St, cross the Otonabee River and turn [R] on Burnham St. Go past the Lions Club building and make a [R] turn onto Dale St following the road into the park. To the left is the

parking lot and to the right are the Quaker Oats Tennis Courts. This is a quiet little park, tucked out of the way, making it an ideal location to safely park a vehicle.

Cycle to the corner of Burnham and Hunter Sts, turn [R] onto Hunter St and ride into downtown East City Ashburnham. Riding through a fairly dense commercial core, cross Mark St and travel past the Mark Street United Church. Just past the church on the left are two cement cairns marking the entrance to the Rotary Greenway. Signal and turn [L] onto this reconditioned Canadian National spur line.

As the trail exits onto Parkhill Rd/Peterborough Rd 4 at a set of traffic lights, turn [R] and climb past the sports field at Nicholl's Oval Park. A short distance past the **Warsaw** Road Bridge is Television Rd and the community of Donwood. Keep to the left to follow Peterborough Rd 4. Land here is difficult to farm, and fields are planted haphazardly on any available flat ground. Just a short distance past the local taxidermist, look for the Warsaw Ostrich Farm. After going under a large hydro corridor, the road begins to climb before descending into the village of Warsaw. First settled in 1834, Warsaw was first known as Dummer's Mills and then renamed Choate's Mills in 1839 after the local mill owner's cousin. On the long, winding downhill ride into town, Peterborough St goes past a couple of interesting old stone homes before it swings to the left. Turn [R] onto Mill St and coast to the [T] intersection at the bottom of the hill.

Before making a [L] turn onto Water St, spend some time ridir

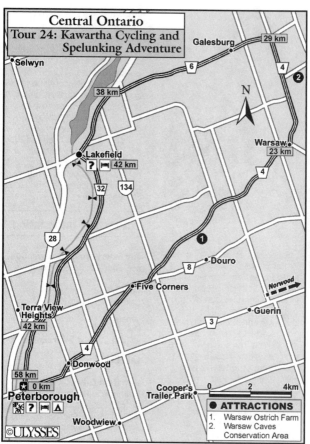

Central Ontario

around the village's back streets.
This can be an interesting diversion before descending into the
darkness of the Warsaw Caves.
Follow Water St/ Peterborough
Rd 4 as it climbs past Quarry Lake
to Warsaw Caves Rd. Turn [R]
and follow the signs as directed to
the Warsaw Cave Conservation
Area. There is a small admission
fee to the park, but it's well worth

When you're done spelunking
and exploring the "kettles," return
to Peterborough Rd 4 and follow
it north to Peterborough Rd 6.
Turn [L] and cycle through the
hamlet of Galesburg to another
[T] intersection at Hwy 28. Make
another [L] turn and ride along
Hwy 28 into the town of
Lakefield. Hwy 28 becomes
Hwy 29 (Queen St) as you get
closer to the downtown core.
Just before crossing the

ever-changing surroundings. At Douro Lock 24, the road follows the river shoreline to the left and then right, swinging once more as it approaches the Otonabee Lock 23 rest area. Upon reaching Trent University, continue following the river as it passes under the university's connecting walkway. Cycle past the old railway swing bridge and the green rowing club building, cross the river and make a [L] turn onto the Rotary Club Trail. Follow the trail past several road crossings before it returns to East City Ashburnham and James Stevenson Park.

Practical Information

Otonabee River, turn [L] onto Water St, which becomes River Rd or Peterborough Rd 32. Lakefield was first called Nelson's Falls after John Nelson, who settled in the area in 1819. It is a charming community that has preserved much of its past. A ride around this Irish town will reveal many interesting buildings and much about the town's early years along the rapids. Today, Lakefield is best remembered as the place where novelist and children's author Margaret Lawrence did most of her writing, and for its Preparatory Boys School, whose pupils have included His Royal Highness, Prince Andrew.

The ride along Peterborough Rd 32 from Lakefield to Peterborough is one of loveliest in the province. Cycling at river level approximately 1km out of town, you will pass a little picnic area and Sawyer Creek Lock 25 along River Rd. Flowing slowly, the river has widened considerably, becoming a continuous mirror that perfectly reflects the

For Peterborough information, see Tour 22: Peterborough

Population:
Lakefield: 2,600

 Tourist Information

Lakefield

Kawartha Lakes Chamber of Commerce, Eastern Region
Box 537, Lakefield, ON K0L 2H0
☎ *(705) 652-6963 or 888-565-8888*
www.kawarthalakes.net

 Special Sights and Events

Lakefield

Lakefield Fair, Literary Festival, Lakefield Winterfest, Lakefield Victoria Days, Annual Busker Festival, Victorian Christmas, Art, Jazz and Craft Festival on the River, Annual Rose Show, flea markets and craft shows throughout the year.

Accommodations

Lakefield

B&B

25. Port Hope to Cobourg and Back (including Part of the Waterfront Trail)

Explore heritage port towns along the shores of Lake Ontario to get a taste of life long ago, as it travelled that long and winding road towards present day. Today, the road includes part of the Waterfront Trail system which is being developed along the north shore of Lake Ontario. Along the way, the two towns encountered still have an attachment to their romantic past and, with a steady hand on the tiller, they have been substantially committed to making the waters and beaches of Lake Ontario cleaner and more inviting.

Return Distance:
46km

No. of recommended legs:
1

Level of Difficulty:

Surface:
Mainly asphalt, some reconditioned rail bed

Villages/Towns/Cities:
Port Hope, Cobourg

Local Highlights:

Port Hope

Historic downtown Port Hope, Ganaraska Trail and Forest, Capital Theatre (Canada's only operating atmospheric theatre), Canadian Firefighter's Museum, St. Marks Church, Dorothy's House Museum

Cobourg

Cobourg Marina, Art Gallery of Northumberland, Victoria Hall, Dressler House, Victoria Park Beach, Waterfront walking trail, Rotary Floral Clock, Barnum House Museum in Grafton

Recommended Bicycles:
Touring/Hybrid/Mountain

Tour Suggestions:
This is a very nice summer's evening ride or, if you start out in the morning, pack a lunch for a picnic at Cobourg's Victoria Park Beach.

How to get there:
From the east or west take Hwy 401 to Hwy 2, Exit 461. A good starting place is the free parking lot at the mouth of the Ganaraska River. Follow Hwy 2/Toronto St and turn left onto Ridout St, which changes to Walton St when it enters the downtown core. Turn [R] at Mill St, cross Hwy 2/ Peter St, and go past the local senior citizens hall and the Canadian Fire Fighter's Museum to the free parking along the river.

It is easy to understand why the site of present-day Port Hope was once home to a Cayuga First Nation village called Ganaraski or Cochingomink. Fishing and hunting was very good at the mouth

Central Ontario

of the Ganaraska River, and by early 1788, the area, then called Pemetaccutiang, was being surveyed for a settlement which became known as Smith's Creek. By 1817, the town was also referred to as Toronto, but to avoid confusion with the new name for the town of York, it was renamed Port Hope after the Lieutenant Governor of Québec.

Itinerary:
On the way to the lake and the Port Hope Marina, just before turning onto Madison St, take note of the East Beach rest area and restrooms. It's a nice ride out to the end of the pier with a panoramic view of the city on the way back.

Immediately after turning [R] onto Madison, the road begins to curve to the left and climb. Turn [R] onto Caldwell St and join the Port Hope Waterfront Trail at the end of the road. The trail becomes a gravel pathway and a refreshing ride along the lake, starting with a quick downhill slope to lake level. This portion of the trail was opened in 1998 and, judging by appearances, has been well used. Head east along Lake Ontario's north shore, keep riding past the Esco Limited offices and plant, but be careful when crossing the two log bridges.

The trail continues to follow the lakeshore and eventually ends at the Gage River parking lot. At this point, take a few moments to explore the single track along the river, which eventually comes to a dead end at the CNR tracks, then follow Lake St out of the parking lot. Travel west through the Port Hope Water Treatment Facility and continue along Lake St

until arriving at the first of two Esco Limited buildings.

A few metres before Esco Limited's large manufacturing facility, on your right, is a long, gated lane that leads to the back of the plant. If the gate is open, proceed up the lane and look for an opening to the right at the end. Cross the CNR tracks via an old walkway. Turn [R] onto Hwy 2 and follow the Waterfront Trail into Cobourg.

If the gate is closed, continue following Lake St past the Esco Limited manufacturing plant and turn [R] at the Esco Limited office building onto Hope St S. At the traffic lights turn [R] onto Hwy 2 and follow the Waterfront Trail into Cobourg.

A great deal of planning went into redeveloping Hwy 2/Cty Rd 2 by incorporating a generous cycling lane, the Waterfront Trail, into the highway. Leaving the city of Port Hope behind, Hwy 2 passes a mall which is home to the local bicycle shop. A short distance after a large conglomeration of gas pipes, owned by Perth Hydro, is the Cumberland Pistol and Revolver Club and the tasty, fresh produce of the Burnham Family Farm Market.

Before Cobourg's Northumberland Mall, turn [R] onto Rogers Rd and follow it to the left as it becomes Carlisle St. At the [T] intersection of Burnham St, turn [R] and follow it past St. Michael's Cemetery, bearing right at the Heath St [Y] junction. Continue along Burnham, past the Burnham Public School, then cross over and under a number of railway tracks. As you cross King St W, a pocket of fresh, lake air streams up Burnham from

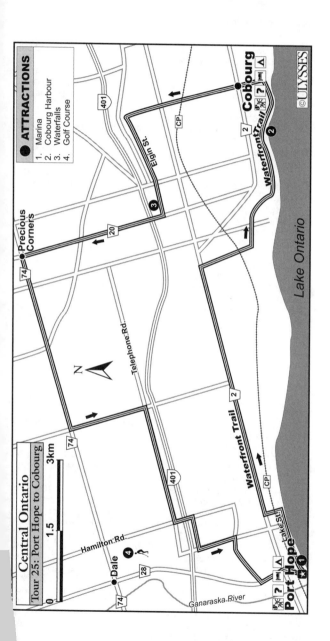

ATTRACTIONS

1. Marina
2. Cobourg Harbour
3. Waterfalls
4. Golf Course

Central Ontario
Tour 25: Port Hope to Cobourg

0   1.5   3km

Lake Ontario

Cobourg

Waterfront Trail

Precious Corners

Telephone Rd.

Elgin St.

Hamilton Rd.

Dale

Ganaraska River

Port Hope

Lake St.

Waterfront Trail

©ULYSSES

Monk's Cove, a small park at the end of Burnham St that overlooks the lake.

Turn [L] onto Monk St and take a few moments to enjoy the beautiful displays of the Northumberland Community Gardens. Monk changes into Tremaine Terrace as it bends to the right.

On your left is the entrance to the Peace Park. Turn [L] to cross Cobourg Creek into the park, and follow the trail as it gracefully bends to the right, exiting onto Clyde St. Continue along Clyde St and cross Ontario St onto Sydenham St. At Durham St, turn [R] and travel towards the lake. The decrepit, abandoned stone building on your left was an 1812 army barrack. Go through a narrow entrance at the end of Durham St, then follow a rocky trail to your left into the marina. At the Cobourg Yacht Club, the surface of the trail turns into interlocking brick. Bicycle rentals are available for boaters who moor at the harbour.

The ride along the promenade of Cobourg's Harbour is picturesque and very enjoyable. In 1829, the first of many piers was built here and welcomed hundreds of ships each year until the decline of lake shipping in 1859. The harbour was also home to the America's Cup Challenger, the Countess of Dufferin and the Steamship Cobourg car and freight ferry. As the harbour pathway exits into a parking lot, take note of the red Coast Guard rescue ship on the right and the entrance to the Victoria Park Boardwalk on the left. The Victoria Beach shoreline is clean and inviting, shade is provided by the

many century-old trees and the view is amazing. Rest areas, play areas, entertainment and camping are all located along the boardwalk. (Cycling is not permitted on the boardwalk.)

Leave the boardwalk at the children's play area and take the time to explore this European-style settlement. Walking-tour brochures are available at the tourist office. Founded in the latter part of the 1790s, the settlement has gone through a number of name changes, beginning with Buckville, then Amherst and finally Hamilton after the township. The locals even nicknamed it "Hardscrabble" before agreeing on its present designation, which commemorates the marriage of Princess Charlotte to Prince Leopold of Saxe-Coburg, Germany. The extra 'o' in the name has been attributed to an error made by the local clerk. The magnificent town hall is one of 70 heritage sites in the downtown core. Victoria Hall is one of Canada's most elegant buildings and was built because the locals mistakenly thought Cobourg would be chosen as the capital of Upper Canada, in 1856.

Rejoin the boardwalk and slip onto the saddle again at Bay St. Turn [R] at the [T] intersection and follow D'Arcy St across King St E/Hwy 2. Cycle several kilometres to the Elgin St stop sign and turn [L]. Follow the truck bypass as it crosses Division St/Cty Rd 45, cycle past a number of fast-food outlets and the Union Cemetery and turn [R] onto Ontario St/Cty Rd 20. Travelling north on Ontario St, the road climbs past the Old Mill Restaurant, the waterfalls and the Cobourg Creek Country Club, and crosses over Hwy 401 to a relaxing downhill descent.

Enjoy a small cycling lane as you ride along this Hamilton Township rural road towards Precious Corners. One of the township's original hamlets, it was named after Joseph Precious and his family, who arrived here in 1829. After turning [L] at the [T] intersection onto Cty Rd 74/ Dale Rd, look for the last vestige of the early settlement, an abandoned cemetery with only eight gravestones.

A short distance ahead of Northumberland Rd 18 is the Dale Rd School, a long downhill and then a stiff climb to the Bethesda United Church of Canada. At Theatre Rd, turn [L] and cycle past the local golf course to Telephone Rd. Turn [R] and follow the road as it runs parallel to Hwy 401, crossing over Gage Creek, turning [L] onto Hamilton Dr at the top of the hill.

Immediately after crossing Hwy 401, turn [R] onto Croft St and go past Viceroy Homes to a [L] turn onto Rose Glen Rd. After Wladyka Park and Trinity College, turn [R] onto Ward St and climb a small hill to the ivy-covered Trinity College. Continue along Ward St, turn [L] onto Mill St and [R] onto Walton St. This area immediately surrounding downtown Port Hope along the Ganaraska River has been designated as a Heritage Conservation District. This is a fine example of a formal main street, because most of the buildings in this area were built in a 30-year period, between the 1840s and the 1870s.

Before returning to the Marina parking lot and Lake Ontario, you

will have noticed one of two significant landmarks. One that should not be missed, because of its size, is the Port Hope stone railway viaduct. Massive in size yet graceful in design, in 1856, its stone arches were part of the longest section of continuous railway in Canada, linking Toronto and Montréal. The second landmark is the limestone Victorian Grand Trunk Railway station, just west and south of the viaduct on Hayward St.

Practical Information

Population:
Port Hope: 17,000
Cobourg: 16,000

 Tourist Information

Port Hope

The Municipality of Port Hope, Tourism Office
20 Queen St, Port Hope, ON L1A 3Z9
☎*(905) 885-5519 or 888-767-8467*
www.town.porthope.on.ca

Cobourg

Cobourg Economic Development and Tourism
212 King St W, Cobourg, ON K9A 2N1
☎*(905) 372-5481 or 888-262-6874*
www.town.cobourg.on.ca

 Bicycle Shops

Port Hope

Proform Cycle and Accessories
RR 4, Hwy 2, Cobourg, ON K9A 4J7
☎*(905) 885-4857*

Cobourg

Sommerville's
84 King St W, Cobourg, ON K9A 2M4
☎*(905) 372-7031*

 Special Sights and Events

Port Hope

Main St (well-preserved 19th-century buildings), The Capitol Theatre, Canadian Firefighter's Museum, Dorothy's House Museum, Ganaraska Forest Centre, Architectural Conservancy of Ontario Biennial Garden Tour and Historical House Tour, Canada Day, Agricultural Fall Fair, Float your Fanny Down the Ganny River Race, A Candlelight Christmas

Cobourg

Great North American Land Yacht Regatta Car Show, All Canadian Jazz Festival, Waterfront Festival, Cobourg Highland Games, three different theatre groups, including outdoor summer theatre, Cobourg Vintage Film Festival

 Accommodations

Port Hope and Cobourg

Hotel/Motel/B&B/Camping

 Off-Road Cycling

Port Hope and Cobourg

Yes, refer to "Off-Road Cycling" at the end of this chapter.

 Market Days

Cobourg

Saturday mornings, May to December

Port Hope

Saturday mornings, May to November

26. Kent Portage: The Oldest Road in Ontario

Cycle back to the past along the Bay of Quinte and several historic routes, including Ontario's oldest road.

Return Distance:
35km

No. of recommended legs:
1

Level of Difficulty:

Surface:
Asphalt

Villages/Towns/Cities:
Trenton, Carrying Place

Local Highlights:
RCAF Memorial Museum, Fort Kente, CFB Trenton Air Force Base, Murray Canal Swing Bridge, Trenton Greenbelt Waterfront Trail, Lock One Interpretation Centre, Bay of Quinte, Mount Pelion Canon

Recommended Bicycles:
Touring/Hybrid/Mountain

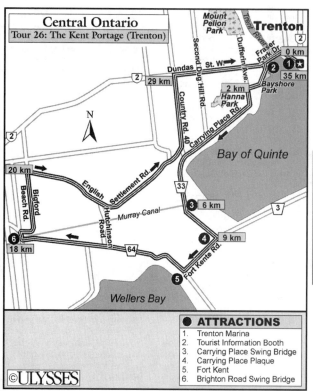

Central Ontario
Tour 26: The Kent Portage (Trenton)

● **ATTRACTIONS**
1. Trenton Marina
2. Tourist Information Booth
3. Carrying Place Swing Bridge
4. Carrying Place Plaque
5. Fort Kent
6. Brighton Road Swing Bridge

©ULYSSES

Central Ontario

Tour Suggestions:
A very nice evening country ride with frequent appearances of local wildlife at dusk.

How to get there:
The tour starts in the city of Trenton at the Trenton Marina. Get off Hwy 401 at Exit 525 and make a [L] turn onto Dundas St W. Cross the Trent River and turn right onto Ontario St and follow it to the marina parking lot.

In the mid-1800s, the Trent River was one of two major trade routes in Ontario. Two communities, Annwood and Trenton,

developed on both sides of the river at the Bay of Quinte. They eventually merged in 1829, and the town became known as River Trent, Port Trent, then Trent Port until 1853, when the formal name of Trenton was adopted. Government influence has long been felt in the area—since 1919, in fact, when a film company was established in the hopes that Trenton would become the movie capital of Canada. Today, the Canadian Air Force Training Base is located here and it is common to see olive-green military aircraft flying overhead.

Itinerary:

Exit onto Ontario St from the Robert Patrick Trenton Marina and turn [L] onto Dundas St W/Hwy 2. Cross the bridge, passing Front St, and turn [L] at the lights onto Albert St. The local tourist information booth is located on your left as you pass Front St. Cycle down Albert St to Quinte St, then turn [R] and immediately [L] onto Creswell Dr. Bayshore Park and the Bay of Quinte should be on the left. Turn [L] at Dufferin Ave/Cty Rd 33 and follow this former loyalist path towards **Carrying Place**.

A cycling lane appears just after rounding a left bend in the road. Road designations can be somewhat confusing, as this road goes by a lot of different names: Carry Place Rd, Queens Hwy 33, The Loyalist Parkway and Cty Rd 33. Catching occasional glimpses of the Bay of Quinte on the left, watch for a unique road name on the right, Second Dug Hill Rd. As you cycle through a wetland area on Cty Rd 33, traffic may be backing up as it nears the Murray Canal Swing Bridge. The canal itself is over 8km long, creating a safe, short and fast water transportation link between Lake Ontario and the Bay of Quinte. Spend a few moments at the information/rest area on the far side of the bridge. There is always water traffic and it's fascinating to watch the swing bridge in action.

Continuing along Cty Rd 33, the old Carrying Place Cemetery on your right warrants some scrutiny. As you approach the flashing light, look for the Carrying Place plaque on your right before turning [R] onto Northumberland

Rd 64. After St John's Anglican Church, built in 1824, the next several kilometres will be spent riding on the oldest road/pathway in Ontario, the Kente Portage. A splendid view of Weller Bay is just ahead after crossing Northumberland 64 onto a gravel surface. To your left is the replica of the 1813 Fort Kente, built by Capt. Coleman's Dragoons. This is not the fort's original location; it was actually built on the opposite side of the road. If the grass has not been trimmed, watch out for poison ivy.

Retracing your steps, turn [R] onto Cty Rd 64, better known to locals as Gardenville Rd. Since this road is fairly flat, good time can be made to another Murray Canal crossing, the Brighton Road Swing Bridge. A short distance away, on the other side of the bridge, make a [R] turn at the variety store onto Bigford Rd and follow it past the Mount Carmel Cemetery. At English Settlement Rd, turn [R] and pass a number of flower wagon displays and the final resting place of Gilligan's *S.S. Minnow*.

At the [T] intersection of County Rd 40, turn [L] and travel towards Hwy 2, passing a large apple orchard on your right. Turn [R] onto Hwy 2 and make your way into Trenton. As you approach the downtown core, a tower and several church spires stand high above the horizon like beacons welcoming the cyclist home. A little time spent exploring the downtown core before returning to the marina parking lot will yield much information about this gateway to the Trent-Severn Waterway.

Practical Information

Population:
Quinte West (includes the former city of Trenton: 17,200): 42,000

 Tourist Information

Quinte West Chamber of Commerce
97 Front St, Trenton, ON K8V 4N6
☎ *(613) 392-7635 or 800-930-3255*
www.quintewestchamber.on.ca

Prince Edward County Chamber of Commerce
PO Box 50, 116 Main St, Picton, ON
K0K 2T0
☎ *(613) 476-2421 or 800-640-4717*
www.pec.on.ca

The Bay of Quinte Tourist Council
PO Box 726, Belleville, ON K8N 5B3
☎ *(613) 962-4597*
www.quinte.on.ca

 Bicycle Shops

Doug's Bicycle Sales & Service
159 College St, Belleville, ON
☎ *(613) 966-9161*

Stephen Licence Ltd.
288 Front St, Belleville, ON
☎ *(613) 966-6900*

 Special Sights and Events

Opening of the Trent-Severn System, Canada Day, RCAF Memorial Museum, Empire Theatre, Walleye World Fishing Derby, Scottish/Irish Festival, Weller's Bay Bass Derby, Amazing Loyalist Country Adventure, Classic Country Music Reunion.

 Accommodations

Hotel/Motel/B&B/Camping

 Off-Road Cycling

Yes; see "Off-Road Cycling" at the end of this chapter.

27. Lake on the Mountain Adventure: Picton and Prince Edward County

Central Ontario

The locals say that the soil is deep and rich in Prince Edward County, and this certainly holds true in more ways than one. Starting in Picton, our route travels along the peaceful back roads of Prince Edward County, following the shores of Prince Edward Bay to a friendly welcome from the folks at the Rose House Museum. As the road rounds Pleasant Point, take a few moments to appreciate the beauty of Prinyer's Cove before ascending to Lake on the Mountain and a stunning view of the Picton Bay area.

Return Distance:
60km

No. of recommended legs:
1

Level of Difficulty:

Surface:
Asphalt

Villages/Towns/Cities:
Picton, Waupoos, Glenora

Local Highlights:
Macaulay Heritage Park, Mariners' Park Museum, Prince Edward County Courthouse, Rose House Museum & North Marysburgh Museum, Sandbanks Provincial Park, Lake on the Mountain, The Exotarium, Regent Theatre

Recommended Bicycles:
Touring/Hybrid/Mountain

Tour Suggestions:
There are no public facilities on this tour. Bring a lot of water and pack a picnic lunch to enjoy a day of leisurely cycling fun.

How to get there:
A number of routes to Quinte County, Picton are available: Hwy 401 from the east and west, and Hwys 7, 30, 14 and 62 from the north and south. The closest international border crossing is near Alexandria Bay in New York; follow the 401 west from there.

Back in 1786, Picton must have been at the centre of a heated controversy. It grew from the merger of two settlements that developed at the head of Picton Bay. The original, financially successful town of Hallowell was a thriving community when Reverend William Macaulay established another settlement on a nearby 20ha of land. He named the property after General Sir Thomas Picton, a major-general in the Napoleonic Wars. Through his position in the community as pastor of St. Mary Magdalene Church, he succeeded in uniting the two communities in 1837. Picton has managed to preserve its past through many of its heritage sites and stories of long ago. One such tale involves Sir John A. Macdonald, Canada's first Prime

Minister and a Father of Confederation, and his rather outrageous escapades as a youth in the town of Picton.

Itinerary:
Start from the convenient Mary St municipal parking lot, which is one block east of the Loyalist Parkway/ Main St at the [T] intersection of Elizabeth and Mary Sts. Exit the parking lot by turning [R] and follow Mary St as it turns into York St. Past the intricate stone work of the original country courthouse and jail, which now contains the County of Prince Edward Archives, York St ends at Church St. Directly in front is the Macaulay Heritage Park. Turning [L] onto Church St, you will pass the Macaulay homestead and St. Mary Magdalene Church. Built in 1825, the church now serves as the county museum. Notice the old cemetery on your right as you reach the stop sign at Union St. Make a right turn onto Union and ascend Prince Edward County Rd 8, going past Macaulay Mountain Conservation Area, Birdhouse City and an old Shooting Star P86 fighter jet.

As the road twists and turns through the county's rolling landscape, you may notice that some of the homes just past Old Milford Rd are flying a Loyalist flag. This flag was created to mark the union of these two thrones in 1606 and is a combination of Great Britain's Saint George flag and the white-and-blue flag of Scotland. This new flag was called the Union Flag and it was under it that the United Empire Loyalists entered Prince Edward County in 1776. Today, the flag is better known as the "Union Jack" (the British flag) and for the better part of 400 years it has flown without

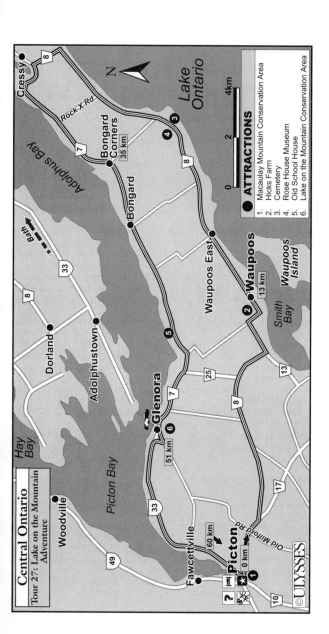

Central Ontario
Tour 27: Lake on the Mountain Adventure

N

Lake Ontario

ATTRACTIONS

1. Macaulay Mountain Conservation Area
2. Hicks Farm
3. Cemetery
4. Rose House Museum
5. Old School House
6. Lake on the Mountain Conservation Area

0   2   4km

Cressy

Rock-X-Rd.

Bongard Corners
35 km

Adolphus Bay

Bongard

Waupoos East

● Waupoos
13 km

Waupoos Island

Smith Bay

Hay Bay

Bath

Dorland

Adolphustown

Glenora

Picton Bay

Woodville

Fawcettville

● Picton
0 km

Old Milford Rd.

51 km

60 km

© ULYSSES

interruption in the commonwealth.

Enjoy the sweet aroma of cedar
and the occasional climb as you
cycle along Cty Rd 8, going past
Cty Rd 25 before arriving at
Prince Edward County Rd 13.
Continue following Cty Rd 8 to
the left as it quickly descends past
a small windmill. It then bends
sharply to the right and begins to
climb as it swings back to the left.
Just around the bend, the unique
crest of the Duke of Marysburgh
Pub comes into view. Occasionally providing views of Smiths Bay
and Lake Ontario on your right,
the road passes the North
Marysburgh Community Hall and
Willow Water B&B on the left. As
the sign says, Willow Water offers
all saddle-sore cyclists a place to
rest for a few moments and the
chance to enjoy some fresh, cool
water.

The grapes that grow in this part
of the county have a robust taste.
Back on the road, just ahead on
the left, is St. John's Anglican
Church and the turnoff for
County Cider Estate Winery.
When looking at the map,
Waupoos, meaning "rabbit" in an
Aboriginal language, looks like a
small community. In reality, it is a
very large hamlet. Beginning at
the junction of Cty Rd 8 and 13, it
finally ends at Rock X Rd. Cycling
past the 200-year-old Hicks
Farm, a red building appears on
the left, in the distance. Simple in
design, the Rose House Museum
is home to a collection of historic
artifacts that tell many stories of
struggle and success in the township of Marysburgh. To the left of
the large silo, opposite the museum, is a road that descends to
the oldest cemetery in Prince
Edward County. This was once
the Rose Family cemetery, and it

preserves the legacy of one of the
island's most respected families.

The road now moves away from
the lake, passing the Vahonneh
Area girl-guide camp as it begins
to climb at Wavey Rd, finally
levelling out at Rock X Rd. Be
prepared for a rapid descent and
keep an eye on the road, as the
view of Lake Ontario can be quite
distracting. Following Cty Rd 8 as
it continues to arc left, now at
lake level, the view at Prinyer's
Cove will elicit some oohs and
ahs.

At this point, Cty Rd 8 changes
into Cty Rd 7, and off in the distance two tall smokestacks peek
above the horizon, in contrast to
Cressy United Church, just a
short distance ahead. Wisteria
vines cover the hydro wires and
are quite a sight when they
bloom. Cycling uphill past a red-
roofed art gallery, this is the first
of five fairly good climbs before
reaching Lake on the Mountain.
Just after the third hill, Cty Rd 7
goes past an old schoolhouse on
the right. This was the county's
No. 3 schoolhouse, probably
built around 1875. The next 5km
go through some pretty bleak-
looking farmland before ascending
through a rock cut to the waters
of Lake on the Mountain.

At the top of the hill, to the right,
is a stunning view of Picton Bay,
Adolphustown and the Loyalist
Parkway. Below, the Glenora Car
Ferry shuttles cars across the bay
all day long. To the left is the
tranquil lake that defies the laws
of nature and is the subject of
many myths and legends, Lake of
the Mountain.

Going past the old Lake of the
Mountain Inn, Cty Rd 7 descends
immediately to a [T] intersection

at Hwy 33. A right turn leads to the Glenora Ferry, which sails across Adolphus Reach to the continuation of the Loyalist Parkway. Turn [L] and follow Hwy 33 past the MacFarland Conservation Area back into Picton. The road descends as you pass the harbour and then begins to climb towards the downtown core. Keeping left at the [Y] intersection, be cautious as you follow Hwy 33/Main St into the city's busy downtown area. At Elizabeth St, turn [R] and return to the Mary St parking lot.

Practical Information

Population:
Picton: 4,700

 Tourist Information

Prince Edward County Chamber of Commerce
(see p 193)

The Bay of Quinte Tourist Council
(see p 193)

 Bicycle Shops

Annie's Pedal & Prop
13559 Loyalist Parkway, Picton, ON K0K 2T0
☎(613) 476-4649

Bloomfield Bicycle Co.
225 Main St, Bloomfield, ON K0K 1G0
☎(613) 393-1060

 Special Sights and Events

Jet Rally, Prince Edward Horse and Pony Show, Art on the Fence, Antique Fair, Art in the Country, Canada Day, Ghost

Tours of Picton, Picton Annual Arts and Crafts Sale, Annual Model Train Show, Prince Edward County Pumpkinfest, Prince Edward Highland Games, Country Garlic Festival

 Accommodations

Motel/Resort/Inn/B&B/Camping

28. Lighthouse and Lookouts

No matter where you ride in Prince Edward County, your excursion is bound to be satisfying. Starting in the hamlet of Milford, you quickly leave its many enticing boutiques behind and ride past the Mariners' Memorial Museum. The highlight of this trip, which ends at the Point Traverse Lighthouse, is a stop at Little Bluffs Lookout. Here you will be rewarded with an inspiring view of Prince Edward Bay and the hamlet of Waupoos.

Return Distance:
56km

No. of recommended legs:
1

Level of Difficulty:
🚲 🚲

Surface:
Asphalt, several kilometres of loose gravel

Villages/Towns/Cities:
Picton, Milford, South Bay, Point Traverse, Salmon Point, Cherry Valley, Bloomfield

Central Ontario

Local Highlights:
Macaulay Heritage Park, Mariners' Park Museum, Prince Edward County Courthouse, Rose House Museum & North Marysburgh Museum, Sandbanks Provincial Park, Lake on the Mountain, Exotarium, Regent Theatre, Black River Cheese Company, Hicks General Store, Scott's Mills Conservation Area, bird-watching at Pt. Traverse, Quinte Educational Museum

Recommended Bicycles:
Mountain/Hybrid

Tour Suggestions:
Pack a picnic lunch to enjoy at the Point Traverse lighthouse or on the beach at Sandbanks Provincial Park.

How to get there:
There are several routes to Quinte County, Picton: Hwy 401 from the east and west and Hwys 7, 30, 14 and 62 from the north. From the south, the closest international border crossing is near Alexandria Bay in New York, from which you follow Hwy 401 west.

Located in an out-of-the-way spot, the pretty little village of **Milford** has developed into a thriving community along the shores of a quiet mill pond. The village's original mill, built by the Clapp family, is still standing. Opened in 1810, the mill, now known as Scott's Mill, continues to operate, serving as a tourist attraction and craft store. Today, Milford is a cyclist's haven, making it a good place to start a day of cycling in Prince Edward County.

Itinerary:
Starting from the Milford Town Hall, located a short distance from the town centre on Prince

Edward Rd 10, exit the parking lot by turning [R] and following Cty Rd 10. Cycle past the fire hall, where the road descends and then climbs back up to the predominately level roads of the South Bay area. At the first [T] intersection, turn [R] onto Prince Edward Rd 13. The false Duck Island lighthouse marks the location of the Mariners' Memorial Museum, which has some *Titanic* artifacts and maps of Prince Edward County that date back to the early 1800s.

Immediately after you turn onto Cty Rd 13, hidden to the left behind some trees, will be the South Bay Cemetery, circa 1820; some of its stones bear interesting inscriptions. Cty Rd 13 descends towards the waters of Lake Ontario, curving around the small hills and taking the path of least resistance.

Just before the tour's halfway point, Cty Rd 13 passes the greenhouses of the South Bay Cactus Farm and the corrals of the South Bay Ostrich Ranch. Don't miss Little Bluffs Conservation Area, which is a great place to stop on the return route. Just ride up the long gravel road and continue along one of the jeep trails to an awe-inspiring view.

Prince Edward County is one of the oldest settled areas in the province and has many old barns and homes that have been left in a state of disrepair. Arriving at the Babylon Rd [T] intersection, turn [L] and follow the road as it bends sharply to the right. Just past the cottage rentals for scuba divers, the surface becomes loose gravel for the next 4km. Ride past School House No.16 and the red Union Church. The beautiful blue sparkling waters of **South Bay** and

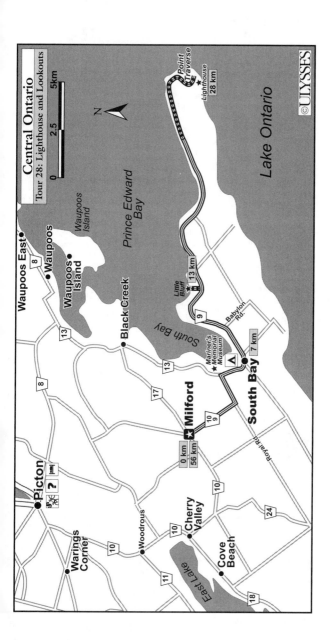

Central Ontario
Tour 28: Lighthouse and Lookouts

0   2.5   5km

N

Waupoos East
Waupoos
Waupoos Island
Black Creek
Prince Edward Bay
Point Traverse
Lighthouse 28 km
Lake Ontario
South Bay
Little Bluff
13 km
Babylon Rd.
Mariner's Memorial Museum
South Bay
7 km
Milford
0 km
56 km
Picton
Warings Corner
Woodrous
Cherry Valley
Cove Beach
East Lake
Royal Rd.

© ULYSSES

the sweet-smelling cedar forest of the Prince Edward National Wildlife Preserve highlight the rest of your trip to the Point Traverse lighthouse. At **Point Traverse** there is a rangers station, the old lighthouse, a boat dock and a number of cottages. Swinging to the right, follow the road around the harbour to the lighthouse and the rocky shores of Lake Ontario. A new battery-operated beacon has replaced the old lighthouse, guiding mariners by beaming out an identifying sequence of flashes.

Retrace your route to return to Milford. Alternatively, continue straight when you reach Babylon Rd (gravel), instead of bearing to the right and following Cty Rd 13. Follow Babylon Rd to a [T] intersection, turn [R] and cycle to a [L] turn onto Cty Rd 13, retracing your original route back into Milford.

Practical Information

Population:
Picton: 4,700
Bloomfield: 690

 Tourist Information

Prince Edward County Chamber of Commerce
(see p 193)

The Bay of Quinte Tourist Council
(see p 193)

 Bicycle Shops

Picton

Annie's Pedal & Prop
(see p 197)

Bloomfield

Bloomfield Bicycle Co.
(see p 197)

 Special Sights and Events

(see p 197)

 Accommodations

Motel/Resort/Inn/B&B/Camping

 Market

Yes, seasonal

 Off-Road Cycling

Yes; see "Off-Road Cycling" at the end of this chapter.

29. Athol Bay, Sandbanks and Sand Dunes

From the relaxing resort town of Picton, follow the undulating roads of western Prince Edward County to the shores of Lake Ontario and Sandbanks Provincial Park. Here you can enjoy the park's white-sand beaches and its many hiking trails. If you're feeling adventurous, a ride on the sand dunes will definitely be an experience to remember! The tour concludes with a visit to the Bloomfield Bicycle Co. and a ride along the Loyalist Parkway.

Return Distance:
50km

No. of recommended legs:
1

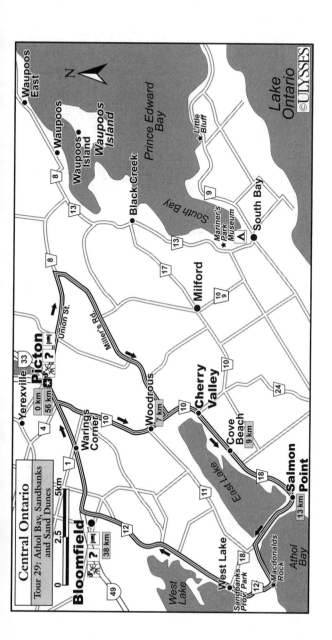

Central Ontario

Tour 29: Athol Bay, Sandbanks and Sand Dunes

Lake Ontario

© ULYSSES

Level of Difficulty:
🚲 🚲

Surface:
Asphalt

Villages/Towns/Cities:
Picton, Milford, South Bay, Point Traverse, Salmon Point, Cherry Valley, Bloomfield

Local Highlights:
Macaulay Heritage Park, Mariners' Park Museum, Prince Edward County Courthouse, Rose House Museum & North Marysburgh Museum, Sandbanks Provincial Park, Lake on the Mountain, Exotarium, Regent Theatre, Black River Cheese Company, Hicks General Store, Scott's Mills Conservation Area, bird-watching at Pt. Traverse, Quinte Educational Museum

Recommended Bicycles:
Touring/Hybrid/Mountain

Tour Suggestions:
Pack a picnic lunch to enjoy on the beach at Sandbanks Provincial Park.

NB: the first 7km of this tour take you along a stretch of road that is fairly busy on summer days. Consider an alternative route by going east on Prince Edward County Rd 8, [R] on Rd 17 and [R] again on Miller's Rd. You will add 15km of wonderful and quiet riding through fairly flat farm roads and rejoin the tour at Cherry Valley.

How to get there:
Take Hwy 401 to Picton from the east and west, or Hwys 7, 30, 14 and 62 from the north. From the south, the closest international border crossing is near Alexandria Bay in New York, from which you follow Hwy 401 west.

Picton is a Loyalist town whose origins date back to the American Revolution, when people of all nationalities settled in the Bay of Quinte region. It is the county's largest city and home to the Bay of Quinte's deep harbour and the oldest fair in the province. Because of its location along the Loyalist Parkway, its streets spread out like the branches of a tree. Some of these roads veer off each other at difficult angles, making turns onto and off them somewhat confusing.

Itinerary:
Start from the Mary St municipal parking lot, located one block east of the Loyalist Parkway/Main St, at the [T] intersection of Elizabeth and Mary Sts. Leave the parking lot by turning [L] onto Mary St and cycle past the large United Church at the end of the street. Built in 1898, this particular site has seen three different churches, including the present one. As you round the bend, Mary becomes Chapel St. Just before the lights at Main St, turn [L] onto Ferguson St. After passing the Glenwood Cemetery and the Letitia Youmans historical plaque, the road becomes Grove St. Turn [L] at Ontario St, then make a [R] turn onto South St. At Spring St, turn [L] and then make a [R] onto Albert St, cycling to a [T] intersection at Lake St, Prince Edward Rd 10.

There is no cycling lane on this busy country road but drivers, for the most part, respect cyclists and generally wait until the road ahead is clear before passing. The road climbs a small hill, enters the community of **Cherry Valley** and then descends past the local convenience store. Continue straight, past the turnoff for Cty Rd 10, and follow Prince Edward

Rd 18 along the south shore of East Lake.

Gradually climbing once it leaves Cherry Valley, Cty Rd 18 passes the Woodland Echos Driving Range, the Woodland Farm silo, a junkyard filled with old farm equipment and a very old church that was built in 1860 and has been converted into an interesting bed and breakfast. Here, Cty Rd 18 widens, becoming a more comfortable road to ride. Every now and then, delightful views of East Lake appear before you descend slowly to lake level and cross a dense wetland area with hundreds of water lilies. Just after passing through Outlet and crossing the East Lake Bridge, Cty Rd 18 arrives at Cty Rd 12, the turnoff for Sandbanks Provincial Park.

Turn [L] and follow Cty Rd 12 into the park. A very busy spot in the summer, this area has textbook examples of a bay mouth sandbar and a coastal sand dune

system. Wild-looking dunes actually tower 25m (six storeys) above you! Continue along Cty Rd 12 and bypass the lineup at the park by swinging right and following the road along the shores of East Lake Sector. On a busy weekend, park rangers line the road, preventing people from sneaking into the park. For a short time, enjoy the cool, stimulating breezes off Lake Ontario. They don't last for very long, however; Cty Rd 12 bends to the right just after passing Macdonald Rock, leaving the water behind. At the Lakeshore Lodge Rd fourway stop, make a [R] turn and pedal through a very dense woodlot. Once clear of the forest, the welcoming beaches of West Lake will appear to your left, as many enticing boutiques line the road on both sides. About 10km past the turnoff for Cty Rd 18 is the community of **Bloomfield**. First called Bull's Mills after the man who owned 12 milling operations in town, it was renamed Bloomfield in 1830 after a veteran of the War of 1812 who was a local skipper and operated ships on the Bay of Quinte. Bloomfield has a main street that seems to go on forever and is bordered by some of the province's oldest maple and oak trees.

Enter Bloomfield on Cty Rd 12, which becomes Stanley St in town. The road climbs to a [R] turn onto Hwy 33. Cycling along the Loyalist Parkway through downtown Bloomfield, be sure to stop at the best attraction in town, the Bloomfield Bicycle Company; the staff at this unique shop always have a friendly smile and warm handshake for fellow cyclists. They will also direct you to some of the county's best off-road cycling.

From here, the road climbs again. Follow Hwy 33 past a working windmill to the historic West Lake Boarding School, which was the first seminary in Canada for the Society of Friends and is a fine example of Loyalist neoclassical architecture. The cycling lane along the Loyalist parkway is wide enough for two cyclists to ride side by side, but it ends at Picton. At the Walton St traffic lights, turn [R] and follow Chapel and Mary St to the Mary St parking lot.

Off-Road Cycling

Public Trails

Bancroft

Hastings City Heritage Trail
(156km)
Surface:
Original rail bed
Beginning:
Glen Ross to Lake St. Peterborough

Hastings County Administration Office
PO Box 4400, 235 Pinnacle St, 1st floor, Belleville, ON K8N 3A9
☎*(613) 966-1319*
www.hastingscounty.com

Minden

Haliburton Rail Trail
(25km)
Surface:
Original rail bed, loose surface
Beginning:
Kinmount to the town of Haliburton

Haliburton Highlands Trails and Tours Network
PO Box 147, Minden, ON K0M 2K0
☎*(705) 286-1760*
www.trailsandtours.on.ca

Lindsay

Victoria Rail Trail – North Corridor
(55km)
Victoria Rail Trail – South Corridor
(30km)
Surface:
Original rail bed
Beginning:
North Corridor: Lindsay to Kinmount; South Corridor: Lindsay to Bethany

City of Kawartha Lakes Tourism Office
26 Francis St, PO Box 9000, Lindsay, ON K9V 5R8
☎*(705) 324-9411, ext 233*
www.city.kawarthalakes.on.ca

Peterborough

Jackson Creek Kiwanis Trail
(4km)
Surface:
Loose surface
Beginning:
Jackson Park and Ackison Rd

Otonabee Conservation Authority
250 Milroy Dr, Peterborough, ON K9H 7M9
☎*(705) 745-5791*
www.otonabee.com

Rotary Greenway Trail
(20km)
Surface:
Loose surface/Asphalt
Beginning:
Beavermead Park

Director of Planning, County of Peterborough
470 Water St, Peterborough, ON K9H 3M3
☎ *(705) 743-0380*
www.county.peterborough.on.ca

Lakefield Trail
(5.5km)
Surface:
Loose surface/asphalt
Beginning:
Water St at the end of the Rotary Greenway Trail

Smith-Ennismore-Lakefield Township
PO Box 270, 1310 Centre Line, Bridgenorth, ON K0L 1H0
☎ *(705) 292-7034*
www.smithennismorelakefield.on.ca

Resort and Conservation Trails

Haliburton Forest
(300km of trails)

RR 1, Haliburton, ON K0M 1S0
☎ *(705) 754-2198*
www.haliburtonforest.com

Bancroft Area

Silent Lake Provincial Park
(20km of trails)

Ontario Parks
PO Box 219, Bancroft, ON K0L 1C0
☎ *(613) 339-2807 or 888-668-7275*
www.ontarioparks.com/english/ sile.html

Haliburton/ Minden Area

Sir Sam's Inn-Eagle Lake
(26km of trails)

Sir Sam's Inn
Eagle Lake PO, Eagle Lake, ON K0M 1M0
☎ *(705) 754-2188 or 800-361-2188*
www.sirsamsinn.com

Peterborough/ Woodview Area

Petroglyphs Park
(13km of trails)

Ontario Parks
General Delivery, Woodview, ON K0L 1C0
☎ *(705) 877-2552 or 888-668-7275*
www.ontarioparks.com/english/ petr.html
www.mnr.gov.on.ca/mnr/parks/ petro.html

Warsaw Caves Conservation Area
(13km of trails)

Otonabee Conservation Authority
(see p 204)

Picton Area

Sandbanks Provincial Park
RR 1, Picton, ON K0K 2T0
☎ *(613) 393-3319*
www.ontarioparks.com/sand.html

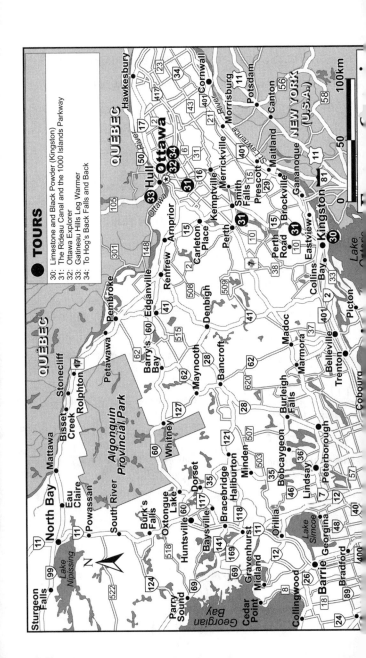

● TOURS

30: Limestone and Black Powder (Kingston)
31: The Rideau Canal and the 1000 Islands Parkway
32: Ottawa Explorer
33: Gatineau Hills Leg Warmer
34: To Hog's Back Falls and Back

Eastern Ontario

is rich in natural wonders. In the south, enjoy the charms of the St. Lawrence River, the cool, clean waters of Lake Ontario and the area's unique attraction, the 1000 Islands.

To the north, along the meandering Rideau River, take in the rolling hills and the spectacular scenery of the Ottawa Valley, home to Canada's capital, Ottawa. Savour the pageantry, history and impressive natural beauty along the Ottawa River and the Ontario-Québec border.

30. Limestone and Black Powder: Discovering Kingston

Cycling around the streets of Kingston is one of the more enjoyable experiences you can have in this province. It is a great way to become acquainted with its past, its culture and the excitement of its daily hustle and bustle.

Return Distance:
40km

No. of recommended legs:
1

Level of Difficulty:

Surface:
Asphalt

Villages/ Towns/Cities:
Kingston

Local Highlights:
Agnes Etherington Art Centre, Bellevue House, Military Communications and Electronics Museum, City Hall, Correctional Services of Canada Museum, Fairfield House and Park, Fort Frederick and the Royal Military College Museum, Fort Henry, Kingston Archaeological Centre, Kingston Mills Lock Station, Marine Museum of the Great Lakes, Miller Museum of Geology and Mineralogy, Princess of Wales Own Regiment Museum, Pump House Steam Museum, St. George's Cathedral, Union Gallery, St Lawrence Cruises, Confederation Tour Trolley, International Ice Hockey Museum, Frontenac County Schools Museum, Murney Tower Museum, Queens University, Brock Street Shopping District, St. Lawrence River, Kingston Mills, Little Cataraqui Creek Conservation Area

Recommended Bicycles:
Touring/Hybrid/Mountain

Tour Suggestions:
This is a trip that will take a complete day so plan for a picnic lunch along the waterfront.

How to get there:
Kingston is halfway between Montréal and Toronto, in southeastern Ontario on the north shore of Lake Ontario. From Hwy 401, take exit 617, one of four exits to the downtown core.

A good starting place is the Via Rail station located south of Hwy 401, west of Division St on Counter St.

In the late 1600s, present-day Kingston was known to the local Aboriginal population as "Cataraqui," which means "rocks standing in water." In 1671, the French built Fort Frontenac, which later played a pivotal role in the Seven Years War for control of French interests in North America. Called King's Town by the first homesteaders, it did not take long for the name to be shortened to its present form. A number of influential people hailed from this city: Canada's first Prime Minister, Sir John A. Macdonald; Molly Brant, who played an important role in communications between the Iroquois and the British in the 1800s; and Ontario's third premier and lieutenant-governor, Sir Oliver Mowat. Kingston was also home to the first school and the first daily newspaper in Upper Canada.

Itinerary:
The best way to become familiar with a heritage city like Kingston is to visit as many of its historic sights and attractions as you can. Leaving the Via Rail station parking lot, turn left onto Counter St and cycle towards Cty Rd 2. Just before the James Reid Funeral Home, turn [R] onto Purdy Cr. Follow the road up a slight grade, turning [R] on Purdy Mill Rd and then [L] into the Cataraqui Creek Cemetery. This is a very old cemetery with some famous names; it could take a few hours to explore. Follow the signs to the burial place of Sir John Alexander Macdonald, the first Prime Minister of Canada.

Retrace your steps by making a [R] turn onto Counter St and then [L] onto Cty Rd 2. Move into the right lane before crossing the CNR railway tracks and descending into the city's small retail area. Cty Rd 2 becomes Princess St. After crossing Portsmouth, past the third set of lights, move into the left lane.

Turn [L] onto Concession St, a multi-lane one-way street. The Kingston water tower is directly in front of you, to the east. After the immense Kingston Memorial Sports Centre, make a [R] turn at the lights onto Alfred St. Cycle to the corner of York St; to the right is the International Ice Hockey Federation Museum, which highlights the contributions of Canadian hockey players to the NHL through displays of personal memorabilia.

Turning around towards Concession St, turn [R] onto Pine St. Cross at the Division St lights to enter a colourful area of old Kingston, where the houses are so close together you could reach out of your bedroom window and shake your neighbour's hand. At the [T] intersection at Patrick St, turn [L] and then [R] onto James St. Cross Montreal St and turn [R] on Baggot St. A short distance ahead, on the left, is Robert Meek School, which houses the Frontenac County School Museum, a living archive of restored educational items from the early 1900s.

Continue past the museum and school and turn [R] onto Ordnance St, then ride past Montreal St and go around the block to take in the spectacular architecture and masonry of the 1861 Providence Manor. Rejoin Montreal St and cross Ordnance St;

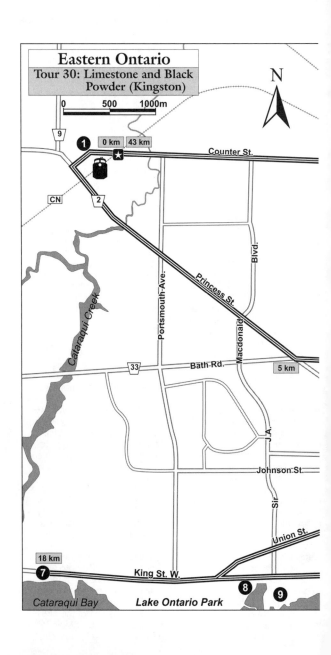

Eastern Ontario
Tour 30: Limestone and Black Powder (Kingston)

N

0 500 1000m

9

1 0 km 43 km

Counter St.

CN

2

Cataraqui Creek

Portsmouth Ave.

Princess St.

Macdonald Blvd.

33 Bath Rd.

5 km

J. A.

Johnson St.

Sir

Union St.

18 km

7 King St. W.

Cataraqui Bay

Lake Ontario Park

8 9

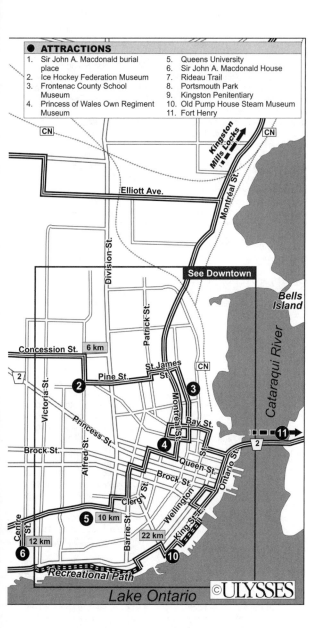

● ATTRACTIONS

1. Sir John A. Macdonald burial place
2. Ice Hockey Federation Museum
3. Frontenac County School Museum
4. Princess of Wales Own Regiment Museum
5. Queens University
6. Sir John A. Macdonald House
7. Rideau Trail
8. Portsmouth Park
9. Kingston Penitentiary
10. Old Pump House Steam Museum
11. Fort Henry

CN

Kingston Mills Locks

CN

Elliott Ave.

Montréal St.

See Downtown

Bells Island

Division St.

Cataraqui River

Patrick St.

Concession St.   6 km

Pine St.

St.James St.

CN

2

Victoria St.

Princess St.

Alfred St.

Montréal St.

Bay St.

4

Queen St.

Ontario St.

2

11

Brock St.

Brock St.

Clergy St.

Wellington

5   10 km

Barrie St.

22 km

Centre St.

12 km

6

King St.

10

Recreational Path

©ULYSSES

Lake Ontario

Artillery Park is on your left. A few feet ahead on the right is the Princess of Wales Own Regiment, a stoic-looking castle-type mansion (museum) that highlights the achievements of the PWOR and its predecessors. The museum also has displays on Canadian citizens who served their country in war and in peace.

After St. Paul's Anglican Church, turn [R] onto Queen St and then [L] onto Clergy St. You will pass some impressive buildings, St. Andrew's Presbyterian Church, Queen Street United Church and, turning [R] onto Brock St, St. Mary's Cathedral. Make a [L] turn onto Barrie St.

Cycle by another very old church, Chalmer's United, and make a [R] turn onto Clergy St W. At Division St, turn [L] and cycle into the heart of Queen's University. The large rock and mineral displays of the Miller Museum of Geology are located at this [T] intersection, in Miller Hall. Make a [R] turn onto Union St and try to imagine that along a good part of this street, in the Queens University Archives, are over 5.5km of manuscripts, photographs, architectural drawings, as well as sound and video tapes, all relating to the university and the city of Kingston.

Continue along Union St, passing the arena, library and registrar's office, one of the older buildings on campus. At Centre St, turn [L] and cycle to the home of Canada's first Prime Minister, Bellevue House National Historic Site.

Return to Union St and follow it west. On the left is the back entrance to St Mary's of the Lake Hospital and on the right is the Donald Gordon Centre, a regional correctional staff college. When Union St meets Front Rd/King St W, keep to your right, following Front Rd uphill past the Church of the Good Thief.

The road descends quickly once you cross Portsmouth St. Go past St Lawrence College and the local golf course. At the bottom of the hill is the Little Cataraqui Marsh. Turn [R] into the Rideau hiking trail parking lot. The Rideau Trail begins in this marshy area on the shores of Lake Ontario and follows the route taken by many pioneers from Kingston to Ottawa in the late 1800s. The 300km trail passes through Westport, Perth, Smith Falls and Bells Corners, ending at Richmond Landing in Ottawa. The trail parking lot makes a very nice spot for a break and the trail into this quiet woodland setting is even rideable for a short distance.

Exiting the Rideau Trail parking lot, turn [L] onto Front Rd/King St W and travel east towards downtown Kingston. At the top of the hill is the Lake Ontario Park and Campground and a Government of Ontario psychiatric hospital. Following the rolling shoreline of Lake Ontario, King St W passes through the historic village of Portsmouth, and climbs past the ominous walls of Canada's oldest reformatory prison, the Kingston Penitentiary. Spend some time exploring Portsmouth, which was settled in 1835; its back streets make for an interesting diversion.

Some striking architecture appears just after the penitentiary. On the right are the Correctional Services Regional Headquarters and on the left is an excellent view of St. Mary's of the Lake Hospital. Just after descending

Kingston
Downtown

Tugwood Park
Railway St.
Duff St.
Fraser St.
Joseph St.
Russell St.
Thomas St.
Stephen St.
Katings-Megaffin Park
Cataraqui St.
Concession St.
Adelaide St.
Rideau Park
James St.
Charles St.
Pine St.
Quebec St.
Riverview Park
Elm St.
Raglan Road
Mc Burney Park
Colborne St.
Queen St.
Artillery Park
Princess St.
Brock St.
Johnson St.
Clergy St. E.
Wellington
King East
Clergy St. W.
William St.
Earl St.
Gore St.
Lower Union
Union St.
Stuart St.
City Park
King St. West
Breakwater
Macdonald Park
Ontario and West St. Park

Belle Park Fairways

N

Lasalle Causeway

Kingston Harbour

Kingston Memorial

York St.

Victoria Park

Queen's University

Lake Ontario

©ULYSSES

● ATTRACTIONS

1. Royal Military College and the National Defense College
2. Fort Henry
3. Kingston City Hall
4. Confederation Park
5. Prince George Hotel
6. St. George's Cathedral
7. St. Mary's Roman Catholic Cathedral
8. Marine Museum of the Great Lakes
9. Pump House Steam Museum
10. Murney Tower Museum
11. Frontenac County Court House
12. Queen's University
13. Miller Museum of Geology and Mineralogy
14. Villa Bellevue
15. Kingston Archaeological Centre
16. Correctional Service of Canada Museum
17. International Hockey Hall of Fame and Museum
18. Kingston Haunted Walk

past the water-purification plant, join the Kingston waterfront trail on the [R] for a pleasant ride along the shores of Lake Ontario. It's impossible to miss the two rectangular metal blocks forming an arch, where 3,000 men crossed from Garden Island into battle, capturing Fort Frontenac from the French on August 27, 1758.

You will have quite a view of the lake as the asphalt path swings towards the water. The huge round tower just past the hospital is the 1846 Moore Murney Tower Museum. Used for defense, it is considered one of the finest Martello towers in North America. Today, this museum houses three floors of military and local artifacts. Continue along the lakeshore path, going past the bandstand and exiting onto Emily St, bearing to the left to rejoin King St E.

Turning [R] onto King St E, make a [R] turn onto West St and follow it as it turns into Ontario St. At the bottom of the hill is the Old Pump House Museum. Home to monster engines and model trains, it also offers an easy access point to Kingston's waterfront. Interesting-looking old steamers can be seen along the path, behind the pump house to the Marine Museum of the Great Lakes. It was here, at Mississauga Point, that Loyalists travelling from Montréal landed in 1784, establishing a camp that eventually grew into the city of Kingston.

Take the time to explore along the channel and inside the marine museum, which contains the original engines and pumps that successfully served Kingston and the Great Lakes shipping industry for almost 68 years. Visit the

Alexander Henry, an old ice breaker that has been converted into a bed and breakfast. Rejoin Ontario St and cycle towards the downtown core. Just past the Canadian Pacific steam engine *Spirit of Sir John A* are the tourist information booth and Confederation Park.

Pass Kingston City Hall and turn [L] onto Brock St to do a circle tour of this area. The Kingston Custom House, the Kingston public market and St. George's Cathedral are only a few of the highlights. After exploring the downtown core, locate Johnston St and follow it back to Ontario St. Travel along Ontario St towards the Lasalle Causeway. The gang plank for the 50-car Wolfe Island Ferry is at Barrack St, to your right.

After bending sharply to the right, Ontario St crosses the Cataraqui River via the La Salle Causeway. When crossing this grated bridge, do not look down. Rather, look to the front, as bicycles tend to bounce around on this type of grated surface. Proceed to the lights and turn [R] onto Duty St. To the right is the entrance to the Royal Military College and to the left is a long climb to Fort Henry and a remarkable view of Kingston's skyline.

At one time, Fort Henry held a major strategic position in Upper Canada. It was rapidly built during the War of 1812 and, as a result, had to be torn down and rebuilt in the mid-1830s. Since then, this 126-room fort has become home to an enormous amount of British and Canadian military history. A great deal of dedication has gone into preserving the furnishings, the appearance and the operation of the fort so that it closely conforms to the time when it was occupied by British soldiers. After briefly stepping back in time, pick up your speed on the downhill descent to the Fort Henry stockade.

At Hwy 2, a [R] turn will take you past the Barriefield Rock Garden Project and Hwy 15. The road levels out just before reaching the Kingston Canadian Forces Base. One kilometre further along Hwy 2 is the Communications Museum and Kingston's Vimy Barracks. At this point, unless you plan to ride the waterfront trail to the MacLachlan Woodworking Museum or Gananoque, retrace your steps to the La Salle Causeway.

Once across the La Salle Causeway and back in the city, keep to your right. Follow the road to the north as it turns into Place d'Armes. Make a [R] turn onto Wellington St and round it to Rideau St. Turn [R] onto Rideau St, cycle past Rideau Park and turn [R] again onto Montreal St. An interesting side trip at this point would be to turn [R] at Belle Park Dr and follow the road through Cataraqui Park and cross over to Belle Island.

Return to Montreal St, continue north and turn [L] onto an undulating Elliott Ave. After crossing Division St, Elliott Ave becomes Leroy Grant Dr as it descends to Counter St. Turn [L] onto Counter St, and go past the Kingston PUC building. After crossing Sir John A Macdonald Blvd, the road descends past Bill Hatchet Park and crosses the CNR tracks to the Via Rail station parking lot.

Optional Kingston Mills Tour (36km):

Before returning to the Via Rail station, why not visit a very picturesque spot just north of the city? The Kingston Mills Lock Station is the first lock on the Rideau as it winds its way north to Ottawa. It is a spectacular place, with the wild-looking rock formations of the Canadian Shield forming a system of four natural adjoining locks. Also on site is the Lockmaster Anglin's House, now a tourist information booth, and the restored 1830 military blockhouse. Continue along Montreal St, now called Battersea Rd/Hwy 11, and cross Hwy 401. Make a [R] turn onto Kingston Mills Rd/ Frontenac 21 and ride along this scenic road to the locks. To return to the Via Rail station, retrace your steps to Battersea Rd and turn [L] and then [R] onto the next road, McAdoos Ln. Cycle through a light industrial area and make a [L] onto the Old Perth Rd/ Division St. Cross Hwy 401, turn [R] at the lights and follow Counter St to the Via Rail Station.

Eastern Ontario

Practical Information

Population:
Kingston: 143,000

 Tourist Information

Kingston Tourist Information Office
209 Ontario St, Kingston, ON K7L 2Z1
☎ *(613) 548-4415 or 888-855-4555*
www.kingstoncanada.com

Bicycle Shops

Frontenac Cycle and Sport
397 Princess St, Kingston, ON K7L 1B4
☎ *(613) 542-4455*

J & J Cycle Shop
675 Bath Rd, Kingston, ON K7M 4X2
☎ *(613) 389-6777*

Cyclepath
339 Princess St, Kingston, ON K7L 1B7
☎ *(613) 542-3616*

Source for Sports
121 Princess St, Kingston, ON K7L 1A8
☎ *(613) 542-2892*

Special Sights and Events

Fort Henry, 1000 Islands cruises, Confederation Tour Trolley, Correctional Services Museum of Canada, Marine Museum of the Great Lakes, Bellevue House; It's Grand Summer - Grand Theatre, Kingston-Buskers Rendezvous, Limestone City Blues Festival, Fanfayre Arts & Craft Show, Women's Art Festival, Chilifest, Kingston Rhythum & Ribs Festival, Taste of Kingston, Sheep Dog Trial, Kingston Haunted walk, Maple Madness, Kingston Jazz Festival, Fall Fair

Accommodations

Hotel/Motel/B&B/Camping

Off-Road Cycling

Yes; see "Off-Road Cycling" at the end of this chapter.

Market Days

Tuesdays, Thursday and Saturdays, year-round behind City Hall.

31. The Rideau Canal and the 1000 Islands Parkway: Kingston, Ottawa and Brockville

Experience one of Ontario's most beautiful and interesting bicycling excursions, where the serenity of the Rideau Canal's many blue lakes and the ingenuity of its lock system can be viewed. You will quickly become mesmerized by the Ottawa River and the mirrored images along the St Lawrence Seaway. Following Old Perth Rd, experience the route taken by wagons of yesteryear as they passed through the villages of Westport and Perth. Join a recreational trail along the Ottawa River and cycle into the heart of the nation's capital. On the return trip, visit the jewel of the Rideau, Merrickville, indulge in fresh chocolate at Smiths Falls and try to find Canada's oldest railway tunnel in Brockville. Finally, after arriving at the Thousand Islands National Park, cycle along the St. Lawrence River into the town of Gananoque and follow the waterfront trail back into Kingston.

Return Distance:
444km (86km, 98km, 82km, 68km, 65km, 45km)

No. of recommended legs:
6

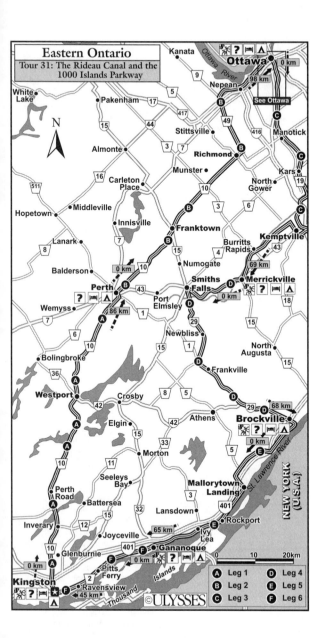

Eastern Ontario
Tour 31: The Rideau Canal and the 1000 Islands Parkway

White Lake

Kanata

Ottawa

Ottawa River

0 km

98 km

Nepean

See Ottawa

Pakenham

Stittsville

Manotick

Richmond

Almonte

Munster

North Gower

Kars

Carleton Place

Middleville

Franktown

Burritts Rapids

Kemptville

Hopetown

Innisville

Numogate

Merrickville

Lanark

Balderson

0 km

10

Perth

Smiths Falls

Port Elmsley

69 km

0 km

Wemyss

86 km

Newbliss

Bolingbroke

Frankville

North Augusta

Westport

Crosby

Athens

Brockville

Elgin

0 km

Morton

Perth Road

Seeleys Bay

Mallorytown Landing

St. Lawrence River

Battersea

Lansdown

Inverary

Joyceville

Rockport

NEW YORK (U.S.A.)

Glenburnie

401

65 km

Gananoque

Ivy Lea

0 km

Pitts Ferry

Thousand Islands

0   10   20km

Ravensview

45 km

Kingston

Thousand

Leg 1 A   Leg 4 D
Leg 2 B   Leg 5 E
Leg 3 C   Leg 6 F

©ULYSSES

Level of Difficulty:
🚲 🚲 🚲

Surface:
Asphalt

Villages/Towns/Cities:
Kingston, Westport, Perth, Franktown, Richmond, Ottawa, Kemptville, Merrickville, Smiths Falls, Brockville, Mallorytown Landing, Gananoque

Local Highlights:
See the related tour information at the end of this tour.

Recommended Bicycles:
Touring/Hybrid/Mountain

Tour Suggestions:
A number of this tour's legs require a solid cycling effort, with five or more hours' riding for each leg. Allow yourself an extra day or two in Ottawa so that you can explore the nation's capital. Please refer to the Ottawa itineraries (Tours 32 and 34) in this chapter.

How to get there:
Kingston is halfway between Montréal and Toronto, in southeastern Ontario, on the north shore of Lake Ontario. Take Hwy 401 to Exit 617, one of four exits to reach the downtown core. A good starting place is the Via Rail station located south of Hwy 401, west of Division St on Counter St.

Sparkling like a diamond necklace, the blue waters of the Rideau Canal invite you to experience the thrill of cycling along their 202km of shoreline and canals. Built over six years by thousands of Irish Immigrants and French Canadians as a supply route from

Ottawa to Kingston, it became a secure way to transport goods during the War of 1812. The canal was a major transportation route until the arrival of the railway. Today, it still sees a great deal of traffic but more for leisure than business.

Itinerary:
Leg 1
(Kingston to Perth, 86km)

Beginning your journey in the historic city of **Kingston**, located at the mouth of the Rideau Canal, leave the Via Rail parking lot by turning [L] onto Counter St. Cycle past the burial place of Sir John A. Macdonald, make a [R] turn onto Hwy 2 and follow it to Sydenham Rd. Turning [R] onto Sydenham Rd/ Frontenac Rd 9, you will cycle past a number of cemeteries.

Cross Hwy 401, then turn [R] onto Bur Brook Rd at the flashing light. Follow this strip to the [T] intersection at Frontenac 10. Turn [L] onto Perth Rd and prepare for a long, gradual climb. Follow the road through the villages of Glenburnie, Bucks Corners and, a short distance past Inverary, enjoy the marvellous view of Loughborough Lake as Frontenac 10 crosses its placid waters.

Cautiously proceed through the flashing light at Frontenac 5, then pass Perth Rd Public School and the fiery red granite rock that towers high above the road. Ride through the village of Perth Rd (not the same as Perth, which is a little further). Frontenac 10 continues to undulate, climbing steeply at times but always twisting and turning its way around the lakes of the Rideau Canal. Keep an eye out for an old goat shed high on a hill to your left, just before Bedford Mills. Once in Leeds and Grenville County after crossing Newboro Lake, the road begins to descend to a [T] intersection at Upper Rideau Lake, one of 33 lakes within 24km.

Turn [L] onto Hwy 42 and enter the town of Westport, originally known as Manhard's Mills. At the large red public school, turn [R] onto Cty Rd 10. As the road descends through town it crosses a small fish sanctuary before going straight up Foley's Mountain. Once at the top of the hill, take a break (you will need it) and enjoy a beautiful view. The entrance to the Foley Mountain Conservation Area is on the right. The kilometres continue to build as the road passes Pike Lake into the county of Lanark, finally arriving in the peaceful town of **Perth**. At the junction of Frontenac 10 and 1, turn [L] at the lights and follow Gore St E into downtown Perth.

Settled in 1815 by 700 Scottish immigrants, this exciting old town on the River Tay was named after Perthshire, Scotland. The town is famous for having made a 22,000-pound cheese for the 1892 Chicago World's Fair. Don't miss the Matheson House and the site of the last fatal duel in Canada, which was fought between two law students in present-day Duel Park. Here, you may get a chance to hear Canada's oldest town band practising nearby, filling the air with music.

Leg 2
(Perth to Ottawa, 98km)

Beginning in the town of Perth, at the corner of North St/Lanark Rd 10 and Gore St E, make a [R]

turn off Gore St onto North St. Lanark 10 passes the historic St. Andrew's Presbyterian Church and crosses a set of railway tracks; the ride for the next several kilometres will be quite dull. After passing through the small hamlets of Richardson and Gillies Corners, turn [L] onto Hwy 15. Travel north through the village of Franktown and make a [R] turn onto Richmond Rd. After riding past a Christmas-tree farm and through the town of Prospect, cross Dwyer Hill Rd/Carlton Rd 3. Watch for golf balls coming across the road from the River Bend Golf Course on the Jock River. After the turnoff for Munster, the road expands as it enters **Richmond**, an early 1800s military settlement.

At Lanark Rd 49, turn [L] onto Eagleson Rd and cycle towards Kanata. Row upon row of townhouses fill the skyline, finally giving way to myriad retail stores. Eagleson Rd, now four lanes, passes the Robertson Rail Trail and the Old Quarry Trails parking lot before crossing Hazeldean Dr. A bicycle lane appears on the road just before it crosses Hwy 417. Be careful after passing through the traffic lights at Campeau Dr, as cars join Eagleson Rd on your right.

Turn [R] onto the next road, Corkstown Rd, and join the paved bicycle path on your left. The path begins as a pretty ride through a meadow, crossing a creek several times. At the first [T] intersection, keep right as you pass under a set of railway tracks, and at the second [T] bear right again. After crossing Water Creek, the path changes to hard-packed calcium and then into hard-packed sand, similar to a jeep road. Continue to follow the

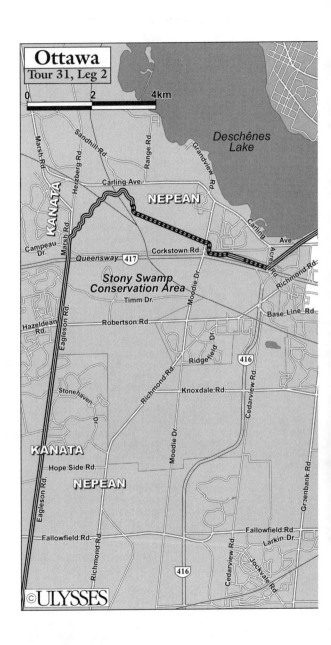

Ottawa
Tour 31, Leg 2

0   2   4km

Deschênes
Lake

KANATA

Marsh Rd.

Sandhill Rd.

Herzberg Rd.

Range Rd.

Grandview Rd.

Carling Ave.

NEPEAN

Carling

Campeau
Dr.

Marsh Rd.

Queensway 417

Corkstown Rd.

Ave.

Acres Rd.

Richmond Rd.

Stony Swamp
Conservation Area

Moodie Dr.

Timm Dr.

Base Line Rd.

Hazeldean
Rd.

Eagleson Rd.

Robertson Rd.

Ridgefield Dr.

416

Stonehaven
Dr.

Richmond Rd.

Moodie Dr.

Knoxdale Rd.

Cedarview Rd.

KANATA

Hope Side Rd.

Eagleson Rd.

NEPEAN

Greenbank Rd.

Fallowfield Rd.

Richmond Rd.

416

Cedarview Rd.

Fallowfield Rd.

Larkin Dr.

Jockvale Rd.

©ULYSSES

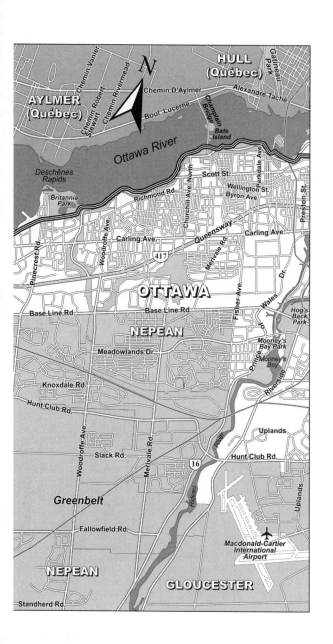

trail as it goes through a set of gates, bearing left as it follows Moodie Dr. The large glass dome on the left belongs to Nortel. Watch for cars as the bicycle path crosses a number of driveways.

When the trail exits onto Carling Ave, cross the street and join the recreational path on the north side. It is not far to Dick Bell Park and Marina, which has a great view of the Ottawa River. Too bad that cycling along the shoreline in this park is out of the question, as "no cycling" signs are posted here. Washrooms and a place to rest are available a short distance past the marina at Andrew Haydon Park. There is another good rest spot further along, just past the large silverdome arena. Make a [L] turn, following the path that leads to Lakeside Gardens and the Ottawa River.

When the main trail reaches Britannia St, it splits into an upper and lower path. Keep to the lower trail as it offers access points to Mud Lake. Coming back along the river, the trail turns sharply to the [R] and then [L] (no bicycles straight ahead) as it goes under the Ottawa River Parkway. Moving away from the river at Woodroffe Rd, take a moment and cross the parkway to the Kitchissippi Lookout.

The trail eventually goes back under the parkway at Bate Island and runs parallel to the Ottawa River for the next several kilometres. The path follows the shoreline of the oldest Trans-Canada thruway, and passes large cement bunker cairns that stand stoically on guard all along the river. These cairns, or *inukshuks*, were traditionally built by the Inuit as landmarks. In the Arctic, they are placed in long rows to drive caribou towards waiting hunters. These particular cairns are primarily the work of one man who cemented these figures together; they make for some interesting conversation.

As you ride past the Lemeus Island Water Purification Plant and under a CN railway bridge, the Ottawa skyline appears on the horizon. The trail exits onto Fleet St just behind the municipal campground, Le Breton. Turn [R] and cross a walkway in front of an old waterworks building, bearing to the left once across. Continue following the trail, and keep right while going past the Trans Canada Trail Pavilion. Ride under the Wellington St Bridge and through a segmented tunnel, turn [L] and then [R], following the trail along the river. This is a confusing section. If you reach the Old Mill Restaurant, just retrace your steps to the pavilion and remember to go under the bridge.

The view from this vantage point along the Ottawa River will take your breath away. The sight of the Parliament Buildings, which seem to merge with the granite cliffs of the Ottawa River, is simply stunning. This leg ends at the Ottawa River Locks, which have eight levels and are located between the Chateau Laurier and Parliament Hill. Continue following the canal as it climbs upwards, going under Rideau St and exiting in downtown **Ottawa** at the National Arts Centre. Days could be spent exploring this city and its surrounding countryside. Take full advantage of everything Ottawa has to offer: exciting nightlife, numerous museums and great cycling everywhere you look! See Tour 32: Ottawa Explorer.

Leg 3
(Ottawa to Merrickville, 69km)

Starting from the Hog's Back Falls parking lot (refer to map of Tour 34), turn [L] onto Hog's Back Rd and [R] onto Riverside Dr. There is no cycling path provided on this multi-lane road, so avoid rush-hour traffic. Go past Uplands Rd and then Hunt Club Rd; on the left is CFB Ottawa. Here, the road narrows to two lanes, just opposite the airport. Going through Cedardale along Ottawa Carlton 19, watch for cattle crossing the road just before Gloucester Glen. At times the canal comes very close to the road, which makes you wonder if it ever floods.

At the [T] intersection of Leeds and Grenville 43, turn [R] towards **Kemptville**. At the traffic lights, make another [R] onto Leeds-Grenville 44. Follow the road and turn [L] before the canal onto River Rd, Leeds-Grenville 23. At the [T] intersection, turn [R] and continue following River Rd, going past Burritts Rapids Rd. If you can spare the time, there are plenty of side trips and interesting places to see and visit along this route. Some highlights are the hamlets of Burritts Rapids, Nicholsons and Clowes Locks, the Oddessy Cow Palace and an old cemetery just before the [T] intersection at Leeds-Grenville 43. Turn [R] onto Leeds-Grenville 43 and cycle into the amazing little village of **Merrickville**, which should definitely be explored and enjoyed.

This lovely village has seen its share of firsts: the first house in Ottawa was built with wood from the town's original mill, the first nursery and seed farm in Ontario was just a few minutes east of the village, and in 1908, Canada's first Boy Scout troop was founded here.

Leg 4
(Merrickville to Brockville, 68km)

Continue following Leeds-Grenville 43 by turning [R] onto Mill St and ride over the the swing bridge across the Rideau River. At the flashing lights, make a [L] turn onto Leeds-Grenville 43, W Broadway St. For the first time during this trip, the canal is now on your left. Once you arrive in Lanark County, a cycling lane appears and makes for a comfortable ride into **Smiths Falls**. Turn [R] onto Hershey Dr and take the time to tour the world-famous chocolate maker. From Hershey Chocolates, turn [L] onto Lorne St and then [R] onto Queen St. At the lights, turn [L] onto Chambers St and make another [L] at the [T] intersection onto Beckwith St. Passing the Rideau Canal Museum and Old Stys Lock, follow Hwy 29/Brockville St by way of a very wide cycling lane, available all the way into Brockville. Located in the village of Frankville is the historic house of suffragette Louise C. McKinny, the first woman in the British Empire to gain a parliamentary seat. When a tall church steeple comes into view, the community of Addison is just ahead and a few kilometres further down the road is the Johnson Wildlife Centre. At Tincap, proceed through the lights and cross Hwy 401 into the captivating city of **Brockville**. First known as Buell's Bay, it went

Eastern Ontario

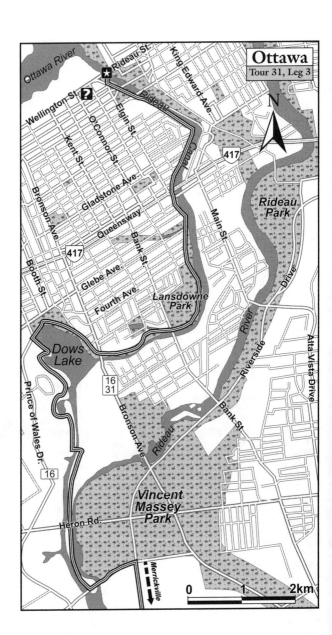

through several other name changes, including Snarlington, before being named after war hero General Sir Isaac Brock. One of the oldest cities in the province, it is the only one in Ontario to have a New England–type town square. It is also home to the oldest railway tunnel in Canada, which runs under the city to the waterfront, and a well-preserved Victorian downtown.

Leg 5
(Brockville to Gananoque, 65km)

From Hwy 401 continue along Cty Rd 29/William St towards downtown Brockville. Turn [R] onto King St/Hwy 2. Travelling west along King St past Rotary Park and Fulford Park, the King's Hwy adopts its new name, Leeds-Grenville 2. At the city limits, just past Lawrence Park, the road picks up an additional two lanes for a short distance. After crossing Jones Creek, look for the lighthouse on the rocks. Much of the exposed escarpment in this area has been enhanced by local landowners with moss and colourful flowers. Continue past the first Leeds-Grenville Rd 5 on the right. Look for a red house and turn [L] onto the second Leeds-Grenville Rd 5. Follow the old Mallorytown Rd over Hwy 401 to the [T] intersection at Old River Rd and the "River of a Thousand Dreams."

Turn [R] onto the 1000 Islands Parkway and cycle into the heart of the St. Lawrence National Park. On the right is the bike path. While the bike path is a nice alternative, the view from the road is even better. The parkway does its best to follow the St. Lawrence River but from time to time it moves away, following the natural lay of the land. The islands are home to many eye-catching cottages; don't forget to keep your eyes on the road! Just past the "Turtle Crossing" sign, the road passes through the peaceful hamlet of Rockport before climbing past Horse Thiefs Bay Rd. At the Hill Island Bridge, the bike path joins the parkway but resumes on the other side.

There is another splendid view on the left, just over the Landon Bay parallel bridges. At Jackstraw Ln, the bicycle path joins the parkway. Follow the road to the right as it rejoins Leeds-Grenville Rd 2/Hwy 2. Turn [L] and go under the welcoming railway bridge into the town of **Gananoque**. To complete this leg, cycle along King St E to the Town Hall and Museum at the Gananoque River. A true tourist haven, Gananoque has several appealing features: live theatre, boat cruises, clean beaches, a rich history and a number of historic buildings.

Leg 6
(Gananoque to Kingston, 45km)

From the Town Hall and Museum, cross the Gananoque River keeping to the right, and follow King St W, which becomes Leeds-Grenville 2 on the far side of town. After passing through the welcoming gates, join the Waterfront Trail and its very wide cycling lane. The road passes the first of two access points for the Howe Island Ferry.

Optional Side Trip:
Howe Island makes for an excellent side trip, at minimal cost. Turn left and make the crossing to the island on the Pitts Ferry. When you return to the mainland, turn [L] onto Hwy 2 and

Eastern Ontario

continue towards Kingston. Turning [R] would take you to the MacLaughlin Woodworking Museum.

At Dear Ridge Dr, the road crosses an imaginary line into the county of Frontenac. A few kilometres ahead is a lovely wetland area and the MacLaughlin Woodworking Museum. The museum is a worthwhile stop, not only for its washrooms and water cooler, but also for its interesting collection of ancient woodworking tools that were used by early pioneers. Leave the museum and cycle up a 2km grade, past the second turnoff for the Howe Island Ferry, Pitts Rd. The road finally levels out just before Hillview Rd and the large sheep operation on the left.

At the St Lawrence Golf and Country Club, enjoy a quick descent to Treasure Island. After the Adoma Community Centre, you will cycle past hundreds of lily pads floating in Abby Dawn Creek before enjoying the last major climb on Frontenac 2. The city of Kingston is quite close when you pass Vimy Barracks and the Museum of Communications.

After a nice downhill ride, cross the l a Salle Causeway back into the city, keeping to the right once over the bridge. Follow the road to the north as it turns into Place d'Armes. Make a [R] turn onto Wellington St and follow it around to Rideau St. Turn [R] onto Rideau St, cycle past Rideau Park and turn [R] again onto Montreal St.

Turn left onto undulating Elliott Ave. After crossing Division St, Elliott Ave becomes Leroy Grant

Dr as it descends to Counter St. Turn [L] at Counter St and pass the Kingston PUC building. After crossing Sir John A Macdonald Blvd, the road descends past Bill Hatchet Park and crosses the CNR tracks to the Via Rail station parking lot on your right.

Practical Information

For Kingston information, see Tour 30: Limestone and Black Powder

For Ottawa information, see Tour 32: Ottawa Explorer

Population:
Perth: 6,000
Ottawa: 316,000 (Capital Region: 1,100,000)
Merrickville: 1,000
Brockville: 21,600
Gananoque: 5,000

 Tourist Information

Perth

Perth & District Chamber of Commerce
34 Herriott St, Perth, ON K7H 1T2
☎ *(613) 267-3200*
www.heritageperth.ca

The Rideau Canal

Rideau Canal
34a Beckwith St S, Smiths Falls, ON K7A 2A8
☎ *(613) 283-5170*
www.rideau-info.com/canal

Most lock stations have washrooms, first aid and picnic facilities. Overnight camping is always available nearby.

Merrickville

Merrickville Chamber of Commerce
PO Box 571, Merrickville, ON K0G 1N0
☎(613) 269-2229
www.merrickville.com/chamber

Brockville

City of Brockville Tourism Office
10 Market St W, Brockville, ON K6V 7A5
☎(613) 342-4357 or 888-251-7676
www.brockville.com

Brockville Chamber of Commerce
3 Market St W, Brockville, ON
☎(613) 342-6553
www.brockville.com/chamber

Gananoque

1000 Islands Gananoque Chamber of Commerce
10 King St E, Gananoque, ON K7G 1E6
☎(613) 382-3250 or 800-561-1595
www.1000islandsgananoque.com

St. Lawrence Islands National Park - Parks Canada
2 County Rd 5, RR 3, Mallorytown, ON K0E 1R0
☎(613) 923-5261
www.canadianparks.com/ontario/stlawrn

 Bicycle Shops

Kunstadt Sports
462 Hazeldean Rd, Kanata, ON K2L 1V6
☎(613) 831-2059

World Class Cycles
1501 Carling Ave, Ottawa, ON K1Z 7M1
☎(613) 728-7960

Merrickville

Bridgman Sports
24 Beckwith St S, Smiths Falls, ON K7A 2A8
☎(613) 283-1339

Brockville

Dave Jones Sports
65 King St W, Brockville, ON K6V 3P8
☎(613) 345-5574

Q J Johnny
198 King St W, Brockville, ON K6V 3R5
☎(613) 342-5543

Racers Edge Pro Shop
6 Delhi, Brockville, ON K6V 4H3
☎(613) 345-2133

Gananoque

T. I. Cycle
7/ 711 King St E, Gananoque, ON K7G 1Z2
☎(613) 382-5144

 Special Sights and Events

Perth

Festival of Maples, Strawberry Social, Canada Day, Stewart Park Festival, Annual Art Show, Glorious Garlic Festival, Authors in the Park, Annual Glen Tay Block Race, Perth Autumn Studio Tour, Art in the Garden, Outdoor Summer Theatre, Perth Fair, Murphy's Point Provincial Park, Inge-Va, Purdon Conservation Area, Duel Park, Matheson House Museum, Hands-on-Garden, Perth Wildlife Reserve

Merrickville

Historic industrial woolen ruins, artists' studio tour, antique and collectibles show, Canalfest, Blockhouse Museum, Merrickville

Lock Station, Smiths Falls Historic Rideau Canal Museum, Hershey Chocolate Factory, Fine Art Festival, Agricultural Fair & Steam Show

Brockville

Multicultural Festival, Celtic Festival, Riverfest, Buskers, Ribfest, Automotion antique cars, spring and fall studio tours, Horsearama rodeo, Harvest Days demonstrations, Old Fashioned Family Picnic, Sunday Concerts in Hardy Park, Gunboat Weekend, Fulford Place Mansion Tours, Brockville Museum, Fright Nights Halloween Haunted Walk, 1000 Islands Poker Run, St. Lawrence Stage Co professional theatre, Railway Tunnel, Seaway Shipviewing, Ghost Walks, Heritage Walking Tours

Gananoque

Festival of the Islands, 1000 Island Boat Cruises, Landon Bay Gardens, Historic 1000 Islands Village, 1000 Island Skydeck, Boldt Castle, 1000 Islands Playhouse, 17km bike path

 Accommodations

Kingston and Ottawa

Hotel/Motel/B&B/Camping

Perth

Resort/Inns/Motel/B&B/Camping

Merrickville

Inns/B&B/Camping

Brockville and Gananoque

Hotel/Motel/B&B/Camping

 Off-Road Cycling

Kingston and Ottawa

Yes; see "Off-Road Cycling" at the end of this chapter.

 Market Days

Perth

Saturdays, May to October

Brockville

Tuesday, Thursday and Saturday mornings, May to October

Gananoque

Saturday mornings, May to October

---

32. Ottawa Explorer: A Full Day in Under Two Hours

A great ride for the first-time cyclist visiting the city, as you will quickly get caught up in the community's hustle and bustle. Cycling along the streets of the nation's capital is perhaps the best way to become familiar with the city's general layout, history, culture and natural beauty.

Return Distance:
28km

No. of recommended legs:
1

Level of Difficulty:

Eastern Ontario
Tour 32: Ottawa Explorer

0   1   2km

● ATTRACTIONS

1. Parliament Hill
2. National Archives of Canada
3. Canadian Museum of Nature
4. Confederation Park
5. ByWard Market
6. Rideau Falls
7. City Hall
8. Rideau Hall
9. Prime Minister's Residence
10. Rockcliffe Park

Eastern Ontario

Surface:
Asphalt city streets

Villages/Towns/Cities:
Ottawa

Local Highlights:
Champlain Lookout, Meech Lake, Pink Lake, Mackenzie King Estate, Parliament Hill, By Ward Market, Canadian Museum of Civilization, Rideau Canal, Sparks St Mall, National Gallery of Canada, Casino de Hull, Canadian War Museum, Notre Dame Basilica, Agriculture Museum, Canadian Museum of Contemporary Photography, Canadian Museum of Nature, Currency Museum of the Bank of Canada, National Archives, National Aviation Museum, National Museum of Science and Technology, Royal Canadian Mint, Laurier House, Gatineau Park, Symphony of Sound, Rideau Hall, Rockcliffe, Supreme Court of Canada, Changing of the Guard

Recommended Bicycles:
Touring/Hybrid/Mountain

Tour Suggestions:
A quick, noon-hour workout or a leisurely after-dinner ride. It can

even be expanded into a full day of sightseeing.

How to get there:
A number of routes lead to Ottawa: Hwy 417 from the east, Hwys 416, 16 and 31 from the south, Hwy 7 from the west, Hwy 17 from the northwest and Hwy 148 (Québec) from the northeast.

Several centuries ago, the present-day site of Ottawa was known as Collins' Landing and then as Bellow's Landing. In 1827, a full survey was carried out and the area was renamed Bytown. Another change was made in 1855 and the town was renamed Outaouak (changed to Ottawa) after an Algonquin First Nation site that held an important position on the nearby Ottawa River. At first, just before Confederation, it was not considered a viable site for the nation's capital. By 1857, it had been discussed for some time as to whether the capital should be in Toronto, Montréal, Kingston or Quebec City. Fortunately for Ottawa, our forefathers passed the buck and let Queen Victoria make the decision. For a number of different reasons, she decided on Ottawa; by 1866, the Parliament Buildings were built and in use. Today, the city has a very clean, well-ordered look to it. It has preserved the past, yet continually moves forward to meet and adapt to the constant demands of its local citizens and the nation. The city thus has numerous green areas, more than 100km of shared recreational pathways, the world's longest skating rink and numerous annual cultural events.

Itinerary:
Start on Parliament Hill, beside the 1967 Centennial Flame,

which was built to commemorate the 100th anniversary of Confederation. The building directly in front is called the Centre Block and is home to the House of Commons and the Senate. The other two buildings, the East and West Block, are used for administration. A ride around Centre Block reveals the Ottawa Locks and a number of interesting commemorative statues. Directly behind Parliament Hill, along the river, is an area known as "Cat Hill"; it is a haven to many a wild cat, racoon and squirrel. If you are in the right spot at the right time, you may see the kind soul with food in hand who comes out to feed the animals each day in their shelters, miniature versions of the Parliament buildings.

Leave Parliament Hill by making a [R] turn onto Wellington St and go past the Confederation Building. At Bank St, as you ride past the Bank of Canada, look carefully for the glitter of gold, as this is where the world's largest gold depository is stored. A little further on are St. Andrew's Church and the Supreme Court of Canada. The National Library and Archives are located on Lyon St.

Turn [L] on Lyon St and [R] on Sparks St. Pass Bay St and the 1932 Christ Church Cathedral, with its impressive green spires. Turn [L] on Bronson St and [L] again onto Queen St. Continue along Queen and proceed to O'Connor St, cycling past the Delta and Marriott hotels. At the lights, turn [R] at O'Connor.

Follow this one-way street past Export Canada and the historic Chalmer's United Church. Cross MacLeod St and go past the three-storied Canadian Museum of Nature. Turn [L] onto Argyle

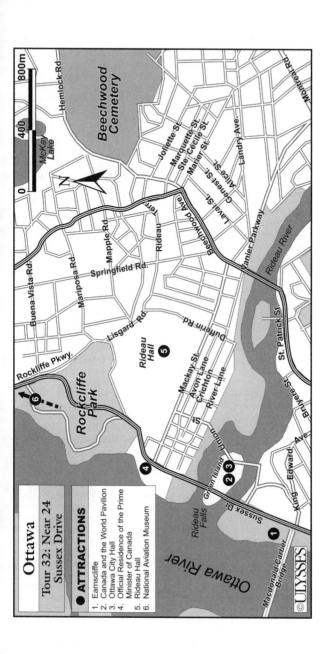

Ottawa

Tour 32: Near 24 Sussex Drive

● ATTRACTIONS

1. Earnscliffe
2. Canada and the World Pavilion
3. Ottawa City Hall
4. Official Residence of the Prime Minister of Canada
5. Rideau Hall
6. National Aviation Museum

Ottawa River

Rideau River

Beechwood Cemetery

McKay Lake

Rockcliffe Park

Rideau Hall

Rideau Falls

Green Island

© ULYSSES

0   400   800m

Hemlock Rd.
Montreal Rd.
Joliette St.
Marquette St.
Ste-Cécile St.
Marier St.
Genest St.
Allée St.
Laval St.
Landry Ave.
Beechwood Ave.
Vanier Parkway
Rideau Terr.
Rideau Rd.
Mapple Rd.
Mariposa Rd.
Buena-Vista Rd.
Springfield Rd.
Lisgard Rd.
Rockcliffe Pkwy.
Dufferin Rd.
Mackay St.
Avon Lane
Crichton
River Lane
Union St.
Sussex Dr.
St. Patrick St.
Bruyère St.
King Edward Ave.
Macdonald-Cartier Bridge

St and make another [L] onto Metcalfe St. The museum, which houses numerous exhibits on prehistoric Canada and creative displays featuring Canada's mammals and birds, is now on your left. At MacLeod St, turn [L] and then quickly turn [R], rejoining Metcalfe St.

Metcalfe St is another one-way road. At Laurier Ave, turn [R] and go past the National Capital Commission. At the corner of Elgin St is the impressive First Baptist Church. Further down on the right, the older building with turrets was the first teachers' college in Canada. In front of it, to the left, is Confederation Park.

Because there is no left turn onto Elgin St, walk your bicycle across the street, remount, then follow Elgin St uphill to Queen St. Get into the left-hand lane and turn [L] at the lights onto Queen St. Ride to Metcalfe, turn [R], and go past the Sparks St Mall. At Wellington St, turn [R] and pass the Parliament Buildings and information centre. Wellington St becomes Rideau St after it crosses the Rideau Canal. Turn [L] at the lights onto Sussex Dr and go past the National Department of Revenue. At York St, turn right into the ByWard Market area. Slow down as this area of town is a bustling, open-air market. Since it was established in the 1840s, it has always been a centre of activity and today is surrounded by streets, houses, cafés, restaurants and boutiques.

The aroma of fresh baked goods fills the air when turning [L] onto William St, which is followed by another [L] turn onto Clarence St. At Sussex Dr, turn [R] and cross St. Patrick St. The large glass building on your left is the

National Gallery of Canada, which houses a collection of more than 45,000 works of art, including a Canadian art history display. On the right is the elegant Notre Dame Basilica. Built in 1841, it is the oldest church in the city and a quick peek inside reveals a beautiful choir stall and many intriguing artifacts. Just ahead is a highly visible military tank that guards the front doors of the Canadian War Museum as well as another nearby building. This second building is the Royal Canadian Mint. At one time the mint struck common Canadian coins, but today it only produces silver, gold and platinum collector's pieces.

Once past the Macdonald-Cartier Bridge, Earnscliffe will be on the left. This is the present-day home of the British High Commission. As Sussex Dr crosses Green Island and the Rideau River, the Ottawa City Hall is on the right. On the left are two waterfalls that are so close together the water forms a curtain as it falls into the Ottawa River. Translated into French, "curtain" becomes "rideau", wich explains how the Rideau River was named.

Over the next kilometre, you will pass some impressive homes. The Prime Minister's residence is just past the falls on the left. To the right, at John St, is the region's first school building. A short distance ahead, around a bend in the road, is Rideau Hall, 1 Sussex Dr. Built in 1838, this Regency-style home was specifically built for the Governor General, the Queen of England's representative in Canada. Today, five rooms and the property's attractive gardens are open for public viewing. Take some time to ride the streets around Rideau Hall; they make for an interesting excursion, passing by many beautiful homes and embassies.

Across from Rideau Hall, a visit to Rockcliffe Park affords a beautiful panorama that encompasses the city of Hull and the Ottawa River. A short distance past Rideau Hall, Sussex Dr becomes Rockcliffe Dr. Continue along the road (bike path on the right) as it follows the river. When it begins to descend, look for a [Y] junction to the right. Keep right, join Acacia Ave and prepare yourself for a pleasant surprise. Opulent older homes abound, all of which look as though they've just had a makeover. Many of these homes are embassies and have incorporated the unique characteristics of their own countries into their design. The streets in this neighbourhood are definitely worth exploring!

Continuing along Acacia Ave, at the Beechwood Ave [T] intersection, turn [R] and continue past the Community Street Church and the Vanier Parkway. Once across the Rideau River, Beechwood Avenue changes into St. Patrick St, passes the Notre Dame Basilica and crosses Sussex Dr.

Turn [L] onto Mackenzie Ave. This one-way street passes the Connaught Building, the Canadian Museum of Contemporary Photography and the one building that dominates all others on the avenue, the unmistakable Chateau Laurier. This is the city's premier hotel, built for the Canadian Pacific Railway in 1912. Its first guest was Sir Wilfred Laurier, a railroad promoter who was elected Prime Minister of Canada in 1896.

Turn [R] onto Wellington St, cross the Rideau Canal and the Ottawa Locks, and return to Parliament Hill. In the summer evenings, from early July to early September, the highlight of this ride will be the "Sound of Light Reflections of Canada: A Symphony of Sound and Light" presentation. This is a sound-and-light show that inspires a sense of unity through the stimulating narration of letters, journals and everyday conversations, all set to music and accompanied by giant image projections and a light show on the Parliament towers.

Practical Information

Population:
Ottawa: 325,000 (Capital Region: 1,100,000)

 Tourist Information

Ottawa Tourism and Convention Authority
130 Albert St, Suite 1800, Ottawa, ON K1P 5G4
☎ *(613) 237-5150 or 800-363-4465*
www.ottawagetaways.com

 Bicycle Shops

Award Cycle and Sports
2280 Carling Ave, Ottawa, ON K2B 7G1
☎ *(613) 596-6665*

Bert's Bike Repair
305 Bronson Ave, Ottawa, ON K1R 6J1
☎ *(613) 567-9117*

Cycle Power
1574 Carling Ave, Ottawa, ON K1Z 7M4
☎ *(613) 722-2453*

Cyco's
5 Hawthorne Ave, Ottawa, ON K1S 0A9
☎(613) 567-8180

Foster's Sports Centre
305 Bank St, Ottawa, ON K2P 1X7
☎(613) 236-9611

Freewheel Cycle and Sports
1890 Bromley Rd, Ottawa, ON K2A 1C1
☎(613) 291-3171

Fresh Air Experience
1291 Wellington St, Ottawa, ON
K1Y 3A8
☎(613) 729-3002

Full Cycle
1073 Bank St, Ottawa, ON K1S 3W9
☎(613) 730-2856

Full Cycle
427 St. Laurent Blvd, Ottawa, ON
K1K 2Z8
☎(613) 741-2443

Full Tilt Cycles
1469 Richmond Rd, Ottawa, ON
K2B 6R9
☎(613) 726-0132

McCrank's Cycles
889 Bank St, Ottawa, ON K1S 3W4
☎(613) 563-2200

Pecco's
86 Murray St, Ottawa, ON K1N 5M6
☎(613) 562-9602

Rebec and Kroes Cycle and Sports
1695 Bank St, Ottawa, ON K1V 7Z3
☎(613) 521-3791

Tommy and Lefebvre
464 Bank St, Ottawa, ON K2P 1Z3
☎(613) 236-9731

 Special Sights and Events

Winterlude, Tulip Festival, National Capital Dragonboat Race

Festival, Canada Dance Festival, Canada Day, Ottawa Chamber Music Festival, International Jazz Festival, Bluesfest, Changing of the Guard, Folk Festival, Odyssey Open Air Theatre, Annual Food and Wine Show, Urban Music Festival, Ottawa Fringe Festival, Capital City Beer Festival, Central Canada Exhibition

 Accommodations

Hotel/Motel/B&B/Camping

 Off-Road Cycling

Yes; see "Off-Road Cycling" at the end of this chapter.

 Market Days

Daily

33. Gatineau Hills Leg Warmer

The Gatineau Hills are an Ottawa attraction that should not be missed. This is a challenging ride along roads and recreational trails that wind their way steadily upwards through the forest to an inspiring view of the Ottawa Valley.

Return Distance:
68km

No. of recommended legs:
1

Level of Difficulty:
🚲🚲🚲🚲

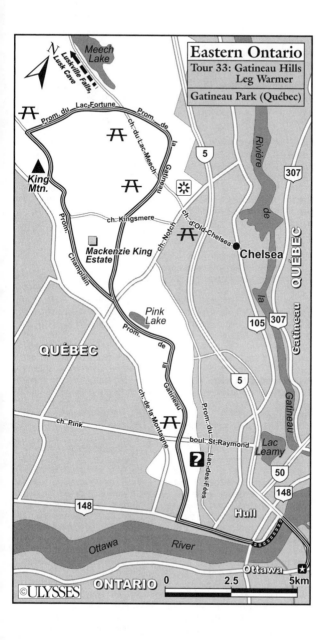

Surface:
Asphalt, road and recreational pathways

Villages/Towns/Cities:
Ottawa, Hull

Local Highlights:
Champlain Lookout, Meech Lake, Pink Lake, Mackenzie King Estate, Parliament Hill, ByWard Market, Canadian Museum of Civilization, Rideau Canal, Sparks St Mall, National Gallery of Canada, Casino de Hull, Canadian War Museum, Notre Dame Basilica, Agriculture Museum, Canadian Museum of Contemporary Photography, Canadian Museum of Nature, Currency Museum of the Bank of Canada, National Archives, National Aviation Museum, National Museum of Science and Technology, Royal Canadian Mint, Laurier House, Gatineau Park, Symphony of Sound, Rideau Hall, Rockcliffe, Supreme Court of Canada, Changing of the Guard

Recommended Bicycles:
Touring/Hybrid/Mountain

Tour Suggestions:
Motorized vehicles are not permitted in Gatineau Park on "Bike Day" Sundays during the summer. Look for the "Tourist Information on Wheels," a bike squad of tourist agents on specially built bicycles, as you near the Canadian Museum of Civilization. Bring lots of bottled water as there are only a few water fountains in the Gatineau hills.

How to get there:
A number of routes lead to Ottawa: Hwy 417 from the east, Hwys 416, 16 and 31 from the south, Hwy 7 from the west, Hwy 17 from the northwest and

Hwy 148 (Québec) from the northeast.

The concept for Gatineau Park was initiated in 1913 by the Holt Commission. By 1934, the Federal Woodlands Preservation League had convinced the federal government to acquire 10,000 acres of land in the Gatineau Hills. Today the National Capital Commission is responsible for approximately 150,000ha within the park. They have developed hundreds of kilometres of hiking trails, maintain 35km of winding panoramic roads and have designated 90km of trail for off-road cycling.

Itinerary:
Beginning at the entrance to the National Arts Centre, at the junction of Queen and Elgin St, make a [R] turn onto Elgin and follow it as it merges with Rideau St. Turn [L] onto Sussex Dr and [L] again onto St. Patrick St. After passing the National Gallery of Canada, join the bicycle path on the left just before crossing the Ottawa River into **Hull**. After the Interprovincial/Alexandra Bridge, turn [L] onto the Voyageurs Path and follow it toward the Museum of Civilization.

This path goes partway around the museum and then descends to the Ottawa River. The Museum is architecturally impressive and a visit inside details the contributions of Canada's Aboriginal peoples, early settlers and other cultures. At the [T] intersection, keep right, cross a wooden bridge and go past a series of water pipes and under a bridge, following the trail as it climbs to a [T] intersection. Turn [R] and follow the trail as it exits onto Rue Maisonneuve at the Portage Bridge. Take this road and turn [L] at the lights onto Laurier, which turns into Blvd Alexandre Taché. Cross Eddy St, which was named after the famous American Ezra Butler Eddy. Eddy played an important role in the development of the area through his connections with the logging industry. His name is still a household word associated with matches, clothes pins and the pulp and paper industry. At the Montcalm traffic lights, rejoin the bicycle path on the left.

The trail passes some rigid-looking wolves and a bronzed boat frame, and crosses a set of railway tracks before going up a slight grade. Keep [R] at the [T] intersection and exit onto the road at the University of Hull. Turn [R] onto Belleau and cross Alexandre Taché, joining the trail on your left.

To take advantage of the park's best vantage points, stay on the road as it ascends to the Champlain Lookout. Once past the reception centre, the road immediately begins to rise and crosses Rue St-Raymond. There are a few downhill rests, but these are always followed by even higher climbs. The Pink Lake Lookout is up past the entrance to Hickory Trails, at the top of the Gatineau Hills' fourth heart-pumping climb.

After Pink Lake, the road rapidly rises and falls. Turn [L] onto the Champlain Parkway. Ride past the set of stairs which are the back entrance of the Mackenzie-King Estate. The road continues to be a leg burner as it passes through several areas of bogged-out forest. The grade of the road becomes even more vertical after Bourgeois Lake and Fortune Ave Parkway. Climbing past two more outlooks, Huron and Etienne-Brulé, the road finally

ends at the Champlain Lookout with an incredible view of the Ottawa Valley.

Once you catch your breath, prepare for a blazing downhill ride back to Fortune Ave Parkway. Watch for white-tailed deer coming out of the forest on the right. Turn [L] and follow Fortune Parkway as it descends and curves to the left before crossing Meech Lake Rd for the first time. For a second time, go straight across Meech Lake Rd and you will see the access points for the mountain bike trails. Upon entering a large open area, note that the parking lot on the left is a convenient place to leave your car if you want to ride the mountain-bike trails another day.

Before you continue along the parkway and go under Kingsmere Rd, an optional highlight at this point (one hour minimum) would be to keep right, follow Kingsmere Rd and visit the gardens and picturesque ruins of Mooreside, the summer home of Canada's 10th Prime Minister, William Lyon Mackenzie King.

Ride past the turnoff for the Champlain Parkway and the Pink Lake lookout. At the bottom of the next valley, look to your left for the well-marked recreational trail access point. Turn [L] onto the trail and immediately climb up a steep little hill. Rises on this trail are always followed by wicked downhills and there are plenty of thrills in store on these narrow paths through the woods. On this part of the ride, the path will come to a number of [T] intersections. Always turn right, and eventually the trail will climb one last time before it exits back out onto the parkway. After passing the reception booth, rejoin the pathway and follow it back to Alexandre Taché. Turn [L] onto the road and follow Taché past Montcalm, then turn [R] onto Maisonneuve. Cross the Ottawa River via the Portage Bridge, turn [L] onto Wellington St and turn [L] into the parking lot of the Old Mill Restaurant. Keep to the right and ride under Wellington St through a segmented tunnel. Turn [L], then [R], and follow the trail along the river past the Ottawa locks before returning to the National Arts Centre.

34. To Hog's Back Falls and Back: Ottawa's Rideau Canal Recreational Trail

For those with only a few hours to spare, this tour is a nice way to spend a warm summer evening or a Sunday afternoon. Following the Rideau Canal from Parliament Hill to a crossing at Hog's Back Falls, the loop is completed via a lesser travelled path along the Rideau River past Rideau Falls back to the National Arts Centre.

Return Distance:
30km

No. of recommended legs:
1

Level of Difficulty:

Surface:
Asphalt and 1.5km of crushed-gravel trail

Villages/Towns/Cities:
Ottawa

Local Highlights:
Parliament Hill, ByWard Market, Canadian Museum of Civilization, Rideau Canal, Sparks St Mall, National Gallery of Canada, Casino de Hull, Canadian War Museum, Notre Dame Basilica, Agriculture Museum, Canadian Museum of Contemporary Photography, Canadian Museum of Nature, Currency Museum of the Bank of Canada, National Archives, National Aviation Museum, National Museum of Science and Technology, Royal Canadian Mint, Laurier House, Gatineau Park, Symphony of Sound, Rideau Hall, Rockcliffe, Supreme Court of Canada

Recommended Bicycles:
Touring/Hybrid/Mountain

Tour Suggestions:
An excellent ride for the whole family or the first-time cyclist. It is also a great tension reliever after a long day on the road or a hard day at the office.

How to get there:
From the north, take Hwy 17; from the east, take Hwy 417; from the south, follow Hwy 416, 16 and 31, and from the west, take Hwy 17. Once in the nation's capital, join the Rideau Canal pathway behind the National Arts Centre, which starts at the junction of Queen Elizabeth Driveway, also known as "The Driveway", and Albert/Slater St by the MacKenzie King Bridge.

Ottawa is probably the only city in Canada where some companies actually pay their employees to bicycle to work. The Rideau Canal was built for less than $4 million, including the construction of its 47 locks. Today, it serves as a pathway for boaters and its banks provide a safe transportation system for many different types of vehicles. In winter, the canal becomes the world's longest skating rink, stretching over 7.8km.

Itinerary:
The canal pathway at Queen Elizabeth Driveway and Slater St is high above the canal but there are plenty of stairs descending down to the water. Eventually the pathway and the canal meet and follow Queen Elizabeth Driveway for quite a distance. The pathway goes under Hwy 417 and the Pretoria Bridge, which runs alongside Lansdowne Park, then climbs away from the canal for a short distance, rejoining it at Dows Lake. At the bottom end of the lake is a very marina/restaurant, and trail directions at this point are not very well marked.

Keep to the canal on the left and follow what looks like a bike path around the lake. The trail changes to crushed gravel after passing in front of the HMCS Carlton/NCS Museum. Cross a little bridge and follow the pathway to the Hartwells Locks. Pick up your bicycle and cross the locks, rejoining the bicycle path at the bottom of the stairs on the other side. Continuing south, go past a golden-roofed mosque under Base Line Rd and Colonel By Dr, to the 450-million-year-old landscape of Hog's Back Falls. An amazing sight! Lock up your bicycle before heading for the best lookouts at the bottom of the rapids. Cross the falls by way of a set of stairs or return to the road rejoining the trail on the east side of the Rideau River. Take the time to look around or relax at the snack bar.

Behind the snack bar, the trail begins again, now following the shoreline of the Rideau River. Descending from the parking lot past the mosque, the land is less developed, more remote and in some ways more visually pleasing. Cycle under Heron Rd through Vincent Massey Park, a well-equipped rest area, and enjoy another downhill ride to the Bronson Ave underpass. The riverside of the Rideau is much more interesting, more rugged and has more climbs. Running parallel to Riverside Dr, the trail goes past the Ottawa Memorial Hospital through a secluded wooded area, then under Hwy 417, the Queensway. Just before the Queensway, notice the dead-end path on the other side of the river, which can be accessed by the old railway bridge on your left. Just past the Queensway, the path comes back down along the river to a set of rapids.

Rejoin the path on the other side of Montreal Rd and cycle through Kingsview Park. Follow the river and go under the St. Patrick St Bridge. The trail turns into gravel by the playground and tennis courts, but quickly changes back into asphalt at the white Minte Bridges at Union St. Cross Union St; the triangular building on the left is the Ottawa City Hall. The bicycle path follows Stanley Ave and ends at Sussex Dr. The Rideau Falls are directly ahead. Cross Sussex Dr and have a look at the falls. While you're there, you can also visit the Canada and the World Pavilion.

Follow the walkway over the falls to a finished park area and lookout, a memorial to the Royal Regiment of Canadian Artillery. Continue across a second

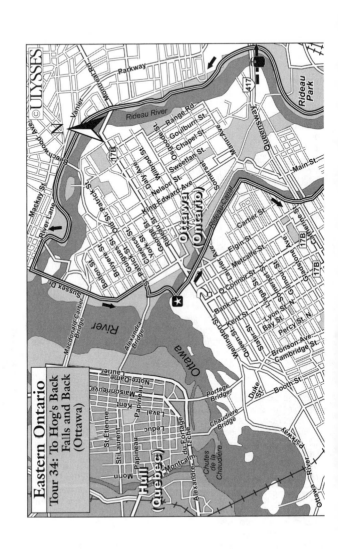

Eastern Ontario

Tour 34: To Hog's Back Falls and Back (Ottawa)

©ULYSSES

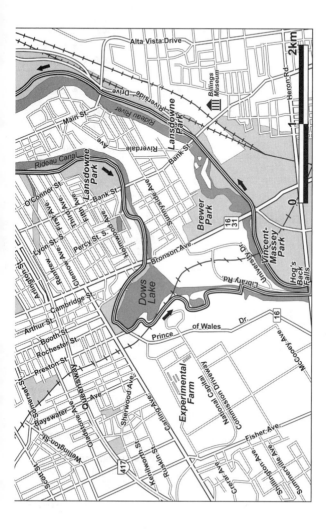

walkway, pass the National Reserve Council's (NCR) Central Heating and Cooling Plant and exit back out onto Sussex Dr. Once past the NRC building, you will come to the Canadian War Museum and the National Gallery of Canada. Bear right onto the Alexandra Bridge Rd and then quickly turn [L] onto the one-way MacKenzie Ave. Do not continue along Sussex as it turns into a one-way street, going in the opposite direction. At Chateau Laurier, turn [R] onto Rideau St and then [L] onto Elgin St and return to the National Arts Centre, at the junction of Queen and Elgin Sts.

Off-Road Cycling

Public Trails

Lanark

K & P Trail Conservation Area
(40km)
Surface:
Original rail bed
Beginning:
Snow Rd (near Hwy 509) and Barryvale (off Hwy 501)

Mississippi Valley Conservation Authority
PO Box 268, Lanark, ON K0G 1K0
☎ *(613) 259-2421*
www.mvc.on.ca

Russell-Ottawa Area

New York Central Fitness Trail
(8km)
Surface:
Asphalt
Beginning:
Russell to Embrun

Township of Russell
717 Notre Dame St, Embrun, ON
K0A 1W1
☎ *(613) 443-3066*
www.twp.russell.on.ca

Resort Trails

Pembroke Area

Forest Lea Trails
(14km of trails)

Ministry of Natural Resources
PO Box 220, 31 Riverside Dr, Pembroke, ON K8A 8R6
☎ *(613) 732-3661*
www.mnr.gov.on.ca

Pembroke/Petawawa Area

Petawawa Fish Culture Station
(6.6km of trails)

Ministry of Natural Resources
(see above)

Ottawa Area

Morris Island Conservation Area
(13km of trails)

Mississippi Valley Conservation Authority
(see above)

Perth/Lanark Area

Palmerston Canonto Conservation Area
(6km of trails)

Mississippi Valley Conservation Authority
(see above)

Rainbow Country

Map of Rainbow Country region:
- Sudbury
- North Bay
- QUÉBEC
- Ottawa ⊛
- Parry Sound
- Kingston
- Owen Sound
- Peterborough
- Lake Huron
- Lake Ontario
- Toronto ⊕
- London
- Niagara Falls
- Sarnia
- Lake Erie
- Windsor
- UNITED STATES

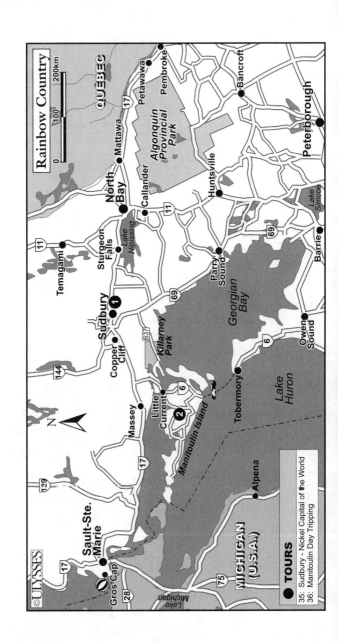

Rainbow Country

QUÉBEC

0   100   200km

Sault-Ste.
Marie

Gros Cap

MICHIGAN (U.S.A.)

Lake
Michigan

Temagami

Sturgeon
Falls

North
Bay

Mattawa

Petawawa

Pembroke

Bancroft

Algonquin
Provincial
Park

Callander

Huntsville

Lake
Nipissing

Sudbury

Copper
Cliff

Massey

Little
Current

Killarney
Park

Manitoulin Island

Tobermory

Georgian
Bay

Parry
Sound

Barrie

Lake
Simcoe

Owen
Sound

Lake
Huron

Alpena

Peterborough

N

© ULYSSES

● TOURS

35: Sudbury - Nickel Capital of the World
36: Manitoulin Day Tripping

Ontario's north

extends from the nearly inaccessible, century-old Algonquin Park, over a land of unspoiled character and rugged beauty crossing hundreds of lakes, wetlands and rivers, to the lands north of Lake Superior.

35. Sudbury: Nickel Capital of the World

A pleasant evening or early-morning ride in the heart of the Sudbury basin. Beginning downtown, follow city streets as they wind their way up and down Sudbury's rolling landscape. Towering reddish-grey rocks thrusting upwards out of a blackened moonscape surface are only eclipsed by the area's immense mining operations and its picturesque and inviting turquoise-blue lakes.

Return Distance:
25km

No. of recommended legs:
1

Level of Difficulty:

Surface:
Asphalt

Villages/Towns/Cities:
Sudbury Region

Local Highlights:
Downtown core, Science North, Cambrian College, Lake Laurentian Conservation Area, Laurentian University and Arboretum,

Sudbury Neutrino Observatory, Ramsey Lake Trail

Recommended Bicycles:
Touring/Hybrid/Mountain

Tour Suggestions:
This is a quick way to get acquainted with the city in a couple of hours. If you are visiting for a day or two it can easily be expanded into a day-long outing

How to get there:
From the south, take Hwy 400 north from Toronto to Hwy 69 N/Hwy 17 E. From the east, follow Hwy 17 W. From the north, follow Hwy 144 S and from the west follow Hwy 17 E.

The Sudbury region may owe its existence to the westward expansion of the Canadian Pacific Railway in 1833, but its continued survival is due to rich mineral deposits beneath the Sudbury basin. A gigantic meteorite collision is now known to have created the basin, and today this area is the largest source of nickel in the western world. As the demand for nickel grew, the area developed in leaps and bounds and the environment became a secondary concern. Back in the early days of the mining industry, large piles of ore and wooden logs would be left to burn for days on end, producing a toxic smoke that killed vegetation and blackened rock. Today, through the efforts of the local population and responsible industry, Sudbury is once again becoming green, slowly restoring the landscape to its original beauty.

Itinerary:
Leave your car at the Sudbury arena, at the corner of Brady and Minto Sts. Facing south, towards the arena, a lovely park will be on your right and will be on your left the Bell Telephone Centre and Tom Davies Square. Between these two buildings is the 13-storey provincial building, which uses solar connectors to heat its water.

Cycling along Minto St, cross Brady and turn [L] onto Elgin St. Once past the train station and the Paris St overpass, Elgin St begins to climb. At the top of Elgin, get off the road and use the Elizabeth St walkway (on your right) to cross the railway tracks. Turn [R] onto Edmund St and [R] again onto Ramsey and continue following Ramsey as it turns into Worthington Cr.

Turn [L] onto Medora St and at the [T] intersection, turn [R] and rejoin Edmund St. Smokestacks should be visible ahead as the road will begin to climb. Travelling through an older section of the city can be interesting. Take particular note of the long set of stairs at the corner of Nicholas and Edmund. Passing huge rocks in the moonlike landscape, be prepared to turn [R] onto Wembley St. Follow it past Wembley Public School, and turn [L] onto Connaught Ave.

After a leg-warming uphill climb, make a [L] turn onto York St. Turn [R] at the [T] intersection of York and Paris Sts. To the left is Sudbury's Centennial Project, the Bell Park Amphitheatre and a great view of Ramsey Lake and Science North. Be prepared to move into the left-hand lane as Paris St descends to the lights at Ramsey Lake Rd.

Turn [L] onto Ramsey Lake Rd. On your right is the Laurentian Hospital, the base for northern Ontario's helicopter ambulance service, and on your left is Science North, a hands-on science establishment. Continue along Ramsey Lake Rd and look for the scenic lookout on the left. The lookout offers a spectacular view of the largest city-contained lake in North America, which is only one of 36 lakes in the area that are over 4ha in size. Farther along are the bilingual campuses of Laurentian University. While in the area, make time to visit the impressive Thornloe Chapel or explore its unique arboretum.

Optional Side Trip:
Continue along Ramsey Lake Rd, turn [R] onto South Bay Rd and follow it (passing the Lake Laurentian Conservation Area) for approximately 5km to a set of gates. Pass through the gates onto the renovated crushed-gravel trail. "Phase One" of this multi-use trail system is underway. When it is completed, it will allow you to go all the way around Ramsey Lake.

Retrace your steps to Science North on Ramsey Lake Rd, just before the street lights at Paris St, turn [L] onto Paris Cr and pass between the two hospital towers. Turn [R] onto Centennial Dr. Cross Paris St and go past a large baseball diamond, turning [R] onto Ramsey View Court. Signal [R] before turning onto Regent St and climbing uphill, past a

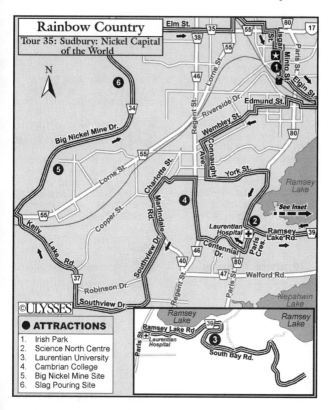

Rainbow Country

Tour 35: Sudbury: Nickel Capital of the World

N

● ATTRACTIONS
1. Irish Park
2. Science North Centre
3. Laurentian University
4. Cambrian College
5. Big Nickel Mine Site
6. Slag Pouring Site

©ULYSSES

Cambrian College residence. At the crest of the hill, move into the left-hand lane as it descends to York St. Turn [L] at the lights, following York St to Bank St to Charlotte St.

Turn [L] at Charlotte St, and [L] again onto Martindale Rd. After a short climb and a quick descent, make a [R] turn onto Southview Dr. Follow Southview to a three-way stop, turning [R] onto Kelly Lake Rd (note: if you continue along Southview Dr, you will encounter some interesting moonscape-type rock, namely Canadian Slick-Rock) which trav-

els through a light industrial area to Hwy 17 (Lorne St, Regional Rd No. 55). Turn [L] onto Lorne St, following the ramp up to Big Nickel Mine Dr and to the Big Nickel Mine entrance. The Big Nickel Mine is temporarily closed; when it reopens in 2003, it will be renamed "Dynamic Earth." Until recently, the mine was home to Sudbury's well-known landmark, the towering "Big Nickel." It has since been moved to Science North.

Exit the Big Nickel Mine by turning [R] onto Big Nickel Mine Dr. As it snakes around mining opera-

Rainbow Country

tions and through natural rock formations, take note of the parking area on your left. In the evening you can watch red-hot slag being poured here. Call ahead to confirm dates and time for slag pouring.

Turn right onto Elm St and follow it down to College St. Turn [L] onto College St, cross Pine St and after passing under the railway bridge turn [R] onto Frood Rd. Turn [L] onto Beech St, then turn [R] onto Durham St. At Elm St turn [L] and then turn [R] onto Lisgar St. Turn left at Larch St. The impressive, grey St. Andrew's Place and the park where your journey began are nearby.

Practical Information

Population:
Greater Sudbury: 164,000

 Tourist Information

Rainbow Country Travel Association
2726 Whippoorwill Ave, Sudbury, ON
P3G 1E9
☎(705) 522-0104 or 800-465-6655
www.rainbowcountry.com

 Bicycle Shops

The Outside Store
2041 Long Lake Rd, Sudbury, ON
☎(705) 522-1755

Cameron Cycle and Services
495 Notre Dame Ave, Sudbury, ON
P3C 5K9
☎(705) 671-2052

Pinnacle Sports
2037 Long Lake Rd, Sudbury, ON
P3E 4M8
☎(705) 523-7400

DeMarco's Source for Sports
25 Elgin St, Sudbury, ON P3C 5B3
☎(705) 675-5677

 Special Sights and Events

Canada Day, Bell Park Concert Series, Northern Lights Festival, Blueberry Festival, Sudbury Gem and Mineral Show, Canadian Garlic Festival, Cinefest International Film Festival, Cavalcade of Colours

 Accommodations

Hotel/Motel/B&B/Camping

 Market Days

Fridays, Saturday and Sundays, April to December, corner of Elgin and Elm Sts

---

36. Manitoulin Day Tripping: Lake Mindemoya, the Bridal Veil Falls and the Cup and Saucer Lookout

---

When you look at an Ontario road map, Manitoulin Island looks pretty small, but don't be fooled. Even if you spend several days cycling on this island, you would be hard pressed to see everything. Starting at Lake Mindemoya, this trip takes you clockwise around the lake to the

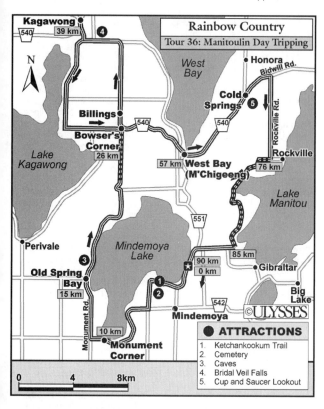

Rainbow Country

Tour 36: Manitoulin Day Tripping

N

Kagawong
540
39 km
4

West Bay

Honora
Bidwill Rd.

Cold
Springs
5

Rockville Rd.

Billings
540

Bowser's
Corner
26 km

57 km
West Bay
(M'Chigeeng)

Lake
Kagawong

Rockville
76 km

Lake
Manitou

551

Perivale

Mindemoya
Lake

3

Old Spring
Bay
15 km

90 km
0 km

Gibraltar

1

2

Big
Lake

542

©ULYSSES

Mindemoya

Monument Rd.

10 km

Monument
Corner

0   4   8km

● ATTRACTIONS

1.   Ketchankookum Trail
2.   Cemetery
3.   Caves
4.   Bridal Veil Falls
5.   Cup and Saucer Lookout

eastern shore of Lake Kagawong. After passing the Bridal Veil Falls and historic Kagawong, it continues along one of the island's main logging roads, and through the West Bay First Nation reserve, now known as "M'chigeeng," to the impressive Cup and Saucer lookout. The loop is completed by cycling along the western shores of Lake Manitou.

Return Distance:
90km

No. of recommended legs:
1

Level of Difficulty:
🚲 🚲 🚲 🚲 🚲

Surface:
Asphalt and gravel

Villages/Towns/Cities:
Mindemoya, Monument Corner, Old Spring Bay, Bowser's Corner, Kagawong

Local Highlights:
Bridal Veil Falls, Cup and Saucer Lookout, Ten Mile Point, High Falls, Providence Bay Beach, Mississagi Lighthouse Museum, Lake Mindemoya, Gore Bay

Rainbow Country

Museum, Little Current-Howland Museum, McLean's Mountain, Assiginack Museum, S.S. Norisle and Heritage Park, Blue Jay Creek Fish Culture Station, Little School House and Museum, South Baymouth Fish Research Station

Recommended Bicycles:
Hybrid/Mountain/Touring

Tour Suggestions:
Accommodations should be booked well in advance as the island is a popular tourist destina-tion. Do not drink the water out of Lake Manitou, even if the locals tell you it is safe.

How to get there:
From the south, take Hwy 6 to the Tobermory Ferry; from the north, follow Hwy 6 to Espanola and the Little Current swing bridge. The tour begins at the Mindemoya government boat dock. Travel north on Hwy 6 from South Baymouth, making a right turn onto Hwy 542. At the junction of Hwy 552, turn right and then left onto old Hwy 551, the first road after the local motel. At the lake, turn [L] and follow the road to the boat docks and the parking lot at the municipal park.

Located in the waters of Lake Huron, Manitoulin Island stretches 129km from east to west and varies from 4km to 48km in width. It is the world's largest freshwater island and has more than eight inland lakes. The name Manitoulin means "Spirit Island," and the Ojibwe, Odawa and Potawatamie First Nations believe that it is the home of the Great Spirit, or "Kitche Manitou."

Itinerary:
Starting from the shores of Lake Mindemoya at the Carnarvon Park pavilion, make a [R] turn off the government boat dock onto the Ketchankookum Trail. Follow the road west as it swings away from the water and climbs past a local trailer park and the Minde-moya Cemetery. At the stop sign, turn [R] onto Lakeshore Rd. The local township sheds will be on the left. As you ride toward Cosey Cove Cottages, on a mix of asphalt and gravel, watch for potholes in this old cedar-lined cottage road. Several kilometres ahead, the road curves back towards the lake. The windy road along the shore of Manitoulin's third-largest lake ends abruptly at the junction of Hwy 542/551. Turn [R] onto the highway and cycle to a small picnic area on the lake, which is 30m higher than Lake Huron. Lake Mindemoya's name comes from the Aboriginals' description of the lake's only island, located to the west of the rest area, which was said to resemble an old woman on her hands and knees.

Continuing west, the highway again swings away from the lake. At **Monument Corner**, also known as the Four Corners or Alexander's Corners, turn [R] onto Monument Rd. Take a few minutes to look at the 1921 statue of a soldier that honours local men who fought and died in World War I. The statue originally stood in the middle of the inter-section, but it was unfortunately damaged by a motorist and its remains were relocated to the southwest side of the highway. Just after you join Monument Rd, it begins a gradual 2km climb before it descends back along the lake into the summer community of Old Spring Bay, or

Cavemount. When the island was bought for just $60 by the MacPherson family of Toronto in the 1880s, over 35 families had settled in this area. Take a few moments to refill your water bottles at the lakefront water pump, which provides safe and cool drinking water.

The ride along the bay is short, and your legs will soon begin to warm up as you ride uphill to the Rock Garden Terrace Resort. The Mindemoya Lake Cave is located here and can be visited for a small fee. The 23m-deep cave was discovered by hunters looking for a fallen duck. The floor of the cave was strewn with 15 skeletons of Hurons who were slaughtered by the Iroquois during the mid-1600s. Back on the road, cycle past the Carnarvon-Billings Line hiking trail to a [T] intersection. Turn [L] onto Jerusalem Hill Rd. At the top of the hill, the road becomes gravel. The next 6km will be spent riding along an old narrow logging road. As you cycle through second-growth forest and past flat dolomite rock, you can still pick out some hardwood trees that were left behind after the last logging operation. Don't be surprised if you encounter fallen trees blocking the road.

At West Bay Rd (Hwy 540), turn [L] and coast downhill to **Bowser's Corners**, making a [L] turn onto Billings Concession 0 Rd. The easy ride to Lake Kagawong (the island's second-largest lake), is followed by a stretch along the lake through rich agricultural land. At Hwy 540, turn [L] and ride past the local variety store to Bridal Veil Falls Park on the right side of the road. Stairs lead down to the bottom of the falls. The more adventurous can walk be-

hind the veil of water that falls 20m from the Kagawong River above.

From the falls, continue straight on the road following it into **Kagawong**, or "Kag", as it is often called. (If you turn [L] on the highway after the falls, you will get to Gore Bay.) The village was originally called Mudge Bay, but the name was changed to Kagawong in 1876 when the first post office was opened. An Ojibwe name, it translates to "where mists rise from falling waters." A walk along the river back towards the falls reveals a reconditioned generating station. After having been out of operation for 31 years, the station once again supplies hydroelectricity to Manitoulin Island. Kagawong's Upper St and lower Main St have a number of excellent turn-of-the-20th-century buildings. Along the bay is the old Manitoulin Pulp and Paper mill, which now serves as the town's community centre. Kagawong has two great lookouts on Maple Point Rd: to get to them, follow the bay road north-west for several kilometres. Cycle past an interesting piece of building art based on the story of Lady Godiva. After climbing up two hills, you will get a fantastic view of Mudge Bay and Capperton Island on your right. The second lookout is only a few more kilometres ahead and to the left.

The uphill climb out of Kagawong will get your heart pounding as you retrace your path back to the Bridal Veil Falls. Continue riding along Hwy 540, watching for unique triangular fences and shingle-sided homes. A short distance after Billings School No.2, is a stone memorial with a bell on top, commemorating the area's first school. The road turns sharply to the left as you pass the familiar Bowser's Corner. Logging trucks groan as they ascend the eight-degree grade to the top of Jerusalem hill. Take a break if you need it to tackle the hill feeling refreshed. About halfway up the hill, you will enter the M'chigeeng (West Bay), the island's second-largest Aboriginal settlement. M'chigeeng means "village enclosed by stepped cliffs."

Limestone rock lines the road as you ride into West Bay. The community was settled by 31 Aboriginals in 1847. Mechecowetchenong, or "hill of fish harpoon," as it was known in the 1870s, became a Roman Catholic settlement for Aboriginals who had converted to the religion. East of Hwy 551 is a new Roman Catholic Church, shaped like a 12-sided tipi, that tries to evoke the feeling of traditional fire pits. Hwy 540 is a slightly winding road that is only 900m long. It has a grade that fluctuates between five and eight degrees, so steady pedalling will get you to the top in no time.

At the Cold Springs Outpost, turn [R] onto Bidwell Rd. The entrance to the Cup and Saucer Lookout is just a few metres ahead on the right. Leave your bike behind and remember to lock up before hiking to the look-

out. The hiking trail has been in existence since 1962 and the hill is the highest spot (351m) on the island. The trail is about 2km long and riding a fully-loaded bicycle along it is not recommended. When you reach the cliffs, climb to the top for an incredible view of Green Bay and Lake Manitou. Follow the edge of the cliff west to take in the spectacular view of West Bay and Mudge Bay. The more adventurous (leave your Lycra behind) can work their way through the rock chimney or along the narrow ledge, gaining access to the "Adventure Trail"—at their own risk, of course! Descending from the highest cliff, continue to follow the sloping trail west along the bluffs; it eventually returns to the parking lot after several hours of hiking.

Turning [R] out of the parking lot, follow Bidwill Rd as it winds its way through a grassy wetland area. Turn [R] onto Rockville Rd. Be careful though, as gravel trucks run up and down this road on a regular basis. Give them a wide berth, as gravel can fly from the trucks and hit innocent cyclists! Descending to a [T] intersection, turn [R] (turning [L] takes you to Rockville) and cycle past the Rockville Community Hall. Follow the gravel road as it swings to the left. Occasional glimpses of Lake Manitou appear to your left. Locals will tell you that you can drink directly from the lake; they may be right but it is always best not to take chances. Turn [R] at the large barn, at Camp Mary Anne, and continue west. Just before reaching Hwy 551, the road changes back to asphalt. Turn [L] onto the highway and ride past the remains of the original highway, which used to run much closer to Lake Mindemoya. At the Idyll Glen Resort campgrounds, turn [R] onto the Ketchankookum Trail. Follow the road back along the island's warmest lake, completing the trip at the municipal parking lot.

Practical Information

Population:
Manitoulin Island: 13,000
Township of Central Manitoulin: 2,000
M'Chigeeng: 900

 Tourist Information

Manitoulin Tourism Association Inc.
PO Box 119, Little Current, ON P0P 1K0
☎*(705) 368-3021*
www.manitoulintourism.com

 Bicycle Shops

Gus' Bicycle Shop
311 Old Webbwood Rd, Espanola, ON P5E 1S1
☎*(705) 869-1346*

The Bike Medics
Mar to Nov
Hwy 540, Little Current, ON P0P 1K0
☎*(705) 368-2193*

 Special Sights and Events

Annual Wikwemikong Pow Wow, M'chigeen Traditional Pow-Wow, Three Fires Music Festival, Annual Manitoulin Island Arts Tour, Canada Day, Summerfest Weekend, Gore Bay Summer Theatre, Haweater Weekend.

 Accommodations

Motel/Resort/Cottage/Camping/B&Bs

 Market Days

Providence Bay, Saturday mornings; Little Current, Saturday mornings, Bank of Montreal; Mindemoya, Saturday mornings; Friday mornings in the Gore Bay Arena, seasonal

Off-Road Cycling

Public Trails

Algonquin Park

Old Railway Bike Trail
(10km)
Surface:
Original rail bed/loose surface
Beginning:
Newlake Campground to Rocklake

Ontario Parks Information Centre
PO Box 219, Whitney, ON K0J 2M0
☎*(705) 633-5572*
www.algonquinpark.on.ca

Parry Sound

Seguin Trail
(61km)
Surface:
Original rail bed/loose surface
Beginning:
Hwy 69 (12km south of Parry Sound) to Fern Glen Rd (6km west of Hwy 11)

Rainbow Country

Ministry of Natural Resources
7 Bay St, Parry Sound, ON P2A 1S4
☎ *(705) 746-4201*

Resort and Conservation Trails

Algonquin Park

Minnesing Mountain Bike Trail
(55km of trails in four loops)

Ontario Parks Information Centre (see above)

Sault Ste. Marie

Searchmont Resort
PO Box 146, Searchmont, ON P0S 1J0
☎ *(705) 781-2340 or 800-663-2546*
www.searchmont.com

Timmins

(45km of trails)

Mattagami Region Conservation Authority
100 Lakeshore Rd, Timmons, ON
P4N1B3
☎ *(705) 360-1382*

Timmins/Porcupine Area

Bart Thomson Trail
(18km of trails)

Mattagami Region Conservation Authority
(see above)

Thunder Bay

Sleeping Giant Provincial Park
(25km of trail)

Sleeping Giant Provincial
General Delivery, Pass Lake, ON
P0T 2M0
☎ *(807) 977-2526*
www.ontarioparks.com/english/slee.html

Index

Abbreviations 30
Accommodations 25
Airlines 18
Attitudes 21
Avonton
    (Southwestern Ontario) . . . 60
Banking 15
Bed and Breakfasts 25
Benmiller
    (Southwestern Ontario) . . . 64
Bicycle Types 30
Big Bay (Georgian Lakelands) 132
Big Chute
    (Georgian Lakelands) . . . 148
Bloomfield (Central Ontario) 203
Bobcaygeon (Central Ontario) 178
Books 32
Bowser's Corners
    (Rainbow Country) 251
Bracebridge
    (Georgian Lakelands) . . . 152
Brockville (Eastern Ontario) 223
Burgessville
    (Southwestern Ontario) . . . 53
Bus 19
Cambridge (Festival Country) 102
Cameron (Central Ontario) . 178
Camping 25
Camping Equipment 28
Car 18
Carlsruhe
    (Georgian Lakelands) . . . 126
Carrying Place
    (Central Ontario) 192
Cataract (Festival Country) . . 85
Central Ontario 169
    Athol Bay, Sandbanks
        and Sand Dunes 200
    Kawartha Cycling and
        Spelunking Adventure . 181
    Kawartha Lakes Adventure 175
    Kent Portage 190
    Lake on the Mountain
        Adventure 193
    Lighthouse and Lookouts 197
    Off-Road Cycling 204
    Peterborough 171
    Port Hope to Cobourg
        and Back 185

Checklist 27
Cherry Valley
    (Central Ontario) 202
Children 28
Circle Check 31
Climate 14
Clothing 27
Conestogo (Festival Country) . 94
Cooking 26
Corunna
    (Southwestern Ontario) . . . 45
Courrier Companies 18
Currency 15
Cycling in Ontario 11
Cycling Laws 21
Cycling Publications 32
Cycling Tours 23
Dehydration 31
Difficulty 30
Directions 30
Documents 16
Dorchester
    (Southwestern Ontario) . . . 70
Downeyville (Central Ontario) 179
Dundas (Festival Country) . . . 86
Durham
    (Georgian Lakelands) . . . 140
Eastern Ontario 207
    Gatineau Hills Legwarmer 234
    Limestone and
        Black Powder 208
    Off-Road Cycling 242
    Ottawa Explorer 228
    The Rideau Canal and the
        1000 Islands Parkway . 216
    To Hog's Back Falls
        and Back 238
Elmira (Festival Country) . . . 92
Elora (Festival Country) 81
Emergencies 16
Environment 31
Equipment 22
Erin (Festival Country) 84
Eugenia
    (Georgian Lakelands) . . . 140
Fauna 13
Fee's Landing
    (Central Ontario) 177

Fenelon Falls
   (Central Ontario) 178
Fergus (Festival Country) . . . 82
Festival Country 79
   Dundas Valley and the
      Niagara Escarpment . . . 86
   Elmira and St. Jacob's
      Countryside Tour 92
   Elora Gorge Adventure . . . 96
   Myths, Miracles and
      Pathways 110
   Off-Road Cycling 120
   Paris to Cambridge
      Rail Trail 100
   Quarries and Cataracts . . . 81
   Welland Canal Explorer . 103
   Wineries and Vineyards . . 115
Flamborough
   (Festival Country) 90
Flesherton
   (Georgian Lakelands) . . . 140
Flora 13
Food 26
Formosa
   (Georgian Lakelands) . . . 128
Fowlers Corners
   (Central Ontario) 179
Gananoque (Eastern Ontario) 225
Geography 12
Georgian Lakelands 123
   Beaver Valley Explorer . . 139
   Breweries, Sulfur Springs
      and Boxing 125
   Cycling the Bruce Peninsula 130
   Cycling to the Big Chute
      and Back 145
   Lake of the Bays and
      Muskoka Hills 149
   Off-Road Cycling 154
Glen Meyer
   (Southwestern Ontario) . . . 53
Glen Morris
   (Festival Country) 102
Goderich
   (Southwestern Ontario) . . . 63
Greater Toronto Area 157
   Off-Road Cycling 168
   Olde Town Toronto 163
   Toronto Islands, Lakeshore
      and Beaches 158
Group cycling 23
Hamilton (Festival Country) . 90
Hardware 27

Harmony
   (Southwestern Ontario) . . . 57
Hawkesville (Festival Country) 95
Heathcote
   (Georgian Lakelands) . . . 142
Holidays 15
Hope Bay
   (Georgian Lakelands) . . . 134
Hotels 25
How This Guide Works 30
Howdenvale
   (Georgian Lakelands) . . . 136
Hull (Eastern Ontario) 236
Huntsville
   (Georgian Lakelands) . . . 150
Independent Cycling 23
Internet Sites 31
Kagawong (Rainbow Country) 251
Kemptville (Eastern Ontario) 223
Kimberly
   (Georgian Lakelands) . . . 142
Kingston (Eastern Ontario) . 218
Kingsville
   (Southwestern Ontario) . . . 40
Lakefield (Central Ontario) . 183
Laws 21
Leamington
   (Southwestern Ontario) . . . 40
Lindsay (Central Ontario) . . 179
Lion's Head
   (Georgian Lakelands) . . . 134
London
   (Southwestern Ontario) . . . 67
Long Point
   (Southwestern Ontario) . . . 52
Maps of Ontario 33
Markdale
   (Georgian Lakelands) . . . 143
Meaford
   (Georgian Lakelands) . . . 142
Merrickville
   (Eastern Ontario) 223
Midland
   (Georgian Lakelands) . . . 145
Mildmay
   (Georgian Lakelands) . . . 127
Milford (Central Ontario) . . 198
Money 15
Monument Corner
   (Rainbow Country) 250
Mooretown
   (Southwestern Ontario) . . . 45
Motels 25

Neustadt
(Georgian Lakelands) ... 126
Niagara Falls
(Festival Country) 113
Niagara-on-the-Lake
(Festival Country) 116
Normandale
(Southwestern Ontario) ... 52
Off Road Cycling 24
Central Ontario 204
Eastern Ontario 242
Festival Country 120
Georgian Lakelands 154
Greater Toronto Area ... 168
Rainbow Country 253
Southwestern Ontario ... 75
Oil Springs
(Southwestern Ontario) ... 44
Oliphant
(Georgian Lakelands) ... 137
On The Road 30
Ontario Cycling Publications . 32
Organized Group Tours 23
Orton (Festival Country) 84
Ottawa
(Eastern Ontario) ... 222, 238
Oxford Centre
(Southwestern Ontario) ... 48
Paris (Festival Country) 102
Pelee Island
(Southwestern Ontario) ... 40
Perth (Eastern Ontario) ... 219
Peterborough
(Central Ontario) 172
Petrolia
(Southwestern Ontario) ... 44
Picton (Central Ontario) ... 202
Plane 18
Point Traverse
(Central Ontario) 200
Police 16
Port Dalhousie
(Festival Country) 104
Port Dover
(Southwestern Ontario) ... 51
Port McNicoll
(Georgian Lakelands) ... 146
Port Rowan
(Southwestern Ontario) ... 52
Port Royal
(Southwestern Ontario) ... 53
Port Ryerse
(Southwestern Ontario) ... 52

Port Severn
(Georgian Lakelands) ... 146
Port Sydney
(Georgian Lakelands) ... 152
Portage
(Georgian Lakelands) ... 150
Preparation 26
Priceville
(Georgian Lakelands) ... 140
Queenston
(Festival Country) ... 112, 118
Radio Stations 14
Rail Trails 24
Rainbow Country 243
Manitoulin Day Tripping . 248
Off-Road Cycling 253
Sudbury 245
Reece's Corners
(Southwestern Ontario) ... 44
Regions 14
Richmond (Eastern Ontario) 219
Road Signs 20
Sarnia (Southwestern Ontario) 42
Sauble Beach
(Georgian Lakelands) ... 137
Sauble Falls
(Georgian Lakelands) ... 137
Severn Falls
(Georgian Lakelands) ... 148
Shallow Lake
(Georgian Lakelands) ... 137
Simcoe
(Southwestern Ontario) ... 51
Smiths Falls
(Eastern Ontario) 223
South Bay (Central Ontario) 198
South Bay
(Georgian Lakelands) ... 147
Southwestern Ontario 35
Down by the
Old Mill Stream 67
Lake Erie's North Shore .. 47
Magical Pelee Island 38
Off-Road Cycling 75
Sarnia Circle Tour 42
Shakespeare's Stonetown . 55
Two Sunsets, a River
and a Trail 62
St. Jacobs (Festival Country) . 95
St. Marys
(Southwestern Ontario) ... 60
Stoves 26

Stratford
  (Southwestern Ontario) ...   56
Taxes   15
Tent   25
Theft   31
Thornbury
  (Georgian Lakelands) ... 142
Thorold (Festival Country) . 106
Tillsonburg
  (Southwestern Ontario) ...   53
Tobermory
  (Georgian Lakelands) ... 135
Toronto 158
Tour Preparation   26
Tour Training   26
Tourist Information   13
Tours 23, 29
Trails   24
Train   18
Training   26
Trans Canada Trail   24
Transporting Your Bicycle ...   16
Travel Documents   16
Travelling to Ontario   16
Turkey Point
  (Southwestern Ontario) ...   52

Vanessa
  (Southwestern Ontario) ...   50
Victoria Harbour
  (Georgian Lakelands) ... 146
Virgil (Festival Country) ... 116
Walkerton
  (Georgian Lakelands) ... 128
Wallenstein (Festival Country) 95
Warsaw (Central Ontario) .. 182
Waubaushene
  (Georgian Lakelands) ... 146
Waupoos (Central Ontario) . 196
Weather   14
Welland (Festival Country) . 108
West Montrose
  (Festival Country)   94
Wiarton
  (Georgian Lakelands) ... 133
Wildlife   26
Winterbourne
  (Festival Country)   94
Woodstock
  (Southwestern Ontario) ...   48
Wyoming
  (Southwestern Ontario) ...   44

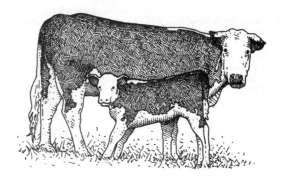

Travel Notes

Travel Notes

Travel Notes

Travel Notes

Travel Notes

Travel Notes

Travel Notes

_____

_____

_____

_____

_____

_____

_____

_____

_____

_____

_____

_____

_____

_____

_____

_____

_____

_____

_____

_____

_____

_____

_____

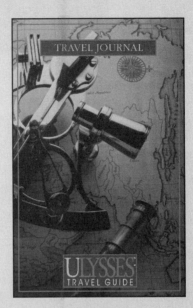

El placer de viajar mejor

e plaisir de mieux voyager

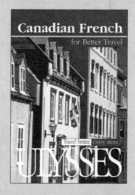

Order Form

Ulysses Travel Guides

☐ Acapulco	$14.95 CAD	$9.95 USD
☐ Alberta's Best Hotels and Restaurants	$14.95 CAD	$12.95 USD
☐ Arizona–Grand Canyon	$24.95 CAD	$17.95 USD
☐ Atlantic Canada	$24.95 CAD	$17.95 USD
☐ Beaches of Maine	$12.95 CAD	$9.95 USD
☐ Bed and Breakfasts In Ontario	$17.95 CAD	$12.95 USD
☐ Belize	$16.95 CAD	$12.95 USD
☐ Boston	$17.95 CAD	$12.95 USD
☐ British Columbia's Best Hotels and Restaurants	$14.95 CAD	$12.95 USD
☐ Calgary	$16.95 CAD	$12.95 USD
☐ California	$29.95 CAD	$21.95 USD
☐ Canada	$29.95 CAD	$22.95 USD
☐ Cancún & Riviera Maya	$19.95 CAD	$17.95 USD
☐ Cape Cod, Nantucket and Martha's Vineyard	$17.95 CAD	$12.95 USD
☐ Cartagena (Colombia)	$12.95 CAD	$9.95 USD
☐ Chicago	$19.95 CAD	$14.95 USD
☐ Chile	$27.95 CAD	$17.95 USD
☐ Colombia	$29.95 CAD	$21.95 USD
☐ Costa Rica	$27.95 CAD	$19.95 USD
☐ Cuba	$24.95 CAD	$17.95 USD
☐ Dominican Republic	$24.95 CAD	$17.95 USD
☐ Ecuador and Galápagos Islands	$24.95 CAD	$17.95 USD
☐ Fabulous Québec	$29.95 CAD	$22.95 USD
☐ Guadalajara	$17.95 CAD	$12.95 USD
☐ Guadeloupe	$24.95 CAD	$17.95 USD
☐ Guatemala	$24.95 CAD	$17.95 USD
☐ Havana	$16.95 CAD	$12.95 USD
☐ Hawaii	$29.95 CAD	$21.95 USD
☐ Honduras	$24.95 CAD	$17.95 USD
☐ Huatulco–Puerto Escondido	$17.95 CAD	$12.95 USD
☐ Inns and Bed & Breakfasts in Québec	$17.95 CAD	$12.95 USD
☐ Las Vegas	$17.95 CAD	$12.95 USD
☐ Lisbon	$18.95 CAD	$13.95 USD
☐ Los Angeles	$19.95 CAD	$14.95 USD
☐ Los Cabos and La Paz	$14.95 CAD	$10.95 USD

Ulysses Travel Guides *(continued)*

☐ Louisiana	$29.95 CAD	$21.95 USD
☐ Martinique	$24.95 CAD	$17.95 USD
☐ Miami	$17.95 CAD	$12.95 USD
☐ Montréal	$19.95 CAD	$14.95 USD
☐ New England	$29.95 CAD	$21.95 USD
☐ New Orleans	$17.95 CAD	$12.95 USD
☐ New York City	$19.95 CAD	$14.95 USD
☐ Nicaragua	$24.95 CAD	$17.95 USD
☐ Ontario's Best Hotels and Restaurants	$16.95 CAD	$12.95 USD
☐ Ontario	$29.95 CAD	$22.95 USD
☐ Ottawa–Hull	$14.95 CAD	$12.95 USD
☐ Panamá	$27.95 CAD	$19.95 USD
☐ Peru	$27.95 CAD	$19.95 USD
☐ Phoenix	$16.95 CAD	$12.95 USD
☐ Portugal	$24.95 CAD	$17.95 USD
☐ Provence & the Côte d'Azur	$29.95 CAD	$21.95 USD
☐ Puerto Plata–Sosua	$14.95 CAD	$9.95 USD
☐ Puerto Rico	$24.95 CAD	$17.95 USD
☐ Puerto Vallarta	$14.95 CAD	$10.95 USD
☐ Québec	$29.95 CAD	$22.95 USD
☐ Québec City	$17.95 CAD	$12.95 USD
☐ San Diego	$17.95 CAD	$12.95 USD
☐ San Francisco	$17.95 CAD	$12.95 USD
☐ Seattle	$17.95 CAD	$12.95 USD
☐ St. Lucia	$17.95 CAD	$12.95 USD
☐ St. Martin–St. Barts	$17.95 CAD	$12.95 USD
☐ Toronto	$19.95 CAD	$14.95 USD
☐ Tunisia	$27.95 CAD	$19.95 USD
☐ Vancouver & Victoria	$19.95 CAD	$14.95 USD
☐ Washington D.C.	$19.95 CAD	$14.95 USD
☐ Western Canada	$29.95 CAD	$22.95 USD

Ulysses Green Escapes

☐ Cross-Country Skiing and Snowshoeing in Ontario	$22.95 CAD	$16.95 USD
☐ Cycling in France	$24.95 CAD	$17.95 USD
☐ Cycling in Ontario	$24.95 CAD	$17.95 USD
☐ Ontario's Bike Paths and Rail Trails	$19.95 CAD	$17.95 USD

Ulysses Green Escapes

☐ Hiking in the Northeastern U.S. $19.95 CAD $13.95 USD
☐ Hiking in Ontario $22.95 CAD $16.95 USD
☐ Hiking in Québec $22.95 CAD $16.95 USD

Ulysses Conversation Guides

☐ Canadian French for Better Travel $9.95 CAD $6.95 USD
☐ French for Better Travel $9.95 CAD $6.95 USD
☐ Italian for Better Travel $9.95 CAD $6.95 USD
☐ Spanish for Better Travel in Latin America $9.95 CAD $6.95 USD
☐ Spanish for Better Travel in Spain $9.95 CAD $6.95 USD

Ulysses Travel Journals

☐ Ulysses Travel Journal $12.95 CAD $9.95 USD

Title	Qty	Price	Total

Name:	Subtotal	
	Shipping	$4.75 CAD $5.75 USD
Address:	Subtotal	
	GST in Canada	
	Total	

Tel: Fax:

E-mail:

Payment: ☐ Cheque ☐ Visa ☐ MasterCard

Card number_____

Expiry date_____

Signature_____

Ulysses Travel Guides

4176 St. Denis Street,
Montréal, Québec, H2W 2M5
☎(514) 843-9447
fax: (514) 843-9448

305 Madison Avenue,
Suite 1166,
New York, NY 10165
Toll-free: 1-877-542-7247

www.ulyssesguides.com
info@ulysses.ca